D0104094

Le Moyne College Library

Gift of
In Memory of Martin A.
Wersing.

JAPAN'S NEW MIDDLE CLASS

JAPAN'S NEW MIDDLE CLASS

The Salary Man and His Family in a Tokyo Suburb

by EZRA F. VOGEL

University of California Press

Berkeley, Los Angeles, London

1971

University of California Press
Berkeley and Los Angeles, California
University of California Press, Ltd.
London, England
© *1963 by The Regents of the University of California*
ISBN: 0-520-02092-8 (cloth)
0-520-02100-2 (paper)
Library of Congress Catalog Card Number: 63-21263
Second Edition, 1971
Printed in the United States of America

HT
690
J3V6
C.3

TO OUR FAMILIES:

Joe Vogels, C. W. Halls, and The Six Families of Mamachi

ACKNOWLEDGMENTS

This study, based on field work which my wife and I conducted in Japan from 1958 to 1960, is an attempt to describe the life of the salary man and his family. In our field work, in order to penetrate beyond superficial appearances and to develop an intimate familiarity with a number of families, we focused particularly on one community where we lived for the last year of our study. We shall call our community Mamachi. Such an intensive study has required the closest co-operation of many Mamachi families. The residents of Mamachi do not take obligations lightly, and we, too, cannot take lightly the fact that we can never repay adequately their kindness and the inconveniences we caused them. We can only hope to prove worthy of their time and effort by portraying their lives as accurately as we know how without sacrificing their anonymity. To these unnamed families, then, we express our deepest thanks.

During the period of field work, the Japanese National Institute of Mental Health provided office space, made arrangements for our field work, made available their case materials, permitted my wife to be the psychiatric social worker for a patient on a regular basis, and accorded us the full privileges of regular staff members. Various members of the staff explained intricacies of their cases, gave and interpreted projective tests to families in our study, and patiently answered an endless number of questions.

I have benefited from the guidance of members of the Sociology Department of the University of Tokyo, the Japanese Psychoanalytic Association, the Group for the Study of the Family directed by Professor Takashi Koyama, and an informal seminar on family studies directed by Professor Yuzuru Okada. Dr. Takeo Doi, a psychiatrist who has practiced in Japan and the United States, generously shared many facets of his deep understanding of Japanese behavior. Professor Tokusaburo Abe of Yamagata University, Professor Tetsuro Sasaki of Tohoku University, and Professor Kenneth Morioka of International Christian University and their staffs and students assisted in the development, distribution, and coding of questionnaires. Professor Tadashi Fukutake and Professor Takeyoshi Kawashima of Tokyo University kindly let me join them on field trips to the country.

At various stages in the work, I have been ably assisted by Hiroshi Satake, Mitsuko Minowa, Michiko Kiuchi, Fumiko Kamiyama Sasaki, Miyoko Sasaki, Hisa Hirada, Yaeko Sato, Sumiko Embutsu, Sumiko Iwao, Tomoko Yagai, Emily Cohen, and Marie Wilson.

Dr. William Caudill first interested me in going to Japan and has been a constant source of support and counsel in all stages of the work. Dr. John Spiegel and Dr. Florence Kluckhohn gave me several years of training in field work and in the analysis of value-orientations and implicit roles, and their study was the model on which I based my research design. Both before and after the field work, I profited from discussions with Professor John Pelzel, who has a uniquely broad perspective on Japan, combining behavioral science theory and methods with an intimate knowledge of Japanese society and history. Professor Ronald Dore's excellent work, *City Life in Japan,* appeared just before the beginning of our field work and provided an invaluable background for the present study.

I have benefited from the stimulation and unselfish guidance of other teachers, particularly Professor Hubert Bonner of Ohio Wesleyan University, Dr. Aaron Beck of Philadelphia, and Professor Talcott Parsons, Professor Robert Bales, and Professor George Homans of Harvard University. The analytic framework for the present study owes much to Dr. Norman Bell and follows closely the outline which he and I developed.* Members of an informal seminar under the direction of Dr. Theodore Lidz of the Yale Psychiatry Department and a seminar in the Harvard Medical School directed by Dr. John Spiegel, Dr. Florence Kluckhohn, and myself gave valuable insight into clinical aspects of the case materials I collected in Japan.

---

* Norman W. Bell and Ezra F. Vogel, eds., *A Modern Introduction to the Family* (Glencoe, Ill.: The Free Press, 1960).

After I returned from Japan, discussions with Professors Masao Maruyama and Takeshi Ishida of Tokyo University on political thought and with Professor Kazuo Noda of Rikkyo University on the structure of the business firm have been particularly enlightening. The final version of the manuscript reflects my indebtedness for the careful reading and thoughtful criticism of an earlier draft by Norman Bell, Robert Bellah, Vin Brandt, William Caudill, Al Craig, George De Vos, Peter Dodd, Takeo Doi, Ronald Dore, Samuel M. Eisenstadt, Sumiko and Coe Embutsu, Takeshi Ishida, Jack Knowles, Victor Lidz, Kenneth Morioka, Yonosuke Nagai, Kazuo Noda, John Pelzel, David Plath, David Riesman, Robert J. Smith, Yonina Talmon, and Kenichi Tominaga. Max Knight of the University of California Press has made preparation for publication painless and even pleasant by being careful in his editing, gentle in his reproach, and expeditious in moving the manuscript through to final form.

The field work was financed by a grant from the Foundations' Fund for Research in Psychiatry, under arrangements with the Laboratory of Social Relations at Harvard. Small grants from the National Institute of Mental Health and the support of the Department of Psychiatry at Yale and the East Asian Research Center at Harvard greatly facilitated the analysis of data.

In many ways my wife Suzanne should be coauthor. She fully shared the problems of planning and carrying out the field work, and the life of a wife-mother-interviewer in another culture was more demanding than either of us might have imagined. Although she did not take part in the actual writing, she has been a patient sounding board, and her concern with individual cases provided a needed balance to my irrepressible desire to paint the broad picture.

E. F. V.

Cambridge, Massachusetts
January, 1963

CONTENTS

Part One

THE SIGNIFICANCE OF SALARY

Chapter I

THE PROBLEM AND ITS SETTING

Among the non-Western nations, only Japan has reached a level of industrialization and urbanization comparable to the advanced countries of Europe and America. From a nation that only one hundred years ago was voluntarily isolated from the developments of the rest of the world, Japan has become an important member of the international community. In a single century, Japan has not only introduced modern technology but kept pace with continuing Western progress. At the same time, modern systems of education, government, business, transportation, and communication have become firmly implanted in Japanese society.

The Japanese people in this century have adjusted not only to these fundamental changes, but to a series of natural disasters and national crises. The contemporary Japanese adult has faced a staggering number of difficulties. The standard of living which was rising in the 1920's was disrupted first by a terrible earthquake and later by the devastating effects of a world depression. The increasing political freedom in the 1920's was gradually stifled by an oppressive military rule which required increasingly severe sacrifices until the end of World War II. During the war, many small children were separated from their parents and sent to rural areas to escape air raids, and many families had their only wage earner killed. After the fighting, many families, already undernourished and short of funds, provided for relatives, friends, and even strangers who returned from the military or the overseas colonies. Not only did they live with severe shortages of food, clothing, and shelter, but they had to renounce their former leaders and traditions and accept new patterns of life imposed by the victors.

In the face of these crises and the rapid social change, it is surprising how successfully the average Japanese has been able to maintain an orderly life free from despair and disorder. In spite of these problems, much publicized by the press, the Japanese have made a successful adjustment, economically, socially, and psychologically. The period of peace and prosperity since World War II has made it possible to consolidate many of the social changes, and for the newly emerging social order to achieve some degree of stability.

An important element in the new social order is the emergence of a large "new middle class." The "old middle class" (the small independent businessman and landowner) has been declining in power and influence and is gradually being replaced by this "new middle class," the white-collar employees of the large business corporations and government bureaucracies.[1] The small independent entrepreneurs who comprise the old middle class have generally played a central role in small local communities because of their influence and power, but their perspective has remained focused within this narrow social microcosm. Although some have profited indirectly from Japan's economic prosperity since 1955, few members of the old middle class have had the motivation, ability, and resources to expand their enterprises to take advantage of Japan's rapid economic growth.[2] They are, rather, being superseded by, or affiliated with and subordinated to large business corporations which have the resources and entrepreneurial skill to play the key role in the recent economic growth. The old middle class has not yet died out by any means, but the trend of the times has been obvious, and many have urged their children to become white-collar workers in the large bureaucratic organizations in the cities. The income of the white-collar worker is less affected by economic fluctuations or by

---

[1] For a brief account of the distinction between the Japanese "new middle class" and "old middle class" see Tadashi Fukutake, *Man and Society in Japan*. Tokyo: Tokyo University Press, 1962.

[2] Cf. John C. Pelzel, "The Small Industrialist in Japan," *Explorations in Entrepreneurial History*, 1954, 7:79–93. Especially since 1955, however, the economic boom in large companies has assisted the development of certain small industries. Although the number of small enterprises has decreased compared to before World War II, the number has remained relatively constant since the war. Many of these small enterprises have been able to survive by affiliating with a large company, albeit in a subordinate position.

the whims of an arbitrary paternalistic employer than that of the employee in the smaller industries. Because the income of the new middle-class citizen is guaranteed in the form of a regular salary, he has come to be known as the "sarari man" (salary man). This word is not used in Japan to include all who receive a salary, but only white-collar workers in the large bureaucracy of a business firm or government office. Although the two words "salary" and "man" are not ordinarily used together in English, the term "salary man" will be used throughout the present work to convey the Japanese meaning of *sarari man*.

The roots of the salary man can be traced at least as far back as the Tokugawa period, for after 1600 when Japan achieved internal stability, the military functions of the samurai withered away and many samurai became, in effect, administrators working for the clan government. With the abolition of samurai class distinctions in early Meiji, many ex-samurai became white-collar workers in government offices and government-sponsored industry. The similarity between the samurai administrator and the salary man has led many Japanese to refer to the salary man as the modern samurai. His brief case is compared to the samurai's swords, his company with the feudal fief, his readiness to uphold his company's interests with the samurai's readiness to do battle for his feudal lord. But the salary man is the product of a different social setting. The concept of the samurai retained a warrior flavor, and the ideal was to be bold, courageous, and capable of independent action. The salary man, being a part of a large bureaucratic organization, is more concerned with complex administrative and technical problems, has less room for independent movement, and is likely to be more cautious and susceptible to influence.

The word "salary man" had already become popular by 1930 although the white-collar class remained relatively small until the rapid expansion of government bureaucracies and war-related industry before and during World War II. During this period, the number of white-collar workers grew rapidly, and this growth has continued with the economic prosperity after the war. Now that the social upheaval resulting from the war has passed and the patterns of the salary man have become stabilized and clearly identifiable, it would seem to be an opportune time to examine the nature of his life.[3]

THE DOUBLE STRUCTURE

The salary man's pattern of life stands out in the Japanese context because of the sharp disparity between the large modern organization where he works and the more traditional small- or medium-sized enterprises.[4] Japanese scholars, struck by the coexistence of the modern bureaucratic patterns of large organizations and the more traditional patterns of the small- and middle-sized enterprises have named this phenomenon the "double structure" of Japanese society.

Although some small enterprises have made technological advances and are offering high salaries because of increasing labor

---

[3] Although no precise statistics are available on the growth of the number of salary men, rough estimates can be obtained from the number of white-collar workers who are not self-employed since most white-collar workers (except those in very small enterprises) would be classified as salary men.

	1920	1930	1940	1944	1955	1959
Nonagricultural labor force	12,575,000	14,933,000	18,291,000	19,275,000	23,600,000	27,810,000
White-collar workers	1,496,000	1,517,000	3,524,000	4,842,000	6,100,000	7,300,000

These data are cited in Solomon B. Levine, "Unionization of White-Collar Employees in Japan," unpublished manuscript.

According to the 1960 census, of the 31,549,800 males fifteen years of age and older, only 6,885,500 earned their living from farming, fishing, and lumbering. If one considers professional and technical workers, managers and officials, clerical workers, and protective-service workers as salary men, there were a total of 5,711,200 salary men. *Population Census of Japan*, 1960, II, part iv, Tables 1 and 2.

[4] Although large organizations are associated with the modern sector of the economy, it does not follow that all small- and medium-sized enterprises are associated with traditional occupations. For the distinction between modern and traditional aspects of the economy, see Henry Rosovsky, *Capital Formation in Japan, 1868–1940*, Glencoe, Ill.: The Free Press, 1961. Some more modern small enterprises have already a fairly high salary scale and are competitive for labor with the larger organizations.

Considering the high prestige, power, and income of salary men in government offices before the war, their position has declined since the war compared to salary men in business firms. The starting salary of salary men in government offices is generally about two-thirds of that in private corporations, but the power of salary men in government remains strong. (For this information I am indebted to Kenichi Tominaga.)

shortages, in the typical small enterprise, the worker tends to have a more diffuse relationship with his employer, a relationship that permeates all his life. The employer has some responsibility for looking after the personal needs of his employees, such as providing housing, helping arrange marriage, or giving special assistance in time of trouble. In return, the employee must be available for work at any time, and his personal life is continually subject to the employer's surveillance and approval. What security he has rests on the good will of the employer, which is not always sufficient because the small enterprises are subject to the fluctuations of the market and offer tenuous prospects for long-term security. Although smaller organizations are more paternalistic, workers are not only less satisfied, but there is a greater turnover of labor.[5] At best the paternalism of the small enterprise is restricting and at worst it is a guise under which an opportunistic owner can pay lower wages and exploit his employees by offering a few personal services.

In contrast, the salary man not only receives higher pay and regular wages, but he has regular hours with time off. His promotions occur to some extent automatically on the basis of seniority and skill, and although responsive to wishes of superiors by American standards, he need not be so responsive as workers in smaller enterprises. Because he belongs to a large, stable organization and the firm is committed to him for life,[6] he knows that his job will be more secure against the fluctuations of the business cycle. When he compares himself to the workers in small organizations, he feels proud and satisfied that he is a salary man.

Until recently there has been almost no movement of workers between the small and large organizations.[7] Fundamental differences

---

[5] Kenichi Tominaga, "Occupational Mobility in Japanese Society: Analysis of the Labor Market in Japan" (mimeographed). For this reason, as Tominaga argues, it is somewhat misleading to link paternalism (which is found in the small enterprise) with the pattern of life-long commitment, a pattern more common in the large organization.

[6] The pattern of life-long commitment of the firm to the worker became prominent in large organizations in the early part of this century because of the problem of shortage of skilled workers, but the commitment did not apply to the larger group of unskilled workers. The salary man has the good fortune to have long-term security as a result of this commitment to the skilled workers. (For this background information I am indebted to Professor Kazuo Noda of Rikkyo University.)

[7] Tominaga, *op. cit.*

in methods of work and the accompanying way of life have made it difficult for an employee of a traditional organization to move to a large one and unlikely for a salary man to want to move to a small one. Even within the large organization there has been a similar barrier between the permanent white-collar workers who form the core of the organization and the temporary and manual workers who may be discharged when the company has economic difficulties. Once a man becomes a manual worker in a large firm, he will not rise to become a white-collar worker. Japanese firms value loyalty and prefer to recruit and train their own white-collar workers who become skilled in the way their particular firm operates rather than to take on employees who have acquired different habits in other firms. With the exception of a few technical specialties, university training is not geared to preparation for a specific vocation. Training for work is generally acquired within a firm and is, therefore, less easily applicable to another firm. Because the supply of young workers has always been plentiful, firms have been able to recruit their employees directly from schools. Therefore, the traditional smaller businesses have been able to continue in operation without fear of losing their workers to higher-paying modern organizations, and the worker who is dissatisfied with being in a small organization concentrates his energies on making it possible for his son to become a salary man. The lack of free movement between small and large organizations has made it possible for a wide gap to exist between these two types of organization.

How long this double structure of the Japanese economy can continue to exist is an open question. In the last few years, since the labor shortage has caused some large businesses to look to the smaller enterprises for employees, there have been signs that the double structure might begin to break down. To keep their workers, the small enterprises may have to raise their salaries and improve their working conditions to match the larger enterprises. Some Japanese social scientists are beginning to talk of a second industrial revolution—one which would destroy this double structure. The first industrial revolution went relatively smoothly because it meant only that large organizations grew up alongside the small, but the second industrial revolution might prove more disruptive because it would mean the collapse of the smaller enterprises. Indeed the economic uncertainty and pessimism that persist in Japan amidst the amazing prosperity and industrial development can be explained partly by the mood of the smaller enterprises which fear destruction because they will be unable to survive the economic squeeze if they are forced to offer higher wages and shorter hours.

In the context of the pessimism of the smaller traditional enterprises, the salary man represents for most Japanese the "bright new life." The salary man's career is not a rapid and glorious rise to such great heights that it appears beyond their reach, but a secure path to moderate success. Able and enterprising young men willing to take risks and look out for their own future have the possibility of rising more rapidly, earning more money, and living more luxuriously by working on their own or joining small firms. But most Japanese have no such confidence in their own talents and long-term economic prospects even if they were to have such an opportunity in the short run. For the vast majority of Japanese the life of the salary man seems to represent as high a standard as they can reasonably hope for.[8] The young Japanese girl hopes to marry a salary man even if his salary were lower because his life is steady, he has leisure time, and she can be free of the anxieties and work connected with independent business. Independent shopkeepers, craftsmen, and farmers complain that they cannot compete with salary men in attracting

---

[8] In comparing essays of 1250 Japanese children with 3750 American children from grades one to eight on what they wished to be when they grew up, Mary Ellen Goodman notes that more Japanese children want to enter government service and business than American children. Furthermore, she reports that the content of what they mean by business is different. American children are more inclined to speak of becoming salesmen or merchandisers of specific products. Japanese children are more likely to speak of becoming a "company man" or an "office man," that is, a salary man. Mary Ellen Goodman, "Values, Attitudes, and Social Concepts of Japanese and American Children," *American Anthropologist*, 1957, 59:983.

Social-stratification studies in Japan have generally focused on occupational ranking rather than size of firm, but occupations which clearly imply connection with a large organization such as newspaper reporter, department-store clerk, professor, and basic-research worker show a higher ranking in Japan while independent professionals such as doctor and dentist show a higher ranking in the United States. Clearly a salaried position in a large organization carries with it high prestige in Japan. Cf. Wendell Dean Baker, "A Study of Selected Aspects of Japanese Social Stratification," doctoral dissertation, Columbia University, 1956. Charles E. Ramsey and Robert J. Smith, "Japanese and American Perceptions of Occupation," *American Journal of Sociology*, 1960, 65:475–482.

desirable brides. The importance of studying the salary man is not
only for understanding this group per se but for understanding the
aspirations of other Japanese.

The community where we studied salary men is a section of a
Tokyo suburb, selected by Japanese social scientists as typically
middle class. From visiting other cities in Japan, from conversing
with and reading works of Japanese social scientists, and from having a draft of this manuscript read by Japanese who have lived on
all four main islands of Japan, I feel confident that the patterns described here for Mamachi are essentially the same for salary men
throughout Japan. Although Japanese are very conscious of variations in regional dialect and custom, Japan is a small country which
has been relatively isolated because of its insular position and hence
has a much more highly unified culture than most countries. Furthermore, the regional differences between salary men are likely to be
less than those of farmers, fishermen, and small shopkeepers where
conditions of climate, land, water, and relative isolation from urban
centers have permitted variations to persist. The standardization of
procedures in large bureaucracies and the fact that these organizations exist in large urban centers has tended to place limits on the
amount of possible variation. Although Tokyo may be considered a
bit more modern than some Japanese cities, about one-tenth of the
Japanese population lives in Tokyo, and since about one-half of the
Japanese population is still rural, at least one-fifth of all Japanese
salary men live in the Tokyo area. Many more were educated there,
and because of its crucial position in Japan (it is, in effect, New York,
Washington, and Hollywood all in one), Tokyo dominates the mass
media and sets the pace for the entire country. Just as the Tokyo
dialect has become the standard dialect, so Tokyo culture is becoming national culture. Some young salary men who live in the center
of Tokyo may consider Mamachi old-fashioned, and some older
salary men in more traditional areas of Japan may consider it too
modern, but compared to vast differences between patterns among
employees in other countries, these variations are minor. While I
have chosen to limit the descriptions to Mamachi because of my
familiarity with a wealth of detail I do not have for other communities, I think it safe for the reader to assume that he is reading
about a way of life found among salary men throughout Japan. In

many cases precise survey data are available showing the similarity between Mamachi and other communities, and in these cases I will present the data in the footnotes.

THE SETTING: MAMACHI

The people of Mamachi think of their neighborhood as *shizuka* (quiet and peaceful), separated from the bustle of Tokyo where most of the husbands work.[9] Until about thirty or forty years ago Mamachi was sparsely settled. Although many new houses have gone up in the last generation, the neighborhood with its narrow paths, large trees, and small gardens still retains an aura of suburban calm.

Virtually all homes in Mamachi are privately-owned, single-storied, unpainted wooden dwellings surrounded by ingenious small gardens, separated from the outside world by high fences. One or two sides of the house, generally facing the sun, have sliding glass doors which can be opened to let in the sun and to air out the house during the day. At night, the sliding wooden doors outside the glass doors will be closed to keep out rain, cold, insects, and prowlers. Construction is generally simple and plain, with thin walls, peaked roofs, small windows, no basement. The homes average perhaps three or four rooms in size, the rooms being separated by sliding paper doors. Many homes have one "Western style" room used for a sitting room or for entertaining guests; it has chairs, a couch and a chest of drawers, and is often decorated in a fashion not too different from American style of a few decades ago. Two or three "Japanese style" rooms covered with soft tatami mats can be used for sitting in the day time and for sleeping at night. In the day time, cushions are brought out to sit on, and a table is set up for meals or for entertaining guests. At night the tables and cushions are put away and bedding is taken out of the large closets and placed over the tatami mats. Other furnishings generally are few and simple: a few chests and bureaus, a television set, a radio, a few pictures, decorations, and perhaps a children's desk and a piano. The kitchen is old fashioned by American standards. A few people now can afford a mechanized American style kitchen or at least a

---

[9] Our field-work procedure is described in the Appendix.

refrigerator, but most families in Mamachi still have only one or two gas burners and a small wooden ice box which they fill with a piece of ice every few days. The kitchen usually is not furnished very attractively and guests are not invited in. One small room contains a small but high Japanese wooden bath tub where the family spends many an evening taking turns relaxing in very hot water. They have cold running water which is safe to drink, and a few families have a little heater to heat water as it comes out of the tap.

The climate of Tokyo is slightly warmer than that of Washington, D.C. with about one snowfall a year and only a few days in winter when the temperature goes below freezing. Because of the style of housing and the high cost of fuel, there is no central heating. In the middle of one of the tatami rooms is a localized heating device known as the *kotatsu*. A portion of the floor is cut out in the shape of a square, and one sits on the floor next to the opening resting his feet on a ledge which goes around all four sides of the opening about eighteen inches below floor level. A few inches below the foot ledge is a place to burn charcoal or install an electric heater. A small table stretches over the opening, and a quilt may be placed over the table and stretched out over people's laps to prevent the heat from escaping. The family eats and spends most of its winter evenings near the *kotatsu* in order to keep warm. The rest of the house is unheated, although many families have a gas or electric stove which they can use when guests come to visit.

Mamachi homes in their simple functional design are pleasant and attractive. In the day time when the sliding doors are opened one can see the choice view of the garden, with its neatly trimmed shrubbery and flowers, carefully swept ground, and, perhaps, some rocks or a very small pond. Although the gardens are small, one has the feeling of being completely away from the rush and pressure of life outside the gates.

Within convenient walking distance from any place in Mamachi are rows of highly specialized small shops which open on to the more heavily traveled streets. There is the dry-goods store, the spice store, the bakery, the sweets store, the canned-goods store, and fruit and vegetable store, the dairy store, the butcher shop, the fish market, the poultry store, the rice store, the tea store, the stationery store, the shoe store, the electrical-appliance store, the store for pots and pans, the Western-clothing store, the store for bedding supplies, the furniture store, the store for medicine and drugs, and perhaps a few more. Intermingled within a short distance are a number of craftsmen's shops such as that of the maker of tatami mats for the floor, the door maker, the bath maker, the repairman for bicycles and motor bikes, the gardener, the kimono maker, and the tailor.

These small shops usually are run by a single family of parents and children with perhaps a live-in hired helper or two who are likely to be treated almost like family members. The family lives behind the wooden floored shop in a small room or two of tatami mats. While most Mamachi families occasionally shop in Tokyo at the large department stores, they do most of their daily shopping at these small shops where they are steady customers. Some shops, like the canned-goods store or the fruit and vegetable store, send errand boys to take daily orders and deliver them a few hours later. More commonly, the housewife goes out daily, basket under arm and perhaps child on back, to select the things she needs. Relations between housewife and shopkeepers or craftsmen are usually pleasant and cordial. However, they are not intimate, for a wide social gap separates the new middle class from the small shopkeepers of the old middle class who have less desirable housing and physical facilities, less money, less security, and less education.

Since Mamachi is not the center of the suburb, it has relatively few public buildings. There is a large two-storied wooden grade school with more than two thousand children, and a somewhat smaller junior high school, both with large gravel-covered playgrounds. Several police sub-stations, with two or three policemen each, keep track of the residents, make sure that everything is peaceful in the neighborhood and give directions to visitors, an important task because of the irregular numbering of houses. Small branch offices of the post office and fire department service the area. A few small shrines and one temple are tucked away among some of the residences. Local buses run down several of the main streets (ending up at the Mamachi train stop), which provides the residents with a rapid and inexpensive route to downtown Tokyo. Most of the men leave early in the morning, brief case and magazine or newspaper in hand, and catch a train to work in Tokyo. Wives occasionally go to Tokyo for shopping and many children of junior-high-school and high-school age attend school in Tokyo.

It was our purpose while living in Mamachi to try to live as other residents did, to try to understand their way of living and their way of looking at the world. While there we took copious notes of our observations and of our talks with the residents of Mamachi. In analyzing the notes after returning to the United States my primary purpose has been to see the world of the residents in the perspective of the social setting in which they live.

Chapter II

THE BUREAUCRATIC SETTING IN PERSPECTIVE

In comparison with most families around the world and with rural families in Japan, Mamachi families are unusually dependent on the husband's salary and personal savings. Most Mamachi families do not feel part of a tight-knit group of friends or relatives to whom they can turn in time of financial distress.[1] Perhaps they are too proud to let their relatives know about money difficulties, or doubt their relatives' ability to help, or fear future family quarrels, or feel the family relationship too distant to be comfortable in making the request. Whatever their reasons, most of these families would undergo great sacrifices rather than call on relatives or friends for financial assistance.

In rural Japan, as in rural areas in most countries, a family derives its security from the land and in time of need a family can turn to relatives or other members of the local community for assistance. In most industrialized countries families in great need can expect to receive welfare benefits from the government, but for an industrialized nation, Japan's welfare services are not well developed. Benefits are small and few, and not given automatically to people who meet standardized criteria of "neediness." As a result, families seeking welfare aid are put in the position of having to prostrate themselves before welfare officials in order to receive even the minimum of aid. While, for example, even a middle-class family in America would not be very embarrassed by accepting aid for dependent children, social-security payments, compensation for in-

---

[1] Even in rural areas, however, mutual aid is not nearly so strong as previously. Cf. Tadashi Fukutake, *Studies in the Rural Community in Japan*, Tokyo University Press, 1959, and Edward Norbeck, "Postwar Cultural Change and Continuity in Northeastern Japan," *American Anthropologist*, 1961, 63:297–321.

dustrial accidents, and the like, the Japanese application procedures are often so humiliating, the chance for receiving aid so uncertain, and the amount of aid so inadequate, that the typical Mamachi family does not expect to seek public help, even in time of need.[2] It is also difficult to obtain loans from banks. Not only are interest rates much higher than in the United States, but banks rarely lend money to individual borrowers, and a borrower may acquire bothersome personal as well as financial obligations.[3] Some families turn to moneylenders, but borrow for only a very short time because interest rates are exorbitant. Although there are several moneylenders in Mamachi and families told us that other families go to moneylenders, no family ever told us that they themselves had used moneylenders. Indeed the stories of people sneaking in to pawn shops sound almost like a criminal escaping the detectives.

The wife of an ordinary middle-class Mamachi family has virtually no chance to earn a living by herself. While some poorer wives are able to take in work like sewing, such jobs are increasingly being done by large industries. Even if a middle-class wife could find such work it would be embarrassing, since few jobs would seem suitable to her status except, perhaps, teaching some housewifely arts at which she was particularly skillful or a special service occupation like hairdressing. Even if another job were available, she would receive a much lower salary than a man in the same position, and perhaps even less than a young girl doing the same job. Ordinarily she would seek work only if widowed, and the income she could earn would probably not be adequate to support herself and her children.

Because of these factors, the father's salary is ordinarily the only source of family income, and there is virtually no alternative in time of trouble. The importance of the father's income is most clearly revealed by the changes in family fortune in the event of the father's premature death or incapacity. An illustration of the common problem of family decline after such misfortune is the case of a second son whose father died when the son was still in grade school. Until

---

[2] Some of the Japanese rules regarding welfare sound as if services were more widespread than they are. For a survey of actual welfare conditions see Eiichi Isomura, Takeyoshi Kawashima, and Takashi Koyama, *Kazoku no Fuyoo* (The Maintenance of Needy Families), Tokyo: Kawade Shoboo, 1956.

[3] For an analysis of problems in borrowing money see John C. Pelzel, "The Small Industrialist in Japan," *Explorations in Entrepreneurial History*, 1954, 7:79-93.

that time the family had been prosperous middle-class people, rich enough to afford a maid. After the father was killed in an accident, the young man's life changed completely. The family had to give up their maid and other luxuries, endure severe economic hardships, and bear the snubs of many former friends. The young man still recalls bitterly the way he felt when he was suddenly without friends. He and his family were not persecuted, but former friends avoided them, apparently fearing they might be called upon for help if they continued to be friendly. Fortunately, the boy's older brother was completing junior high school and soon started work. Although he could not earn enough to keep up their former standard of living, the family never had to worry about having enough to eat. As a result, however, the older brother could never pursue higher education, and only with great sacrifice was the family able to save enough to keep the second son in school.

Furthermore, it is difficult for divorced or widowed women to find new husbands or to obtain help from relatives.[4] It is especially difficult for women with children to remarry because men want children of their own and few earn enough money to support large families. But perhaps more important is the tradition of family loyalty. Sons are expected to continue the family name and line of a dead father, and widows are still admired for remaining loyal to their dead husbands. Men feel that a wife who was properly devoted to her first husband would have difficulty transferring that devotion to another man, and a wife who was not properly devoted to her first husband would be less likely to make a good wife for anyone.[5]

In addition to the financial difficulties a widow or divorcee must face, her children are discriminated against when they begin looking for jobs. Mamachi residents report that if two young men of

---

[4] In 1956, only 6.1 percent of marriages in Japan were of women who had been married before, but 10 percent were of men who had been wed before. *Fujin no Genjoo* (The Position of Women), Tokyo: Roodooshoo Fujinshoonen Kyoku, 1959, p. 55. In the United States, between January, 1947, and June, 1954, 19.9 percent of marriages were of women who had been married before. Paul C. Glick, *American Families,* New York: John Wiley, 1957, p. 141. This difference is too large to be explained by the difference in the divorce rate.

[5] For a widower, however, it is not only considered advisable but necessary to remarry in order to have someone care for the children. Since the children would remain in the father's line, this is not seen as causing any serious problem.

roughly equal qualifications are seeking employment, one whose home includes a father and one whose home does not, the job would go to the boy with a father. This preference continues today even in corporations which select employees by examination. It is assumed, first of all, that a fatherless boy would not have been given proper disciplinary and moral training. Even if he did receive such training, companies feel that he is more apt to be dishonest, for his greater need for money might tempt him to embezzle or in some way cheat the company for personal and family needs. Furthermore, since he is partly responsible for the care and protection of his mother and siblings and since a firm ordinarily assumes some responsibility for the welfare of its workers and families, the firm is cautious in taking on this extra burden. Although the firm may not contribute enough to make a really easy life for the employee's family, nevertheless, the degree to which it is expected to help could be an added burden on the company.

The almost total reliance of the wife and children on the husband's income is further reflected by the late age of marriage (in 1955, in cities, 47.5 percent of men and 23.6 percent of women 25 to 29 years of age were still single) and the importance of the husband's health as a factor in the decision to marry. A girl is reluctant to marry a man until he is fully established in a place of employment and his health and life expectancy are openly and carefully discussed by his fiancée and her parents. A young man who has had tuberculosis or another serious disease has more difficulty finding a wife not only because people want healthy descendants but because the wife's family wants some assurance that the young man will live long and be able to support his wife. Today increased longevity makes health less problematic than formerly, but it is still one of the major criteria of a desirable husband.

The death of the husband undoubtedly is the most serious blow to a family's livelihood, but the loss of his job is almost as serious. Not only are good jobs hard to find, but because of the policies of Japanese firms, a man who loses his job probably will have to start again at the bottom, with a low salary and with little hope of rapid promotion. Hence, many people consider the stability of a job more important than the amount of income.

The significance of the Japanese salary man lies, therefore, not only in the fact that he is a nonmanual worker and an organization man, but in the fact that he has a measure of economic security which most Japanese do not have. In a nonaffluent society where one has no place to turn in time of need, and welfare is provided by neither the government nor the family nor personal connections, the large firm assumes a critical importance because it provides security as well as income. The fact that a firm provides this security has many implications for the life of the salary man, but the meaning of working in a bureaucratic setting comes not only from the man's relation to the firm but also from the position in the community that derives from his work. To see the bureaucratic setting in perspective it is necessary to compare the salary man in Mamachi with families of the old middle class in the same community with whom he compares himself: the successful businessman, the independent professional, and the small shopkeeper.

THE SUCCESSFUL BUSINESSMAN

Above salary man families in Mamachi are a small number of families known as "burujoa" (bourgeoisie), a term used in Japan to describe only very successful businessmen. These families gain their status from the style of life made possible by family enterprises which may have as many as five hundred employees.[6] Generally their offices are in Tokyo, but they are very influential in Mamachi affairs and are treated with respect by other Mamachi residents. These families do not need to rely on a large firm, because they have ample security from the financial standing and success of the business and the fact that the husbands' entrepreneurial abilities and friendships with other influential people would be in demand even if the present business failed. Some of these men are from business families and have acquired these skills over many years, but even those who inherited old family firms have guided their companies successfully through enormous change and development in the past few years. The combination of long training, recent success, influential friends, and high standard of living provides them with ample basis for self-confidence and pride. Yet they are intensely concerned with the business competition, the rapidly changing

---

[6] Large industrialists generally live in Tokyo. To my knowledge, none live in Mamachi.

markets, and the general pressures on small business, and they devote their boundless energy toward making the business even more successful.

Their position in Mamachi society is not based only on financial standing and is secure enough to withstand temporary business reverses. They are continuously called upon for leadership in Mamachi organizations, campaigns, and celebrations. It is thought that without their co-operation and support, if not their active guidance, no organization in Mamachi could be successful and no important matter could be satisfactorily resolved. The successful businessman is effective in local organizations, not only because he can be counted on for a sizeable financial contribution but because he can pinpoint the basic problems, deal with them frankly and directly and, by his broad range of contacts through business and the community, effectively mobilize the support necessary to implement his opinions. While he can express his convictions freely, many others reserve judgment until he has spoken and then accept his suggestions. Although he is capable of showing consideration for others, his manner commonly reflects a sense of superiority and others generally accept this as natural and proper. In striking contrast to the typical salary man, he need not indulge in self-effacing modesty and may even boast about his income, the size of his firm, and the scope of his responsibility.

By virtue of his position, he and his family have a feeling of noblesse oblige toward other members of the community. Indeed, the problem which worries him most is the time and energy required for dealing with the many requests from friends and acquaintances for introductions and assistance in finding their children schools, work, and the like. His response to requests may be determined by the legitimacy of the need, the degree to which he is obligated to help the other person, and the difficulties involved, but even if he refuses, he feels it necessary to give some evidence that he has tried to help. He pays a heavy price for his prominence in the community.

Although responsive to praise and honor, the successful businessman often evaluates his participation in community affairs on the basis of its compatibility with his primary interest: business success. At times he feels it incumbent upon him, because of his community prestige, to participate in activities unlikely to help his business. More often, however, he will sidestep responsibilities in these activities by offering financial help or services which require little time but will participate vigorously in activities which might have indirect business advantage.

Just as business is combined with community activities, so it is combined with recreation and personal activities. It is often difficult to distinguish working time from leisure time, and the businessman often entertains his clients by a trip to the golf course or a party with entertainment by geisha girls. He may do so without any specific business problem in mind, but at other times he clearly uses the informal atmosphere for business ends. One of the businessmen explained that when he has important business, he first lays the groundwork by providing a good atmosphere with a private party, and at the peak of good will he subtly mentions his business plan and completes the arrangements while everyone is still in good humor. Many evenings are spent in just such parties, and many Sundays and even week days are spent at the exclusive golf clubs, combining business and pleasure. Even if there is no specific business purpose, these activities are paid for by the business expense account.

Business expense accounts also are used to cover a variety of family expenses. Although the businessman may not draw much more salary than a highly paid manager, the extras, paid for by the business, make his style of life very different from that of the salary man. For example, he typically has at his disposal at least one or two chauffeured cars. He is chauffeured to and from work and to any place else he wishes to go; when he is not using the car, it is at the disposal of his wife. If the wife should require household help, in addition to her regular maid, she can call on her husband's employees, and their wages will be paid by the company payroll. A young girl in the company may even be used as a part-time maid. As in the United States, company expense accounts have the virtue of avoiding income-tax payments, but in Japan the scope of company expenses is broad enough to include more personal expenses. Since business is so closely intertwined with family affairs and recreation, it is sometimes difficult to distinguish business and personal expenses.

Just as company expenses extend into areas which Americans regard as personal, so employer-employee relationships go far beyond contractual work relationships. While genuinely interested in his employee's welfare, the successful businessman is very aware of the business utility of offering benefits in lieu of higher salaries. He provides employees with personal services, not because he loves them as his children, but because he realizes that this keeps up the workers' morale and productivity. He knows, for example, that discharging an employee without good reason would have a serious effect on the morale of other workers. The problem is that granting favors on an individual basis can be very bothersome and time-consuming. Because some employees may learn of special considerations given to others and because there are no standard rules about how these benefits are to be given, the special arrangements between employer and recipient can lead to a complicated and entangling network of special secrets and plots. Rivalries between employees who received different favors are sometimes almost unavoidable.

Occasionally the wife of the successful businessman helps employees with their personal problems. The worker would go to the employer to discuss financial problems, but if he had a close relationship with his employer he would probably make at least a formal call on the wife to discuss marriage plans or family problems. For this reason, the husband discusses personnel relations with her, and typically she has a fairly clear idea of the inner workings of her husband's business. Even if the assistance she gives the employees in solving problems is merely perfunctory, it serves to reinforce the closeness of the employer-employee relationship and to guarantee the continued loyalty of the worker.

The wife may also give special free courses in sewing, cooking, flower arranging, and the tea ceremony to help female employees with wedding preparations. With her husband, she also officiates at employees' weddings, company festivities, anniversaries, sports contests, and parties honoring new or retiring employees. Such activities are, in effect, a wife's job and constitute a contribution both to social welfare and to her husband's business.

Not only the wife but several relatives may be working in the same family business. Relatives do not necessarily occupy high positions, and some distant relatives may even be hired as low-level manual workers. Business families are known for the close ties among relatives in the business, but tensions and conflicts often arise between relatives as to the position and pay each should have. Work relationships often require authority and obedience which seem incompatible with the close relationship of relatives, and it is often a matter of dispute as to whether the worker should be treated primarily as a relative or as an employee. The solution to these problems is not always clear, but there is no question that competence is important in determining the tasks to which relatives are assigned.

The distribution of top positions depends, however, to some extent on kinship position. It is hard to imagine, for example, a younger brother as president with a father or elder brother as vice-president. If he is in the same firm as an elder brother, a younger brother may not be given much room for independent maneuvers, and his wife may take a less active role in the business than the older brother's wife. In larger organizations, an employee works up gradually, but in a family firm the businessman may have the same position for many years, depending on the constellation of relatives in the business. However, if a senior executive dies or if the company expands rapidly, a relative suddenly may be given weighty responsibilities.

Although family and business are closely connected and a wife may often go with her husband to business or ceremonial functions and help promote his work through skillful use of friendships, the businessman is almost completely removed from home affairs. He often arrives home as late as eleven or twelve at night, and sometimes even spends the night in Tokyo. As a result of this full schedule he sees little of his family, and although he may be fond and proud of his wife and children, he is likely to know little about their daily lives. Typically he enjoys playing with his children when they are small, but this interest generally does not carry over into the daily activities of the children in grade school and high school. While the older children may still be awake when the father comes home at night, younger children may go several days without seeing their father. The wife may go to sleep before the husband returns, waking up to greet him briefly on his arrival. A husband may arise after the children have left for school, talk with the wife briefly at breakfast, and then have the chauffeur drive him to the office. Although he may have a joking relationship with the children and may, for example, talk freely with a favorite daughter, his wife and children generally assume that there is a considerable distance between his life and theirs. They may joke with the father or tease him about his work, his associates, or his activities, but they generally assume that he will not understand or have much interest in their own activities except as they relate to the crucial decisions of education, career, and marital partner.

At times the businessman's wife feels lonely and complains that her husband is not home enough. Some wives are particularly distressed about the husband's visits to his favorite bars and geisha house where he receives special attention because of his prominence and the size of his expense account. Sometimes, although she does not readily admit it, the wife may be jealous of his affection for special girls in these bars. Usually she knows little about the details of her husband's leisure activities and though she may try to learn more about them and may in some cases know the husband's girl friends, she is not likely to interfere unless the husband fails to give her the money and facilities she desires for the home. She feels that she has much to be thankful for. Her husband provides well for her and the children, and she is treated with honor and respect in the community. She particularly appreciates their luxurious style of life for she enjoys electrical appliances, an automobile, and other material benefits still not available, even in cheaper versions, to the average salary man.

Because her husband knows so little of the children's interests and activities, and the maid performs only the simpler tasks, the wife must take over almost completely the care and management of the children, and she turns to them for companionship. She is concerned that her children uphold the family position in the community. Because of the societal stress on success, she helps the young children with their homework and hires tutors for the older children. If the children have difficulty passing entrance examinations on their own merits, she may send them to private schools where they can escape open competition with the salary man's children. She knows that even if a son fails difficult examinations, he still can assume a position of importance in his father's firm.

Capable children, who pass difficult examinations to universities, will have a choice between becoming high-level salaried employees or members of their father's business. While the bulk of the family fortunes will remain in the business, there is no difficulty providing generous financial help to all children, including those who become salary men. Indeed there is no problem in providing equal inheritance to all children.[7] As long as there is a successor in the business the parents usually will not raise serious objections if a child chooses to work for a good company or for a government bureau. If, on the other hand, there is only one son or if an elder son is already working elsewhere, there will be pressure from the parents for the boy to take over the family business. Not only will this solve the practical problems of providing a place of activity for the elderly father and permit the parents to continue the same style of life in their old age, but it gives them the satisfaction that their efforts will continue to bear fruit in the coming generation.

If two or three sons are interested in the business, they can divide the responsibilities within the firm. While the elder son may have more power than younger sons, it is not the exclusive power that accrues to the family head in the traditional rural family. If a family has no son, the daughter is likely to be married to an enterprising and talented young man who would be competent enough to take over the business and continue the family line. But while the concept of the family line remains strong, it is probably not so strong as in the rural areas and is closely tied to the interest in continuing the family firm. Business families do not make sharp distinctions between the elder brother who continues the family line and all other children who are outsiders, but they do distinguish all children who enter the business from those who do not.

Indeed, even the responsibility of looking after the elderly, keeping up the family plot, the family graveyard, and the family treasures is likely to go to the child or children who remain in the family business. Those who remain in the business consider family tradition important, much more so than do most salary-men families. Indeed, business families usually have more in their family history which they can point to with pride. Sometimes these families have

---

[7] In rural areas, where division of a family farm into smaller parts would often make it impossible for anyone to make a living, the postwar law requiring equal inheritance has created serious problems, and various informal techniques have been developed to try to avoid dividing the property. Because these businesses are large enough to absorb all sons, there is no such problem.

a particularly distinguished ancestor or a family line which has been kept intact for many generations. Sometimes they have swords, festival dolls, ornaments, prints, scrolls, or books of calligraphy which have been passed down as family treasures for several generations. These heirlooms and family rites for the departed are important because they are symbols of the prominence of the family, distinguishing it from the "ordinary" families in the community.

THE INDEPENDENT PROFESSIONAL

Since most college graduates, including law-school alumni, are employed in large organizations, the only independent professionals in Mamachi are doctors and dentists. There are no specialists within dentistry, but most doctors specialize in either internal medicine, surgery, pediatrics, or obstetrics-gynecology. In Tokyo, many doctors work for large hospitals, but the doctors in Mamachi are in private practice, with their offices and a few hospital beds attached to their homes. Because a doctor in private practice ordinarily does not have an affiliation with an outside hospital, these beds are necessary to perform operations or look after patients who require constant care; the Japanese word usually translated as "doctor's office" (*iin*) actually denotes both the office and these facilities for the patient to stay overnight.

Ancillary professions are not well-developed, but the doctor generally has one or two assistants who perform the combined duties of nurse, medical technician, and cleaning lady, or, in the case of the dentist, the duties of dental technician and maid. In some establishments, the wife may perform the more professional aspects of the work, and an assistant may also serve as the maid in the family household as well as the nursing assistant. In others, assistants may perform all of this work. The doctor's relationship with these assistants is likely to be very close and paternalistic, and the assistants may even live with the family.

The independent professional has neither the heavy financial reserves of the successful businessman nor the large organizational backing of the salary man. His security rests entirely on his skill in building up a large practice. He generally establishes a practice in his neighborhood and maintains a close personal relationship with his regular patients. Patients are likely to select their doctor on the basis of convenience of location, his general attitude and reputation, and the introduction of friends. The Mamachi doctor's business interests are more overt than those of his American counterpart. He dispenses drugs to his patients for a profit, and he may also operate his ward at a profit. He is permitted to advertise, and at the least he has a billboard calling attention to his location. Since the financial security of his family depends on his practice, he tries to accumulate some savings. Some professionals have formed mutual-benefit groups to help a member's family in case of need, but usually they cannot equal the security offered by the large organization in times of economic recession, accident, sickness, or retirement.

Setting up a private practice poses considerable financial risks because it requires a sizeable outlay of initial capital for machinery, much more so than a few years ago. With the standardization of medical education through medical schools, the cost of education has risen, and the age at which one can begin earning has also risen. It may take many years of practice before a young doctor can build up a practice, repay his debts to benefactors, and earn a comfortable living. Only a few decades ago it was common to serve a long period of apprenticeship with another doctor or dentist and then open a practice with the help of the older doctor and the savings accumulated during the apprenticeship. Most middle-aged practitioners of Mamachi got their start this way and now have no difficulty making an adequate living. Indeed, their income tends to be much higher than that of the salary man.

The basic problem confronting the older practitioners is that of assimilating the technical advances introduced from the West since the war. Some have not kept fully abreast of these changes, but other conscientious doctors have enrolled in special courses in addition to reading professional journals and attending special lectures or demonstrations sponsored by their former university or by the medical societies. The amount of skill required for such technical work and the individual responsibility for pursuing training while engaging in practice have made this problem particularly acute among the professionals.

Unlike the successful businessman who has broad responsibilities in community affairs, a doctor's activities, with few exceptions, are limited to his relationships with his patients, relatives, and professional colleagues. So much of his time is spent in his office or calling on his patients, that he has little time for outside activities. His professional relationships are more likely to be determined by the school he attended than by the community in which he now lives. Not only do fellow alumni have professional relationships but together they may engage in the full range of leisure-time activities, including drinking, group games, parties, and trips. Some doctors feel competitive with other doctors in Mamachi, but they generally do not feel competitive with fellow alumni. However, because of professional ethics and a steady clientele and income, doctors and dentists do not compete as bitterly as, for example, small shopkeepers.

Like successful businessmen, doctors rarely make a sharp separation between work and leisure hours, and to some extent working hours are determined by the arrival of patients. Most offices are open until eight or nine in the evening, and even in non-emergency situations, patients sometimes call the doctor at later hours. It has not been customary to schedule appointments, but now some doctors are attempting to set up regular appointments. The doctor-patient relationship is now coming to resemble the more contractual business-like arrangements between doctor and patient in the West, but even now, some patients bring presents and pay on a more informal basis than in the West. As one dentist jokingly remarked, he was starting to charge his customers standard prices just as if he were running a department store. For doctors, the standardization of prices has been greatly accelerated by the national health insurance which has set up a regular scale of fees. Nevertheless, doctors often do engage in informal visiting with a patient, provided there is no pressing work.

Because of the physical proximity of office to family, the doctor-husband spends considerable time at home, eating and visiting with the family between patients. Hence, he knows more about family activities, and exercises more authority in the home than the salary man or the businessman. For example, he may decide when his nurse or office assistant will help his wife with housework. If his wife is also his nurse, bill collector, and drug mixer, she is likely to be under her husband's constant supervision. Even the wife who does not help in his office and has a maid for the home does not have the freedom from her husband's wishes that wives of salaried employees or of successful businessmen have. Concurrently, the wife is likely to know more about the activities of her husband, and he can have few monetary secrets from her. She has less reason to worry about her husband's recreational activities and expenses than the wife of the businessman, but she may get tired of her husband's tight supervision of her daily activities and may even wish that he spent less time at home.

Because professionals typically have more money than salaried employees, they are more likely to own the household articles they desire. Nevertheless, the decision to purchase may create more anxiety and worry than in the family of the salary man. Since professionals feel they must rely on their own savings in case of emergency, they are likely to put a large portion of their income into savings for emergencies and every purchase detracts from security. Despite the concern over savings, however, the successful private practitioner is likely to have a better house and furnishings than the average salary man.

To assure themselves of continuing income in old age, most professional families strongly encourage one of their children to take over the practice. The nature of family succession makes the independent professional family pattern most similar to the traditional farm family system. Just as the farm family often had too small a plot of land to divide among several sons, so the independent professional has a practice too small to divide among his children. One son is likely to inherit not only the practice but the home as well, and often this son and his wife and children continue to live with the parents even after the father's retirement. The son who inherits the father's practice is likely to be closer to his parents even before he goes into practice and to be allowed more participation in family decisions and arrangements. The other sons are then forced to go elsewhere and receive less financial help from their parents. Since passing on a practice to a son is a psychological and financial advantage to the father and an even greater financial advantage to the son, it is not surprising that a large percentage of dental and medical students are children of professionals who intend to take over their fathers' practice, or children of nonprofessionals who hope to marry a girl whose father has a practice to pass on. For these reasons, the stem family remains a viable form among independent professionals.

For the son who succeeds to the father's profession, entrance examinations for a particular school are not overly important; as long as the son can get into any medical or dental school he will be able to continue his father's practice. For other sons who are likely to become salary men, examinations are more important, but professional fathers can finance private education more easily than salary men and therefore examination pressure on their sons is not so great.

Since the independent professional has little hope of being as powerful a community leader as the successful businessman, he is more likely to compare himself with the salary man. He has neither the security nor the short regular hours of the salary man. His style of life tends to be more comfortable than that of the salary man, and he can avoid the long daily commuting. If commuting time is added to working hours, the salary man probably puts in almost as many hours as the professional. The independent professional generally feels that his real advantage lies in his freedom to work when and how he pleases without having continually to strive to satisfy his superiors.

THE SHOPKEEPER

Mamachi has few factories and craft shops compared to some suburbs, and the lower groups on the social ladder consist mostly of shopkeepers. Because the shops carry a limited range of goods, they require little capital or training and offer little security. Because of the difficulties in accumulating capital, obtaining loans, or getting customers beyond easy walking distance, their opportunities for expansion are relatively limited.

The shopkeeper family depends upon a small daily income and must continuously struggle to make ends meet. At the present time, as department stores take over an increasing proportion of retail trade, many small shops are failing, and others are afraid of failing. Because of this fear, even the more successful shopkeepers live on a very tight budget which allows them only the barest necessities.

Although sales are small, shopkeepers work long hours for very little profit. There are some agreements among certain kinds of shopkeepers to close one or two days a month, but competition is still relatively uncontrolled by any association of shopkeepers so that no one dares to close earlier or remain closed one day a week for fear that some of his business might go elsewhere. Most shopkeepers work a seven-day week, closing for only two or three holidays a year, opening as early as eight every morning and remaining open until ten or eleven in the evening. The work itself is not difficult, and between customers the shopkeeper can relax in his home; but the economic pressure is unrelenting.

Because of these long hours, there is little opportunity for any activity unrelated to the work. Some husbands may go out for recreation at times, if the wife and children can remain to care for the shop. The wife and children may try to prevent his outside activities since it may burden them with extra work and since the husband may spend part of their small income on a whim of his own.

While the relationships with customers are usually cordial, the relationships with other merchants, even between shops in different lines of business, tend to be unfriendly.[8] In general, shopkeepers seem to feel that the other neighbors, like themselves, live a miserable existence and do not wish to associate themselves with such a life.

Because they can operate the business in his absence, the wife and children are not so completely dependent on the husband for income. In contrast to the small craft shops which require physical labor and ordinarily can be operated only by men, a number of shops are operated by widows and children.

Since the husband and wife normally work together most of the time, they have a much closer relationship than any of the other occupational groups, but not necessarily a happier one. Family pleasures are sacrificed for business considerations, and the wife particularly feels harrassed by the pressures of work and the lack of time for herself or her children. She is envious of salaried men's wives whose days are devoted to the home while she must care for her children only in odd moments. She often carries a small child on her back while working in the store or even nurses between customers. Older children may be left alone in the living quarters while the mother is called out in the front to take care of a customer. Because they are almost always together, the husband has even

---

[8] In sentence-completion tests given to shopkeepers in another community, the responses to items about neighbors were almost universally critical and bitter.

more opportunity to give orders to his wife than the independent professional does, but shopkeepers' wives, feeling that they make a major contribution to family income, are often free in expressing their opinions to the husbands.

Although the general economic level of shopkeepers is much lower than that of professionals or salary men, some successful shopkeepers with several assistants or boarders from the country can have a style of life not too different from that of independent professionals, except that they have less security and the wife has less time for her children and for community activities.

The poor long-term economic prospects offer little motivation for passing the shops from one generation to the next. Many shops have been opened by migrants from the country who had no contacts for a better job, and a few of them have been opened by elderly people who had no other opportunity for making a living. Even if the business continues long enough to have a successor, it is not large enough for more than a single successor, and there is little enthusiasm for having a child follow this unsatisfactory way of life. If a son is capable enough to get a good job in a factory or to pass school examinations despite the lack of assistance from the family, the parents are pleased and honored. However, because the parents lack the educational background, time, and interest to help a child with his homework and because the children themselves are often busy working in the store, the likelihood of such children doing well on examinations is much less than that of children of salary men of equal intelligence. Many shopkeepers regard their present work as temporary and dream of getting a better job in a small firm or office. Yet they have little basis for expecting that their dreams will be realized, and in the meantime they cling to what little they have.

THE SALARY MAN

The salary men,[9] who dominate Mamachi both in spirit and num-

---

* No attempt has been made in this chapter to trace in detail all variations of occupational groups living in Mamachi but only to highlight certain major patterns. However, one pattern not discussed separately because of its over-all similarity to the salary man requires special mention because of its numerical frequency: the white-collar worker in the small company.

In contrast to the salary man, the white-collar worker in the small company lacks

bers, range from high-level managers to humble office clerks, from the powerful elite to servile office boys. But whatever the variation, they all tend to live an orderly life, made possible by long-term membership in a large and stable bureaucratic organization. A salary man receives his pay regularly and can predict within a close range his position and salary of five, ten, fifteen, or even twenty years hence. He may not be able to name the department of the company in which he will work, but he can predict with such accuracy when he will become section head that he will be bitterly disappointed if he receives even a small promotion only a year later than he had originally expected. Business fluctuations affect the size of his bonus, but they are likely to have little effect on his salary because the company continues to meet its commitments to him even in time of economic difficulty. A typical salary man never receives an offer from another firm, but even if he were to receive an attractive offer from elsewhere, his long-term interests are best served by remaining in the same firm because his salary and benefits rise sharply with the number of years of service and he knows that he will be dismissed from his own company only for the grossest incompetence or misbehavior.

In addition, he knows that in the event of sickness, accident, or retirement, he unquestionably will receive welfare benefits. The

the security that comes with a large organization. His wages are generally lower than the salary man's, and the company is not able to provide so many fringe benefits. While he may have a personal relationship with his employer, he is more likely to have changed companies, either because the previous business failed or because he was dissatisfied with the benefits he received. While some small promising concerns attract talented men and are able to advance them more rapidly than the more routinized large organizations, generally the workers have less education and have attended less-well-known schools than the salary men. There is great variation in these small organizations—more than between the standardized and routinized large organizations. It is therefore more difficult to generalize about the white-collar worker in the small concern than about the salary man. Frequently, however, the white-collar worker in the smaller concern is essentially a lower-ranking and less secure salary man, and many comments in the present volume apply to large groups of these men as well as to salary men.

The worker in the large factory, while of lower class standing, has many of the characteristics of the salary man: he has security and regularity, and his family affairs are relatively isolated from company affairs except when he lives in a factory-sponsored apartment house.

To heighten the contrast, I have included small shopkeepers and successful businessmen. There are also middle-size businessmen in Mamachi who fall somewhere in between and are perhaps closer in style of life to the independent professionals than any other group described here.

successful independent businessman can provide his own security against sickness and injury by his large income and savings; the independent professional must save carefully for such contingencies; the small shopkeeper has almost no hope of being able to cope with such emergencies. The salary man has security, not through his own savings or power, but through the company which, in effect, gives him a guaranteed income and insurance against various kinds of difficulties that he and his family might encounter.[10]

The salary man, then, has security, but his stipend is, after all, rather small in comparison with the successful businessman or even in comparison with the independent professional. Hence, he must carefully control his spending. Perhaps the greatest financial difficulty he will face is the period after retirement. His company will provide some retirement benefits, either in the form of a lump sum or pension, but generally these are small, barely enough for minimum subsistence. The salary man usually is required to retire as early as fifty-five or sixty years of age; afterward, to supplement his company's retirement benefits, he must turn to his savings, supplementary income, or his children, although sometimes his company will help him find a part-time job after retirement. A retired teacher, for example, may get a job as a part-time consultant to a book company. A man with rich relatives or friends may get a part-time job working for them. Some of the less successful may open a small shop. Many have no choice but to live with their children.

The daily life of the salary man is the essence of regularity. Although commuting trains generally run to Tokyo every five or seven minutes, the salary man knows precisely on what train he leaves in the morning. Theoretically, he is expected to work overtime with little or no extra compensation whenever his firm requests it, and

---

[10] In our sentence-completion tests given to other suburban areas of Tokyo, one of the questions concerned sickness. The answers show that the salary man was much less anxious about sickness than the small shopkeeper who has no such security. In case of sickness, 33 of the salaried respondents simply said they would go to the doctor, 4 said that they would be more careful, 7 said that this would give them an opportunity to rest up, and 5 said it would give worry to their family. Of 69 small businessmen, no respondent said he would simply go to a doctor; 23 said that they would be worried, extremely anxious; 9 said that their families would be depressed, and 12 others said that they would be worried about money. The remaining replies covered a wide range, but they generally reflected a much greater concern among the small businessmen about sickness and accidents than among the more secure salaried groups.

he is reluctant to take all the free time to which he is officially entitled. For example, he may be given ten days or two weeks annual vacation, but he ordinarily would not take this much time off. If he were to request his full vacation time, he would be regarded as selfish and disloyal by his co-workers and by his superiors.[11] However, at the same time companies find it increasingly difficult to ask their salary men to work overtime. The salary men have become used to regular hours and regard overtime work without extra compensation as an encroachment on their freedom. They have no objection to working their eight or nine hours a day Monday through Friday and until mid-afternoon on Saturday. But they resent being made to work longer hours.

It is the salary man who makes the sharpest distinction between working time and free time. In contrast to the businessman who mixes business and leisure, to the small shopkeeper who has almost no leisure, and to the independent professional, whose leisure is determined by the absence of patients, the salary man, like his child in school, generally has set hours so that he knows he can plan certain hours of the day and certain days of the week for himself and his family.

In addition to regularity, security, and free time, the companies provide various side benefits which constitute the joy of living. The salary man attends parties, athletic meets, and even trips sponsored by the company. At least once or twice a year, the company treats its employees to an overnight trip to the country, and on other occasions employees take up voluntary collections for company trips.

The salary man usually cannot afford such luxuries as a car or expensive entertainment, but occasionally he can use the company expense account for such privileges. To an American, an expense account may give added comfort, but to the Japanese salary man it means enjoying pleasures he otherwise could not hope to afford. Even on a personal trip, he can often stay at an inn at a discount obtained through his company. Some government bureaus and large businesses or their unions own inns which can at times be used by

---

[11] Such practices make it difficult for Japan to enforce "maximum working hour" laws. Even if a firm officially sets a maximum number of hours, the worker would be afraid to complain if the firm in fact required him to work more hours.

employees. If a salary man wishes to entertain his family on a festive occasion, he may use company contacts to rent inexpensively a room in a *Kaikan,* a special building for just such purposes. (*Kaikan* are used for meetings and entertainment, much as American hotels are, but since Japanese homes are not considered adequate to entertain a group of any size, *Kaikan* are used more widely than hotels in America.) Depending on the nature of the company, the salary man can get goods or special services at a discount. A worker in a large electrical industry, for example, can get a big discount for his family and friends on electrical equipment. A man working for Japan Airlines may be entitled to as many as five free rides for himself or a family member per year. Although such benefits are not always available to the average salary man, the fact that the large organizations offer more benefits than smaller enterprises helps explain the enthusiasm which the salary man feels toward his organization and which he manifests by wearing a company badge, carrying a company brief case, and using a company emblem as a tie clasp.

Foreign observers have described Japanese firms as paternalistic since they look after so many aspects of the employee's life. Yet large firms, in at least one fundamental respect, are much less paternalistic than the traditional small enterprises. In the large firm, privileges are established by routine procedures or rules; they are less determined by a particular relationship to an employer, the whims of superiors, or the fluctuation in the company's financial condition. Rather, they tend to be awarded universally to all members of the organization on the basis of seniority and ability.

The salary man's contacts are largely restricted to his work associates and to his own immediate family. He lacks the prestige to have important community positions and the money for anything but the simplest entertainment. He spends many evenings at home with the family, and may go on Sunday with the family to the city, perhaps to visit a large park or a department store. For week-day recreation, he and his work associates stop off after work at their favorite bars, tea or coffee houses, or snack bars. Because he expects to be in the same organization all his life, his closest relationships are with work associates and he considers it of utmost importance to keep their friendship.

The salary man is essentially free when he returns home; home is a place to relax. In some cases the salary man, in contrast to other husbands, may even help his wife, albeit not as much as his American counterpart. He may know how to make his own tea and, in extreme cases, he may even know how to cook. He occasionally may help the children with their baths, fold up his own bedding, do a few shopping errands, and go for walks with the children.

However, the wife generally knows little and cares less about her husband's daily activities at the office. She has virtually no opportunity to go out with her husband to meet other men in the company and their wives. The husband's assignments in the company generally are limited, and the problems in which the husband is interested at work have little meaning to the wife. Even if a curious young wife expresses an interest in her husband's work, he has difficulty explaining his work in a way that she can understand and hence he gets little satisfaction in telling her about the details of his work. Because she is so completely separated from the husband's daily world and he knows so little about her community activities, the area of mutual interest tends to be the children and the relatives.

Although the salary man's wife does not understand precisely what her husband does, unless she has unusually high ambitions she is usually satisfied with her husband's position in a large company. From her point of view, the major advantages of her husband's job are the regular hours and wages. She can count on his being home certain hours and she can count on his income. It is possible for the wife to manage household expenses without worrying about how much the income will be next month, or where it will come from. In comparison to the shopkeeper's wife and even to the independent professional, she is happy that she does not have to subject herself to the indignities of long hours of hard work. She can take care of the children and devote herself to them as she wishes. In comparison with the wives on the farm or the shopkeepers' wives, she lives a life of freedom and luxury. She does not have the same desire as her American counterpart to go out and get a job on her own and she does not have the same kind of feelings about being "just a housewife." She is delighted that she can devote herself to her family with so few outside demands.

In planning the children's future it is the salary man and his family who are most dependent on entrance examinations. Unlike the independent professional or the businessman, who can take the children into his own work regardless of the educational institutions the children attended, and unlike the shopkeeper who has lower aspirations for his children, the salary man's children are dependent upon entrance examinations to universities and companies. Hence, they generally place more pressure on their children and spend more time and energy to prepare them for these examinations.

The salary man's family is likely to be limited to parents and children.[12] Association with relatives has nothing to do with business and tends to be based more on mutual liking than on reciprocal obligations. In the businessman's family, there is often a business tie with relatives which keeps the children and the parents together. The son who takes over his father's professional practice is also likely to have close business ties with his parents. Children of shopkeepers help their parents when young, and occasionally one child may succeed to the shop. In the salary man's family, however, there is no such economic bond between parents and children. Because a son's life is more determined by his education and the organization to which he belongs than the size of his inheri-

---

[12] While not analyzed precisely in terms of the occupations mentioned here, the following data, given by the Ministry of Health and Welfare for 1960 is at least suggestive since there is a heavy overlap between "employee" and "salary man." Takashi Koyama in Robert J. Smith and Richard K. Beardsley, eds., *Japanese Culture*, New York: The Viking Fund, 1962.

Type of household	Agriculture	Owner-Manager	Employee
		in percent	
Nuclear family only	37.6	68.4	73.5
Includes relatives in direct line	53.5	24.4	19.4
Includes other relatives	8.8	7.2	7.0

The number of children also tends to be smaller in the salary-man family. In 1952, the Institute of Population Problems in the Welfare Ministry noted a national average of 3.5 children per family. Physical laborers averaged 4.7, farmers 4.1, people in commerce and industry 3.2, and white-collar workers 2.9. Cited in Yoshiharu Scott Matsumoto, *Contemporary Japan: The Individual and the Group*, Philadelphia: The American Philosophical Society, 1960.

tance, and the daughter's marriage more dependent on her training and character than the size of the dowry, parents devote themselves to preparing their children properly for work and marriage rather than to accumulating a large inheritance.

Distinctions between the first son and the second son tend to lose significance in the salary man's family. No son succeeds to family headship in any meaningful economic way so that the postwar regulations requiring that inheritance be divided equally among the children poses no problem for the salaried man. Inheritance of family ritual objects generally goes to one son, but a more important problem which leads to a partial preservation of the stem family is the location of elderly parents after retirement. Retirement payments are minimal, and parents usually find it necessary to live with the children if they are to retain the same standard of living after retirement. In addition, elderly couples ordinarily have few opportunities to be integrated into a community except through their children. All children may share the financial responsibility, but the retired parents, and especially a widowed mother, ordinarily continue to live with only one of the children.

The salary man cannot hope to match the style of life of the successful independent businessman. But psychologically he derives a feeling of power by belonging to the large organization. The fact that in Japan a person is so closely identified with the group to which he belongs gives the salary man a backing which enables him in important respects to look down on the businessmen and independent professionals, who have more real power in the local community.

With this brief perspective on the significance of working in a large bureaucratic organization, it is now possible to take up in greater detail the various facets of the life of the salary man. We may begin by considering the process of becoming a salary man, the preparing for and taking of examinations, and the impact of this process on the family. We may then describe the relations between the family and the major subsystems of Japanese society, the internal family processes, and finally consider some implications of the present study for the problem of maintaining order in Japanese society.

Chapter III

THE GATEWAY TO SALARY:
INFERNAL ENTRANCE EXAMINATIONS

No single event, with the possible exception of marriage, determines the course of a young man's life as much as entrance examinations, and nothing, including marriage, requires as many years of planning and hard work. Because all colleges and high schools, and many private junior high schools, grade schools, and even kindergartens use entrance examinations to select only a small proportion of the applicants, and because examinations are open to all,[1] the competition is fierce. Passing examinations to a good school seems as difficult to the Mamachi resident as for a camel to pass through the eye of a needle. There is virtually no limit to how much one can prepare for examinations. The average child studies so hard that Japanese educators speak of the tragedy of their school system which requires students to sacrifice their pleasures, spontaneity, and sparkle for examination success. These arduous preparations constitute a kind of *rite de passage* whereby a young man proves that he has the qualities of ability and endurance necessary for becoming a salary man. The Japanese commonly refer to entrance examinations as *shiken jigoku* which literally means "examination hell."

The Mamachi youth is willing to endure these tortures because if successful he will be able to join a large successful firm where he can remain for life.[2] To be admitted to such a firm, one must

---

[1] This is in contrast to many developing countries where for reason of race, language, ethnic discrimination, or financial requirements, the opportunities are limited to certain groups in the population.

[2] Abegglan argues that the key differences between Japanese and American factories is the Japanese factory's life-long commitment to the employee. James G. Abegglan, *The Japanese Factory: Aspects of Its Social Organization*, Glencoe, Ill.: The Free Press, 1958.

Recent evidence indicates that there is in fact considerable mobility, even of

attend a good university, and to attend a good university one must pass the entrance examination. To pass the entrance examination for a good university one must have good training, and to acquire the good training one must pass the entrance examination to a good high school. In the final analysis, success is determined not by intelligence tests, nor by the school record, nor by the teacher's recommendations but by entrance examinations.

Although it seems a tragedy to the participants, there is a certain logic in how the examination system works. Because the firm commits itself to a young man for life and because business in contemporary Japan is highly competitive, the firm must be careful to select men of unusual promise and ability. The number of men a large firm takes in each year is so large and the number of personal connections of company officials so great that it would be impossible to use personal evaluations as the primary basis to select applicants. One need only imagine the problems of large numbers of company employees each urging the company to support his favorite candidate, to understand the convenience and value of a more universalistic basis of judgment. Because there is such wide agreement in Japanese society as to which universities are most desirable, firms consider the university attended as important or even more important than their own examinations for selecting salary men. Not only the university's relative standing, but even its style of life, has considerable stability over time, because of the practice of inbreeding. Nearly all professors at a major university have received their

---

people working in large firms, but it has greatly declined since the war. Kenichi Tominaga, "Occupational Mobility in Japanese Society: Analysis of the Labor Market in Japan" (mimeographed, 1962). Also, Koji Taira, "Characteristics of Japanese Labor Markets," *Economic Development and Cultural Change,* 1962, X:150–168.

Even if there is mobility, however, it may be to a company affiliated with the original company or through arrangements made by people within this company.

Even new or expanding firms prefer young people. One Mamachi industrialist opening a new plant kept expanding for three years before the plant reached full size. The new employees were admitted annually, immediately following graduation from high school or junior high school. He felt, like most Japanese employers, that he would have a greater likelihood of getting competent employees this way than by recruiting older people from elsewhere.

The age of Japanese farmers at time of entering a master's service was historically important in determining whether they would be granted highly desired semi-independent status. Those who entered service at a younger age were more likely to be rewarded with such status. Cf. Thomas C. Smith, *The Agrarian Origins of Modern Japan,* Stanford, California: Stanford University Press, 1959.

training at the same institution, and it is almost unthinkable for a professor to move from one major university to another.[3] Organizations add to this stability by selecting applicants according to the university's reputation. Young applicants know which universities the firms prefer and choose their university accordingly, thus perpetuating the emphasis on the university attended as a basis for selecting competent young men.

A large company ordinarily hires older workers only when absolutely necessary and even then gives more security and more rapid pay increases to younger employees. Here again, there is a self-fulfilling accuracy to the company's predictions. People who do change companies tend to be opportunistic and less devoted to the company's interests, and the company feels justified in hiring workers directly from college making work experience irrelevant as a criterion.

From the view of the outside observer entrance examinations involve an intensity of affect which cannot be explained only by the desire to obtain a good job. Although the search for security has rational components, as mentioned before, it has been heightened by the many upheavals in the lifetime of the average adult and by the difficulty which the contemporary urban parent had in finding a long-term livelihood when he was young. For the urban resident, a job in a large corporation is as close as one can come to the security that country relatives have by belonging to a household firmly attached to land and the local community. Just as obtaining land is thought to secure the future of a family even in the next generation, so does a job in a large corporation provide long-range security and insure that one's children can be given a proper position in life.

There are now opportunities in Japanese society for adventurous and talented young men, especially in new fields like electronics, advertising, entertainment, and foreign trade. New small companies in these fields can offer higher salaries than larger organizations, but

---

[3] They may, however, move from this major institution to smaller institutions, and then from there to better universities or back to this major university. It is unlikely, however, that they would ever move to a major university other than the one they attended.

most young men are unwilling to take this risk of less security; however, those who do not pass the entrance examinations to a good university may have no other choice.

But even if one wants to work in a smaller company, attending a good university makes it easier to get a good job and even to change jobs at a later time.[4] Once a student has passed an entrance examination to a first-rate university, he has no worry about graduating because the university is committed to his success and would dismiss him only for extreme misbehavior or incompetence. Compared to American state universities, which dismiss a large proportion of first-year students, the number of students failed from Japanese universities is negligible. Moreover, students do not transfer from one university to another. Being admitted to a given university becomes, in effect, a basis of ascription which provides fairly clear limits to one's later mobility.

Although students in a good university may still be concerned about being accepted by the best possible organization, the range of differences in status between the corporations or government bureaus they will join is relatively narrow. The room for achievement within the company is also relatively minor compared to whether one attended an outstanding university and whether one was admitted to a large reputable organization. To a large extent advancement within the firm depends simply on the date of entry into the organization. All new members of a company are admitted on the same day each year, go through the same general training program, and are treated as equals in most matters, such as salary and position. Even when employees begin to get different functional assignments, seniority remains relatively more important than skill and ability in determining rank and salary. An employee's standing vis-à-vis outsiders is determined when he enters the firm, and is little affected by the minor differentiations of status within the firm.

Even if some students from a lesser university are admitted to a

---

[4] The importance of the university attended is clearly greater for a salary man than for independent professionals or independent businessmen. The success of the young man who takes over his father's practice or business is determined not by the school attended but the size of his father's enterprise and his own ability. However, if family prestige or tradition is tied with a given university, it may be important for prestige purposes to attend that university regardless of economic significance.

good company or government office, they still may be at a disadvantage compared to those who attended the better universities. While some say that cliques of graduates of a given high school or university are weaker than before the war, fellow alumni of the same university are known to show preferences for their fellow graduates. It is assumed that those who attended a certain university (and sometimes even a certain department within a university) will feel mutual loyalty and share similar attitudes, making it possible for them to work together harmoniously despite differences of opinion and temperament. Especially in large government bureaus, acceptance in informal circles and even rate of advancement may be affected by the university one attended.

This analysis has focused on the boy and his problem of entering a large organization, but similar considerations apply to girls even though their career is marriage. Girls generally worry less about examinations than boys. Some people even question whether a girl who has attended the most competitive coeducational universities will make a good wife, and many girls prefer not to go to a co-educational school where they would have to study harder to keep up with the boys. But the better girls' schools are regarded as highly desirable, and these schools also require entrance examinations. Marital choice even in urban Japan is still decided in large part on the basis of objective criteria rather than simply on the diffuse relationship between a young man and a young lady, and the university or school attended has become an even more important criterion than ascriptive considerations like family background. Indeed, a boy's family proudly speaks of marrying a girl who attended a well-known girls' school just as her family will speak proudly of a young man who attended a good university. Thus, examinations are crucial to the girl's as well as to the boy's career.

In the view of the Mamachi resident, one's station in life is not predetermined by birth, but it is determined by the time one has his first job. For those who aspire to the new middle class, the opportunities for mobility are highly compressed into one period of life, late adolescence. The intense concentration of pressure for finding one's position in life during this brief time is undoubtedly related to the fact that Japan is the one country in the world where the suicide rate is high in the late teens and early twenties and declines during middle age.[5] Success or failure in finding the right opening at the time of college admission is considered permanent, and failure or fear of failure is disturbing even to the most talented.

PREPARING FOR AND TAKING EXAMINATIONS

Mamachi residents are careful in their selection of schools, and the range and variety of possible choices are enormous. At the apex of educational life are the great national universities, such as Tokyo University, and the well-known public high schools, such as Hibiya and Shinjuku, which students of all social classes can afford to enter if they pass the examinations. Next are the good private universities and the attached private elementary, junior, and senior high schools. Entrance examinations for these schools are almost as difficult as those for the best public institutions but tuition is higher, so that only well-to-do students can attend. Thirdly, there are public and private schools of lesser quality ranging from expensive schools which few salary men can afford, to public and less expensive private schools widely attended by children of salary men. At the bottom of the scale are the local public elementary and junior high schools, the only schools which do not require entrance examinations.

All students are required by law to complete junior high school, but any student who wishes to go beyond must take examinations. (The length of compulsory education is not determined by age but by number of years [nine] of schooling. No student is failed. One might speculate that failing students would arouse the same kind of threat to group solidarity as discharging a man from a firm.) It is assumed that once a student has been admitted to a junior or senior high school or college, he will remain in the same school until he graduates, but it is possible to change school systems at the time of each graduation. Although normally a student takes examinations in order to continue after each successive graduation, certain school systems, known as *escareetaa* (escalator) schools since students can

---

[5] It is not claimed that pressure to find the proper job or marriage opening is the only cause of the high suicide rate, but in the minds of Mamachi residents and in the popular press, there is a large connection between the two. On the basis of projective tests, Professor George De Vos has suggested that suicide in Japan is also closely related to the feeling of loneliness as a result of breaking the intense parent-child bond at the same age.

move up within the same system from kindergarten to college, have only nominal examinations for students within the same system. When a child is admitted to an outstanding kindergarten such as those associated with Keio University (private) and Ochanomizu Women's University (public), he is thought to be on the *escareetaa* and established for life. Thus, a heavy premium is placed on getting into the kindergarten of the *escareetaa* schools, and the schools charge higher tuition for kindergarten than for the upper levels. The applicants to the best kindergartens are so numerous that difficult examinations cannot sort out the applicants adequately, and a lottery also is required to select the favored few. Recently, special schools have been opened in Tokyo to prepare three- and four-year-olds for the kindergarten entrance examinations.

Occasionally a Mamachi child takes these difficult kindergarten examinations, but the chance of passing is so slight, private-school costs are so high, and the daily commuting to Tokyo on public transportation is so taxing for mother and child that nearly all Mamachi children go to the local kindergartens and elementary schools. Mamachi families then concentrate on preparing their children for entrance examinations for the better junior and senior high schools and colleges, which are, by and large, in Tokyo.

Junior and senior high-school entrance examinations are not thought to be important for their own sake, but because they permit a child to get the better training that makes it easier to pass an examination to a difficult college. Because college entrance is considered so crucial, many students who fail the examination the first time may choose to wait a year and try the examination again. These students, not attached to any school or university, are called *ronin*, the name formerly used for the lordless samurai. Some persistent young people who have their hopes set on a certain school and whose families can afford to continue supporting them, may attempt the examinations several years before being admitted, in the meantime attending special preparatory schools.

Examinations, by and large, measure educational achievement. Because they must be given to large numbers, they consist mostly of objective factual questions of the multiple-choice variety. At the kindergarten level they may test the child's knowledge of the Japanese syllabary, perhaps a few characters, and elementary arithmetic.

Junior-high and high-school examinations generally test science, Japanese language and literature, mathematics, history, and English. College examinations are similar but require more technical and specialized knowledge, especially in foreign languages.

A student ordinarily begins to prepare seriously about a year or two before the examinations that take place in January or February before the new school year begins in April. He studies several hours after school every day, and in the summer vacation preceding the February exams, he spends most of the day and sometimes part of the night in study. He often gives up movies, hobbies, and other recreation during this year of preparation. Athletes usually are advised to drop their sports activities, and music and dance lessons ordinarily are suspended.

In the year preceding the examination the mother spends much time investigating expenses, entrance requirements, and the schools' records in successfully placing their graduates. She visits schools, reads advice columns and books, and gathers information from friends. In addition, she spends much time consulting with her child's teacher and other parents in order to assess her own child's abilities. Naturally she wants her child to get into the best possible school, but this requires strategy and risk-taking. A child can take as many as three or four examinations if they are not offered on the same date, but it is seldom possible to take more. If a child fails all these, he may be out of luck. In addition, the process of taking examinations is tiring for the student and his mother, and they frequently require money payments. If a student tries to take three or four examinations during the same season, he may be so exhausted and discouraged from the first ones that he will not perform well on the later ones. Hence it is important for the mother to assess her child's abilities accurately and have the child take the most appropriate examinations.

The mother does most of the ground work but she must make sure that the father and the child approve her choices. The child's veto of a school is usually final, for while the mother often persuades a child to accept her choice, without his co-operation and hard work, the mother can have little hope of success. The mother does not want to risk being solely responsible for the choice of schools in case the child fails, and she is likely to consult with the father.

Indeed, the family is likely to have frequent and sometimes heated discussions during the period of decision-making.

By late January these initial decisions are made, and the process of application begins. A candidate can apply only during an allotted two or three days. The mother applies in person, taking health certificates, school records, and the entrance fees. At almost every school on the first day of applications, there will be a few mothers who have waited in line overnight with their small snack and cushions, so that they will be among the first to apply. These mothers know that schools state that arrival time makes no difference. But apparently they hope that they may impress the school administration with their seriousness of purpose, that the low number on the application blank may be lucky, or that their child may be called for the examination early in the day and hence be somewhat fresher in taking the examinations. Their early arrival simply may reflect anxiety and excitement and a desire to get the application process over with. While most Mamachi mothers think it somewhat foolish to wait overnight, nevertheless many start out on the first train leaving Mamachi, at about four o'clock in the morning, on the day when applications are due. Even then, there may be a long line when they arrive, and those who have enough courage to come later in the day may have a wait of several hours before filling out the application. A mother who is going through the application procedure for the first time or who is applying for her only son is more likely to be among the first in line. If a woman is a "beteran" (veteran) she may be confident enough to come much later.[6] Sometimes it is necessary for the children to go along with the mother for applications, but for a college application the child probably will go by himself. This same standing in line may be done three or four times, depending on the number of applications a person is making.

If a personal interview is required at the elementary and junior high school age, the mother and child will be concerned about the impressions they make. It may be desirable to bring along letters of introduction from people who have important positions or some

---

[6] One is struck by the similarities between the mother's attitudes about giving birth and about having her child take an examination. In both, there exists a great amount of folklore and advice constituting a special subculture passed down from veteran to newcomer. In the examination, however, one's odds for success are much lower, and the amount of effort required is much greater.

personal connection with the faculty, administration, or Parent-Teachers Association. Although a mother and child carefully plan what to say during this interview, it is not uncommon for the child to be frightened and to have difficulty expressing himself in the interview. Even if the mother and child consider the examination more crucial than the interview, they approach the interview as if it were of the greatest importance.

The month or so before and during examinations is commonly known as "examination season." The child studies very long hours, and if the family can afford it, a tutor comes to the house regularly. The child's household responsibilities are taken over by his brothers and sisters who are warned not to interrupt his study. In extreme cases the mother may bring him meals on a tray, sharpen his pencils, and stand ready to serve his every need. His father may come home from work early to help with the studying if the tutor is not available. The family is collectively on tiptoe for fear of disturbing the young scholar. They become almost hypochondriacal, and the slightest sign of a cold is taken seriously as a possible hindrance to examination success. Community activities and social visiting come to a complete halt, so absorbed are the families in their children's preparation. On street corners, at the neighborhood shops, in business offices, and at the dinner table, conversation revolves about the one topic of most immediate concern to all—examinations.

During the weeks around examinations, mothers of applicants try to avoid meeting other mothers and friends. Usually they leave their homes only for necessary shopping or to make arrangements for school applications. If they should meet an acquaintance accidentally, they attempt to steer conversation away from the delicate question of their child's examinations. Since a family will be embarrassed if it becomes known that their child has been refused by a school, the mothers usually do not identify the schools to which they are applying. If it is obvious to the other party, they explain that they do not expect to succeed for they have not prepared properly and they really are trying to get into another school (to which they are almost certain to be admitted). Sometimes a family denies that their child is taking a certain examination only to be discovered on the scene of the exam by the very friend who questioned them.

Children also watch closely to see who is missing from school on an examination day to ascertain which schoolmates are taking which exams. On the whole, children are more open and direct in talking about examination plans than their parents, and they often report their findings to their mothers.

Mothers accompany children to all but the college examinations to give them moral support. If the father can take off from work or if the examination is early enough in the day, he may accompany the child in place of the mother. There is a waiting room close to the examination room where parents can sit while the children are taking the examination. A number of mothers reported that they were unable to sleep on the night before the examination. By the end of a series of two or three examinations over a period of eight to ten days, mothers as well as children are so exhausted that they often have to go to bed for a few days.

There is a hiatus of several days before the results of the examinations are announced. If a child takes examinations for two or three different schools, he may hear the results of the first examination before he takes the last. Since the report of the first examination is the first real indication for the family of the child's standing, the results have an exaggerated importance. The mother whose child has passed the first examination generally is jubilant. Conversely families with a failure are extremely gloomy and pessimistic. Tensions increase as families await the results. Most people will not telephone or communicate with examination families until after the results have been announced. A few mothers and children cannot resist talking about the examinations, and worries are at least shared and discussed within the family and among some friends and relatives. Some mothers have said that there is such an ominous weighty feeling during this time that they would almost prefer to hear negative results rather than continue the uncertainty.

The dramatic climax comes with the announcement of the results. Usually grades are not mailed, but the names or code names of successful candidates are posted at the school. Sometimes the names of successful candidates for well-known schools and universities are announced on the radio. Even if a family has heard the results on the radio they also check the posted list to assure themselves that there has not been an error.

The date the list is posted usually is known long in advance, but the time of day often is indefinite. Crowds gather as much as twenty-four hours before the auspicious hour. Frequently parents will go because children might have difficulty controlling their emotions in public. Even the father may take off a day or two from work at this time to check the examination results or to be of moral support to the mother and children. People concerned about controlling their emotions go to see the bulletin board during the night. Some, attempting to be casual, wait several hours after posting to check the results.

If a child has succeeded, he and his parents are only too glad to tell the results, although they will attempt to show the proper reserve. They may whisper the result saying "please don't tell anybody else," but their smiles are irrepressible and there can be no doubt about their satisfaction. If a mother looks troubled, friends do not ask the results. Indeed, the mother of an unsuccessful candidate may cry and sleep for several days before going out to face friends. Although to my knowledge there has been no suicide in Mamachi in recent years as a result of examinations, stories of juvenile suicide as a result of examination failure are widely publicized in the mass media and well known by all those taking examinations.

Because there are so many schools in the Tokyo area and because suburban children attend so many different schools, it is rare for more than two or three students from the same grade school to continue to pass examinations for the same junior high school, high school, and college. Even if two friends should intend to take examinations for the same school in order to continue together in junior high school or high school, if one passes and the other fails, the one who succeeds will not let friendship stand in the way of attending the better school. While at first they may attempt to keep up the friendships while attending different schools, the difference in status leads to embarrassment, and the ties generally become less meaningful.

Since a large portion of Japanese universities is in Tokyo, many ambitious children from all over the country come to stay with relatives in Tokyo and Mamachi or other suburbs while taking the examinations. Although it may take forty-five minutes or an hour to commute from Mamachi to Tokyo for the examinations, inn houses are expensive and relatives in Mamachi can take the responsibility for comforting the child and seeing that he gets sufficient food and rest. The niece, nephew, or cousin probably will come to Mamachi a few days before the examination to get accustomed to the new environment and to have a good rest for a night or two before taking the examination. He may also stay on a few days after until he learns the result, but he usually is encouraged to return to his parents immediately after the examination to comfort him in case of failure. Some of the universities, at the request and expense of the student, are willing to send a telegram, indicating whether he has passed or failed. This telegram usually does not state the examination result directly, but in code. For example, a telegram indicating failure might read something like "The cherry blossoms are falling." Despite the attempt to state the result in as nice a way as possible, failure is none the less hard to bear. In other cases, the suburban family will find out the result and then telephone the rural relatives. Several families have indicated the sorrow they felt when they telephoned to pass on the news of failure, and found the phone answered by the applicant who had been waiting beside the phone.

Even families whose children are not taking the examinations cannot avoid the excitement of examination season. Notices of examinations appear everywhere in the newspapers and the weekly magazines. News reels show pictures of applicants waiting in line or taking examinations. Experts appear on television to give advice to parents or to evaluate the implications of the examination system for Japanese society. Desks, study supplies, and guides to examination success are widely advertised. Statistical reports in newspapers and in magazines indicate precisely how many students from which high schools enter which colleges. Any middle-class parent can rank the first few high schools by the number of their graduates admitted to Tokyo University, and also the leading junior high schools by the number of graduates who enter the best senior high schools. Advice columns for mothers of younger children give hints ranging from ideas for room arrangements to suggestions for motivating the child to study and for dealing with the accompanying tensions. Some people cut out these articles and save them.

Even when no child in a family is taking examinations, the parents may be called upon by relatives, friends, and even acquaintances for assistance in getting a child admitted to a good school. Because of their influence, friends of school-board members, principals, prominent school teachers, PTA officers, and alumni of a particular school, employers or superiors at work are particularly likely to receive such requests. Usually they try to be helpful to close friends and to others for whom they feel some fondness or obligation, and even if they refuse a request, they usually make at least a token effort to help. Knowing the difficult problem of gaining admission, they generally want to be as helpful as possible although they resent requests from some people who never feel the obligation to return favors.

Families with means may employ students from the most famous universities to tutor their children for examinations. Tutoring younger children provides college students with their best and most common opportunities for *arubaito* (part-time work, from the German word "Arbeit"). Students at lesser universities are less in demand and may have to be content with smaller fees. Wealthy families may use several students as tutors, each in his special field, while the ordinary salary-man family at best is able to afford a tutor only one or two nights a week. Nevertheless, even the middle-class family tries to find a tutor specializing in the subject in which their child plans to major. The tutor is generally of the same sex as the student and often provides a kind of role model, but the focus of their discussion is on preparation for examinations. Families which cannot afford a private tutor for a year or two before examinations will try to hire a tutor just before examinations or at least to join with other families in hiring a tutor for a small group of children preparing for the same examination. College students in need of money are pleased to find work as tutors since it is related to their field of study, and they generally have more free time once they themselves have been admitted to college.

When confronted with the question of why examination pressure is so intense, many Japanese respondents answered that it is because Japan is a small crowded country with few opportunities for success. This answer unquestionably highlights a factor of crucial importance, but it does not explain everything. There are many universities in Japan which are not difficult to enter, and there are opportunities for success aside from examinations. There are other crowded countries where opportunity is limited but examination pressure much less severe. Implicit in this response is the feeling that one's opportunity to achieve security and social mobility is highly compressed into one brief period of life, and many explicitly recognize that the best way for a commoner to rise on the social ladder is to enter a famous university. At least two other social systems, the family and the school, seem important for understanding the full force of this pressure. The importance of these two systems, like the life-time commitment to a firm, are further manifestations of a striking characteristic pervading Japanese social structure: the high degree of integration and solidarity within a given group.

THE FAMILY'S CONTRIBUTION: MATERNAL INVOLVEMENT

Success or failure on examinations is not only the success or failure of an individual but of his family. The self-sacrifice, anxiety, excitement, and happiness or sorrow that attend examinations are fully shared by the parents and siblings. It is assumed that a child is successful in large part because of his parents' help, and community recognition for success or failure is accorded to the parents as much as to the child himself. But beside the applicant himself, the most involved person is the mother. In listening to a mother describe examinations, one almost has the feeling that it is she rather than the child who is being tested.

Beginning in first grade a child brings a book bag home every day so that he can get his mother's help with the daily homework assignments. Even if a tutor is hired for brief periods, the ultimate responsibility for helping with (or, from the child's view, hounding about) the homework is the mother's. The work usually is sufficiently difficult so that the child cannot do it without his mother's assistance, and the typical mother cannot do the work without some preparation on her own. Because most Mamachi mothers have completed only elementary school, or at most the prewar "girls' school" (equivalent to eleven grades under the new system), and because postwar educational reforms brought great changes in course content and methods, it is not easy for mothers to help children with homework, even in elementary school. Many mothers read their children's books and study other books while the children are in school, and others consult with tutors or school teachers to keep up with their children's work. It is a challenge for the mother to keep one step ahead of the child—a challenge these mothers take seriously.

The mother wants the child to succeed not only for his sake, but for her own sake. At school meetings, in front of an entire group of mothers, a teacher often will praise or criticize a mother for her child's performance. On certain occasions a mother is expected to stand behind the child while her child performs and other children and mothers look on, and the comments about performance are as likely to be directed to the mother as to the child since it is expected that the mother will see that the child follows the teacher's instruction when practicing at home.

In formal and informal gatherings of mothers, children's performance often becomes the focus of attention. Most children wear uniforms of their school, which signify status as clearly as military uniforms. Some schools post on a bulletin board the class position of all students or seat students according to rank. But even if schools make no such announcement, most parents have a good idea of the relative standing of their children. When mothers of classmates get together, they generally know roughly the academic standing of each other's children, and mothers whose children are doing poorly are likely to listen carefully to mothers whose children are doing well. Mothers of successful children, even when discreet, indirect, and modest, have difficulty refraining from bragging about their children's successes. They may, for example, mention casually that their child is planning to specialize in a certain field since his teacher has praised him; or they may describe some technique in dealing with the child which seems to have worked since the child is doing so well; or they may encourage another mother, describing how their child once reacted negatively to mother's pressure but then suddenly began performing well.

The importance of the child's performance for determining the mother's status is reflected, for example, in the problems that schools have faced in trying to introduce special classes for retarded children. The parents have been resistant to sending their children to special classes because of the stigma attached. They have made special appeals for permission to allow their children to attend regular classes, because it would be so embarrassing to them to have their children attend special classes.

Even the families of high social standing are not immune from competition between mothers over children's success. In some ways it is even more difficult for upper-class mothers since they expect their children to do better than other children. Some have withdrawn their children from music lessons rather than face the wound to their pride when their children were not doing as well as some lower-status children.

While some status adjustments are required of mothers as a result of their children's examinations, these adjustments are usually minor since the family and community, through rank in class and practice examinations, already have a fairly good estimate of how a child will do in his examinations. Nevertheless there are always surprises, and mothers always entertain the hope that their child will be admitted to a difficult school, and that their community prestige will rise accordingly.[7]

So closely are mother and child identified that it is sometimes difficult to distinguish the child's success from the mother's success or even the child's work from the mother's work. During summer vacation grade-school children are required to do daily assignments and given optional projects to hand in when school reopens. It is common knowledge that good projects praised by teachers are done in part or almost entirely by the mothers. Although most mothers are critical of "mother's projects," still they feel they must keep up with the Gombeis (Joneses) by helping their children. The danger, clearly recognized by many mothers, is that the mother may exert herself so much that education may be more for the mother than for the child. Many thoughtful mothers are concerned lest their children become too dependent on them for assistance with homework and lose their own initiative. However, most mothers do not

---

[7] It may be argued that because the mother's status depends so much on the success of the child, the status gap between the mother and the child is never permitted to become large. The problem sometimes found in the United States, where the status gap between a lower-status mother and a higher-status child has created serious strains in the mother-child relationship, would seem to be less likely to lead to a break in Japan where the mother usually continues to adjust to the child's new position and keeps in close contact with his associates.

think that helping the child with homework interferes with the child's learning. They feel, rather, that the child needs guidance and that their assistance makes it possible for the child to learn more adequately and rapidly.

While the conscientious mother is very ambitious for the child, she is aware that if she pushes too hard, the child will resist. Yet some mothers become so anxious to be praised before a group that they will drive their children in order to achieve rapid success. Even if the mother uses more subtle techniques and tries to strike a balance between her own ambitions and the child's ability, there is no question that her enormous involvement in examination success will get communicated to the child.

The School's Contribution: Teacher Involvement

The Japanese Ministry of Education contributes indirectly to examination anxieties by pressing schools to raise their standards, and the schools in turn pass the pressure on to the families. At least since the Meiji Restoration, the Japanese government has stressed the importance of education in the development of a modern nation. The Ministry of Education continually compares Japan's level of educational achievement with that of other countries and has set high standards in an effort to make her students' achievements as high as those of any in the world. Thus, all students are expected to study a foreign language (generally English) in junior high school; a mathematics student is expected to complete calculus in high school.

One of the most lively public issues in recent years has been the question of whether there should be teacher-rating systems. Although the origins of and interest in the issue are partly in the realm of politics, its supporters have been arguing that in order to raise the standards of education, it is necessary to rate each teacher's competence. Many teachers have complained that this would permit school authorities to evaluate teachers by their political attitudes under the guise of efficiency ratings. Regardless of the political aspects of the question, this also reflects the seriousness with which the government considers the problems of raising the level of education.

In order to raise standards, many educators have encouraged the publication of materials evaluating each school's performance record, and newspapers and magazines diligently publish this information. Even educators who lament the enormous pressure placed on the children have recognized that posting of such results is useful in getting the schools to do the job more adequately.

Especially in private schools both teachers and students feel closely identified with their school. Since the students in the urban areas can choose between a number of junior and senior high schools and colleges, there is intense competition, especially among private schools, for better students. Schools enjoy a feeling of importance derived from people clamoring to gain admission, and a school without large numbers of applicants standing in lines would be regarded as a school of little consequence. This competition between schools tends to be more open than in the United States, and competition on the athletic field pales in comparison with the competition in placing graduates. Indeed, just as the American football coach is judged on the basis of the number of games his team wins, so the Japanese high-school principal is judged by the proportion of graduates who go on to the better universities; he in turn judges the teachers by the same standards.

The Japanese teacher does not make a sharp distinction between specific classroom duties and a general responsibility for his pupils. In a sense, he is required to take his troubles home with him. School teachers are expected to be available during vacations, and the school principal has the right to require them to report for work at any time. Even during summer vacation, a teacher will be expected to come to school at least two or three times to evaluate the progress of children's homework, and to take his turn supervising children's play activities.

The teacher to some extent is held responsible even for the safety and behavior of a child outside school. For example, one school principal said that a major share of his time is spent in handling children who get in trouble in the community. In the mind of Mamachi residents, the parents are partly to blame for a delinquent child, but the school is also responsible for not having provided better moral training. Although most parents are opposed to the reintroduction of formal moral training, the school does have a responsibility for inculcating basic moral virtues. For example, the teacher must see that girls do not wear make-up, that they have simple hair-dos and no permanents, that they wear proper uniforms, and, at some private schools, that they do not walk with boys. The teacher sends memos to parents, particularly at vacation times, outlining the procedures the parents should follow to insure that their child has a healthful vacation and listing places considered inadvisable for the child to visit. It is only natural that the teacher's responsibility extends to cover examination success.

On the numerous occasions when the mother goes to visit the school, she shows respect for the teacher and takes his advice seriously. Many a mother, relatively calm before going to a PTA meeting, returned concerned about whether she was doing enough to help the child and resolved to follow the teacher's advice more closely. She will, of course, show deference to the men teachers, who comprise as much as one-half of the elementary-school staff and an even larger proportion of the co-educational junior and senior high school staffs. But in addition, because the mother's own education is often inadequate, she must look to the teacher for guidance in helping her child. While mothers collectively may complain that certain teachers are not giving their children adequate training, by and large they feel grateful for the teachers' help, especially for the many teachers who provide extra tutoring in preparation for examinations. Mothers express their appreciation often, sometimes by means of presents. Knowing how much they depend on him and how important examination success is to a child's career, a teacher cannot help but feel a keen sense of responsibility to the mothers and children he advises.

When we asked families about the importance of teachers' recommendations for university admissions, we were told that they carry almost no weight since it is assumed that the teacher will be trying to push his own pupil ahead. His recommendation is more likely to be an exercise in flattery than an objective appraisal. It would be almost like asking a parent to write a recommendation for his own child.

The school teacher who wants to please his superiors and who takes seriously his responsibility for his pupils' futures will want to do everything he can to insure the child's success. This inevitably means that he will advise the mother to have the child study harder and to sacrifice other activities that might interfere with studying.

MITIGATING THE HARSHNESS

The cause of examination worry is not only the finality of the results but the fact that examinations are impersonal and therefore unpredictable. The generation which came to the city from rural areas relied on personal contacts as a basis of finding positions, and Mamachi parents still consider personal contacts a much safer way to find a good job. By having properly placed friends and keeping up a good relationship with them, one previously could be virtually assured of success. But there is no such assurance when one is evaluated on the basis of competency by some impersonal authority. Examination questions might be different from what one had anticipated, or one might not feel well, or one's nervousness might inhibit performance.

Some families, unwilling to take this risk, try to find other paths to success. Genuine alternatives to examinations are, however, extremely few. One alternative is enrolling a child in a private "escalator" school permitting him to advance from kindergarten or elementary school through a reputable university with only nominal examinations. But these private "escalator" schools are so expensive and require close family connections with such prominent people that virtually no Mamachi salaried family has given this possibility serious consideration.

Another alternative is for a family to arrange for their son to be taken directly into a large organization regardless of educational background. Most schools leave a few openings for students who do not pass the examinations, and the selection of these students is generally made by a committee of prominent people in the school; and this permits a few students to be admitted on the basis of particularistic claims on the school, either because the parent is an alumnus, has contributed financially to the school, or has a friend influential in school affairs. However, there is considerable competition for these openings. The family's strategy is to get the person most powerful in the selection committee to make the most forceful appeal for the admission of their child. To do this the family tries to do anything it can to increase the influential person's personal motivation, because of personal liking or feeling of obligation, so he will make this vigorous appeal to the committee. A standard way to establish such a *kone* (connection) is to get one's friends who know such influential people to try and persuade them to help out. Often parents bring presents to influential school officials. Some junior and senior high-school principals receive two or three presents for every opening, and even if they announce that they accept no presents, they often find it difficult to refuse. Parents are thoughtful in selecting unique, appropriate, carefully wrapped gifts and presenting them in a polite way. School officials try to avoid any feeling of obligation to these families, but they do honor some obligations, especially if the applicant also is relatively competent. While principals and important teachers or school officials sometimes derive substantial economic gain from such presents, there were no indications of their misusing their position for purposes of personal gain. The responsibility they incur as a result of receiving presents causes considerable discomfort, and there is undoubtedly a large measure of truth when they say they prefer not to receive them.

The foresighted mother sometimes begins courting potentially influential people years in advance, offering generous presents and a variety of personal services. If such a friend later gives assistance in getting a child admitted, the mother feels an obligation and expresses appreciation for many years afterward.

To be really influential these claims on particularistic relations must be more than simple introductions because any salary man can get some kind of introduction. But even with the most influential friends who will exert themselves most forcefully, one cannot entirely escape the importance of examinations. The lower the examination score, the more difficult for an influential person to get his favorite candidate accepted by the rest of the committee, and if the examination score is too low, no introduction will help. Furthermore, the child who enters with a low examination score is often at a disadvantage vis-à-vis his classmates, and some children who could use connections prefer to study hard and take the examinations so they will not be accused of succeeding because of their family's wealth or influence.

Money, like introductions, can be used to supplement examination results, and within a limited range may be used instead of examination scores. A student who did fairly well on examinations can attend a private school which has a high entrance fee and tuition and is comparable in quality to a public institution which has slightly more difficult examinations.

Some wealthy parents who wish to avoid possible embarrassment by open competition with ordinary families often plan to use private schools and connections from the beginning. But salaried families cultivate these ties only as an alternative in case the child does not pass the more difficult examinations at a public school.

If a family cannot afford the better private schools, there is still the possibility of sending the child to a local public school which happens to have an unusually good reputation. Since a local public school is open only to children living in that particular school district, sending a child to a school in another district is, strictly speaking, illegal. Yet this practice is so common that principals from different school districts occasionally meet to discuss the problem of some school districts bearing the burden of financing the education of children in other districts. Various informal estimates suggest that in certain school districts, one-tenth or more of the students actually reside in another school district.

It happens that Mamachi's elementary school is known as a fairly good school so that some parents in nearby school districts enroll their children in the Mamachi elementary school, but some Mamachi mothers similarly enroll their children in such a public junior high school in Tokyo. Even though the differences between these local schools may be minor, they are treated as if they were major since just such small differences may determine whether a student passes or fails a later examination. It is rare for a family to move to one of these school districts, but it is common for the mother and child to register as living at the home of some friend, relative, or acquaintance in that school district.

Many school officials and teachers feel sympathy for the earnest young children desiring to get ahead and are reluctant to raise objection to illegal crossing of school districts. In contrast to the city officials, school officials may be pleased about the desirability of their school and willing to take these ambitious children, so long as city officials raise no objections. At times, city officials concerned about the heavy school expenditures will carry out an investigation and ungraciously send the child back to his own school district.

Although most people are aware of the problem of crossing of school districts, and although high registration rates of mothers and children of certain ages in well-known school districts are sufficient evidence of the problem, investigations are relatively rare. If there were to be a search, the mother would probably explain that due to domestic quarrels or illness, she and her child have in fact taken up residence apart from the husband in that particular school district. The family will have left clothing, a school uniform, and some school supplies with friends and relatives whose address they are using in case a law officer came to investigate. While this practice makes it more difficult to prove violations, many potential violators are caught at the time of registration, and many run the risk of being thrown out and then having difficulty entering another school.

At the college level the only alternative for a student who fails his examinations is to become a *ronin* for a year or so. It is not especially embarrassing to be a *ronin* for one year, and many famous universities have stories of students who entered on their fifth, sixth, or even tenth attempt. But because the typical salary-man family has difficulty supporting the student for the extra year while studying for examinations, some *ronin* must compromise by working part-time while preparing for examinations. The status of a *ronin* is filled with anxiety. The student who has already failed one entrance examination generally feels somewhat more desperate, and doubt about success overshadows the entire period of *ronin*ship. Many families will take a second failure as clear indication that a child will not make a first-rate university, so that a first-year *ronin* may feel that he has only one more try. As a consequence, few families are able to tolerate and afford more than one year of *ronin*ship, and a student reluctantly may enroll in the university which was his second or third choice rather than become a second-year *ronin*.

It should be clear, then, that it is difficult for a salaried family to escape entirely from judgment by examination. A higher-status family, by wealth and community prestige, can often manage to pave the way to success for a child who does not perform well on examinations. But the typical salaried family lacks the resources to command these alternatives. At best it can use its savings and personal contacts to enable the child to attend an institution slightly better than he would by relying solely on examinations. The salaried family is more likely to concentrate its most valuable resources, the mother's time and the family's savings on helping to prepare the child more adequately for examinations.

THE HYPERTROPHY OF EXAMINATIONS

From an analysis of the various institutions and practices associated with entrance examinations, it is possible to understand why entrance examinations should receive such emphasis. Yet Mamachi residents feel that it has gone entirely too far and that they have become enslaved to the system. They feel sorry for the child who is forced to lead a restricted life deprived of jovial fellowship, music appreciation, sports, hobbies, movies, television, and pleasure reading. One girl, for example, a year before taking a college entrance examination, said that her leisure time activities consisted of occasionally stopping off at a department store for a few minutes on the way home from school. This asceticism, so closely associated with the traditional peasant's outlook, is endured because of the hope of living an easier life later. Preparation for examinations is painful not only because one must make such sacrifices but also because until one has finally passed entrance examinations there is always the anxiety and fear that one may not make the grade.

There is no question that during this period of asceticism these students absorb an amazing amount of facts. Not only do they master their own language, literature, and history, but they also learn to read English and become familiar with the history and culture of Europe and America. Course requirements in mathematics and science are at a higher level than those of comparable American schools.

But at the same time, students must sacrifice types of scholarship not measured by entrance examinations. For example, since the examination is written and not oral, a pupil studying English does not practice ordinary conversation, but concentrates on reading, on fine points of grammar, and, in some cases, on pedantic expressions which are likely to appear on the examination. High-school teachers complain that they cannot get students interested in laboratory work connected with science because the examinations measure only what can be read and answered. Since examinations cover a full range of subjects, a child who begins to show a strong interest in one field usually will be encouraged by his teacher and his parents to broaden his interests so that he can get fully prepared also in other subjects. Since multiple-choice examinations cannot measure original and creative thought, the emphasis is placed on memorization.

Even if the students who do not take entrance examinations imitate the study patterns of examinees, they feel relatively deprived —falling behind their peers in preparation for success in life and neglected by the teachers at school. Since no students are failed, poorer students are supposed to be given special supplementary classes. The poor students often complain that, instead, supplementary classes are given to good students preparing for difficult examinations. While the schools are supposed to help students who wish to get part-time jobs and to help them find employment after the ninth grade, those students likewise feel that they are slighted because the school is more interested in placing the continuing students. Even those who do not complain are distressed that their children will not have such good chances of becoming salary men.

In most modern societies, the task of educating the youth is performed not in the home but in the school system. For these salaried families, however, education is performed by the school *and* the home. In a sense, parents become assistant teachers, checking frequently with the regular teachers about the work the parents should be doing to help educate and train their children. Therefore to a large extent the parent-child relationship is the relationship of teacher and student. The mother must supervise her child, give him assignments, check the work, and impose necessary sanctions to see that he performs the work adequately. Whereas, in some industrialized societies, the mother-child relationship is more strictly limited to primary socialization and to providing affection, among these salaried families it must also take on in addition a task orientation in which the mother and the child prepare for examinations.

ACHIEVEMENT WITHOUT RIVALRY

The prominence of examinations in the life of Mamachi salaried families reflects an acceptance of the principle that success should be determined by competence as judged by a universal standard. The path of success is not determined primarily by birth or connections but by superior capacity as demonstrated by performance. While Japan is sometimes described as a particularistic society, at the time of examinations particularistic relations clearly give way to these universalistic standards. One of the dangers of open competition, however, is that rivalry may prove disruptive to groups.

Yet the extent of disruption is very limited in groups to which Mamachi residents belong because within the group competition is carefully controlled. Once a child is admitted to a school, grades are not given great importance, and there is a strong feeling of group solidarity which serves to inhibit competitiveness between the students.[8] Once in the firm, one's success has been assured, and rivalry is kept in bounds by the primacy of seniority which is non-competitive and the common interest in the success of the firm. Since schools and firms do not drop members for poor achievement records, there is no feeling that one's remaining in the group depends on another's leaving.

Even in taking entrance examinations, a person plays down competition with friends. A person ordinarily hopes that all in his group of friends will be among those who pass. Even if friends are separated and pursue different paths as a result of examinations, there usually is no feeling of acrimony. In a sense, the one who did not get in feels that the position he hoped for was filled not by his friend but by a stranger.

Achievement patterns also do not disrupt family solidarity. In the United States, for example, where achievement is defined as an individual matter, the child who goes beyond his parents in achievement level often feels that his parents have difficulty understanding the kind of world in which he lives. Among the Mamachi families,

---

[8] This pattern appears to begin at an early age. Miss Kazuko Yoshinaga who taught in middle-class kindergartens in both Japan and the United States reported that in kindergartens American children are much more openly competitive than Japanese children. Even about matters of age and size, Japanese kindergarten children rarely engage in comparisons and are less interested in who is bigger and older.

however, the child's success is more directly a family success. The mother continually keeps close to the child and his work. Even if the child does not need his family's introductions, he will require the family's help in preparing for the examinations. While disparities between achievement of siblings may create some problems, brothers and sisters are also so involved in each other's success and share in the community respect awarded to a family that examinations serve usually to unite siblings as well as other members of the nuclear family.

Under conditions of competing with strangers the achievement pressures are least controlled. Just as considerations of politeness do not prevent the shoving of strangers getting on a subway, so competitiveness is accepted as natural at the time of entrance examinations. In this way, the entrance-examination system operates to preserve the distinction between friends and strangers because blatant competition is concentrated at the time of admission when one competes with strangers. Once admitted, competition is subordinated to loyalty and friendship within the group. Thus the phenomenon of entrance examinations operates to maintain universalistic standards in such a way that it minimizes the threat to group solidarity. The cost to the individual is the anxiety and pressure which he must endure at the crucial point of admission.

Part Two

THE FAMILY AND OTHER SOCIAL SYSTEMS

Chapter IV

For the rest of Japan the people who have been able to become salary men are symbols of the *akarui seikatsu* (bright new life), the life with leisure time, travel and recreation, and few binding obligations and formalities. Because he has security from the firm he may steadily acquire the new consumer goods without fear of being without income and going into debt. For the person who aspires to be a salary man, the bright new life is indeed a rosy picture. For the salaried family each glamorous new purchase is the result of careful planning and many sacrifices. To an affluent American, the bright new life appears orderly but ascetic, and he finds it hard to share the anticipation with which the Japanese salaried family awaits each new acquisition.

Before the war, electricity, the sewing machine, irons, and the radio were already widespread, but all other electric equipment, like refrigerators, heaters, toasters, washing machines, fans, and the like, which had spread through the United States and Europe in prewar days, have become common in Japan only in the last decade. In the immediate postwar period, Mamachi residents, like other Japanese, were concerned with getting the barest necessities of food and shelter. They were accustomed to great economic deprivations, to long food lines, to trips to the country for food. Even their beloved small flower beds and rock gardens were turned into vegetable patches. In the last decade, this picture has changed drastically. Large numbers of machines which formerly they had seen only in foreign films were imported, and later, as Japanese business began to recognize the importance of the consumer market, they were produced at home. The excitement of the consumer has been enormous. These new goods were at first available only to the wealthy, but now they are within the reach of the average salary man. Mamachi residents relate with pleasure how they first saw the machines and how they heard about them. They still tell funny stories about the mistakes and misunderstandings in their first attempts to use them, and they talk with great delight of their most recent purchases.

Only partly in jest, Mamachi families talk about wanting the "Three Imperial Treasures," by which they do not mean the three treasures which are traditionally handed down in the Imperial Household (jewel, sword, and mirror) but three new pieces of electrical equipment. Indeed, those who get machines for the first time behave almost as if they were acquiring the Imperial Treasures, and the enthusiasm remains even while the content of the list changes as former treasures become more widely available. Several years ago listings might have included TV sets and electric rice cookers, but newer ones might include a refrigerator or an electric washing machine.[1] The same kind of enthusiasm is shown for the latest models of cameras, transistor radios, hi-fi equipment, electric heating devices, and the newest clothes styles from abroad. Garbage-disposal and central-heating units and dishwashing machines are still almost unknown, and cars still are too expensive for the typical salary man. While all Mamachi families have had running water for many years, other modern plumbing facilities like flush toilets and sewers, already common in some areas of Tokyo, have not yet reached Mamachi.

As yet these families have little critical judgment in making their new purchases. For example, a family buying its first refrigerator probably would not look into the number of cubic feet, the size of the freezer unit, or the location of the door handle, as long as it was produced by a "big maker." Japanese advertising reflects a lack of critical public judgment, for it includes almost no details. Many Japanese consider it bad manners to ask a salesman many detailed questions and then not purchase a product. Now consumers generally are interested only in the appearance, the price, and the *meekaa* (maker), but critical standards of judgment are beginning

---

[1] In a national survey in 1959, 72 percent of city wives had sewing machines, 97 percent radios, 44 percent washing machines, 40 percent TV, 28 percent refrigerators, and 6 percent electric vacuum cleaners. In Mamachi, with a higher standard of living, the percentages would be much higher.

to develop rapidly as people acquire experience using various products.

THE ORDERED LIFE

Because the salary man's income is limited, he has been relatively slow but steady in acquiring new goods. Since future income can be accurately predicted, he can plan when he will be able to afford what machine. He knows that on his limited salary he cannot hope to acquire all desirable machines, but he adjusts his expectations to his salary and hence is never subject to serious disappointments. His salary is even more predictable than that of his American counterpart whose salary may rise appreciably with new assignments or with a change in companies. To a family which has lived through such serious disruptions as depression, war, acute shortages, and spiraling inflation, living according to plan seems highly desirable. The salary man thus develops a measured optimism, and, under present circumstances, there is every reason to expect that his limited dreams will come true.

Long-Range Planning

Since these salaried men, in contrast to farmers or businessmen, do not depend on inheritance for their livelihood, they usually do not worry about saving money to pass on to children, but if they do not plan carefully they may lack even the necessities after retirement. In less extreme cases, planning can make the difference between a miserable and a moderately comfortable existence, a difference more crucial than the distinction between shades of comfort one would have in the more affluent America. On the small income of the salary man, every bit of savings requires sacrifice.

In rural Japan, where one child usually is designated as the heir, he naturally assumes the responsibility of caring for his parents in their old age. But in Mamachi filial responsibility is not so clearly assigned, and many parents want to be financially independent in their old age in order to avoid feeling a burden on their children and to prevent conflicts with daughters-in-law or sons-in-law.

Since retirement from most large companies and government offices is at fifty-five or sixty, since retirement benefits are minimal, and since a man at fifty-five can expect to live about eighteen more years, families try hard to put aside savings for old age. This is often difficult because of the expense of educating the children. If, for example, the bread earner is thirty-two when his last child is born and supports this child through college to the age of twenty-three, the bread earner may be retiring the same year the child finishes college. This means that while some families may attempt to save for old age, they may have to choose between the children's educational expenses and savings for retirement.

Education is the primary goal and major expense for most families. While children who attend college live at home and commute, admission fees and tuition can be fairly high, and the expenses of food, transportation, and incidentals through college years require planning. One advantage of having a bright child is that he can qualify for a public school and public university, which are inexpensive but of high quality. Indeed, while sending a child to private school is a possibility for salary families, it requires serious sacrifices. The entrance fee and one year tuition at an acceptable private university may be as much as a third of the annual salary of a typical middle-aged salary man. Since many of these families try to send their children to private junior and senior high schools as well as to college, education imposes a financial burden especially if there are several children. While the father's salary will be higher in middle age, he still must budget carefully.

Educational expenses are also likely to occur about the time when a girl is given in marriage. In rural areas, a large dowry, perhaps equivalent to several years of the family's earnings, was usually given to the bride to take with her when she married. Since she ordinarily. received no inheritance, a daughter's dowry, in effect, constituted her inheritance. In spite of the fact that salaried families have reduced the amounts given to a bride, still they are expected to cover a large part of the marriage costs. They also are expected to give their daughter enough new clothing to last many years and enough furniture to set up a household. Although part of these expenses will be covered by the gift of money from the groom at the time of engagement, most of the expenses must be met by the bride's family. Since relatively little furniture is required in a Japanese home, furniture may include only a chest of drawers, bedding, linens, a table, cooking equipment, dishes, silverware, and perhaps a sewing machine and other electrical appliances. Sometimes the bride's family may not give the furniture at the time of marriage, but promise to give it when the young couple is able to buy a home several years later. The husband is expected to pay for everything else and for current living expenses from his own salary. The wife ordinarily does not work after marriage or, at the latest, after her first child is born. It is true that some "modern" couples originally introduced through friends at work or school will set up a household more inexpensively with almost no help from their families, but most parents in Mamachi still try to have enough money to supply the furniture and clothing which their daughter will need to begin housekeeping.

Virtually no homes in Mamachi are for rent, so that couples unable to make the down payment on a house are likely to rent in Tokyo and move to Mamachi a few years later. Before large apartment projects were developed, it was more common for a newly married couple to live at the home of one of the parents for a few years or perhaps even in housing provided by their company until they were able to afford a down payment on their own home.

Mamachi homes are generally constructed inexpensively of wood so that a middle-class family can build a comfortable house for four or five thousand dollars. A public agency provides standard loans for seventeen years' duration if the couple can make a down payment of about one-third. This payment may be the equivalent of about two years of the husband's salary, and may take many years to accumulate. Immediately after the war, war damage, the lack of wartime home construction, and the return of soldiers and citizens living overseas, created housing shortages and considerable movement from one household to another. Although the acute housing shortage in the immediate post-war period has eased, the lack of availability of good housing often requires several moves on the part of a young couple until they find adequate facilities. Once a family makes a down payment on a home, they are likely to live in the same home all their lives. Generally they will have completed paying for the house before the beginning of the heavy expenses for the education and marriage of their children.

Thus a typical life pattern is roughly as follows: at the time of marriage a couple sets up housekeeping with the furniture provided

by the wife's family, the rent or housing facility provided by the
husband or his family. In the early stage of marriage they may live
in a small apartment or with in-laws while saving for a down payment on a house. Having made this payment, they then begin saving for their children's education, for their daughter's dowry, and
for their own retirement.

The general pattern of savings may be similar to that of the American middle class, but the difficulty in obtaining loans and saving
enough money to meet later expenses, the early retirement age,
and the small size of stipends after retirement, all require the
Mamachi family to be more cautious in spending, to plan more
carefully, and to put aside a comparatively larger proportion of
savings.

During the inflation immediately after the war, savings that had
required years of sacrifice were reduced to virtual worthlessness. At
that time people tried to save by buying stock, real estate, or durable
goods. In the last few years, however, with the stabilization of the
value of the yen, families have been increasingly willing to save
money. Many families deposit small amounts into post-office savings
accounts or banks, and purchase stocks of real estate only if they
accumulate sizeable sums.

Short-Range Planning

Generally budgeting is on a monthly basis since the husband receives his pay monthly. The monthly pay is usually divided into
three parts, one for the husband to use for spending money, one
for the wife to use for the household, the children, and herself, and
one for savings. An average husband may be allotted perhaps ten
dollars or so (with a buying power perhaps comparable to twenty
or thirty dollars in the United States) for all monthly expenses. In
addition he may be entitled to a small expense account because of
his position in the company.

By far the largest part of the monthly income, however, is man-
aged by the wife. Even if she does not keep a budget, she will have
some idea how much money is left at various stages during the
month, and she may cut down expenses toward the end of the
month if she sees she is running short. She will purchase most food
items from the same places with little variation from day to day.

Most wives use little, if any, of their money for their own pleasure. In addition to household expenses, they must provide for the children's school supplies, school lunches, clothing, and spending money. Most salaried families cannot afford a maid, but if they have one, the household account will be used to pay her salary.

Except for "modern" young people, most couples make a sharp separation between money allotted to the wife and money allotted to the husband. Although the husband may ask the wife for more money, the wife is reluctant to ask the husband for more even if she does not have enough money toward the end of the month. They rarely inquire about each other's use of small amounts of money, and in some cases, there is mutual secrecy and some deceit about the amount of money spent. Not every wife knows exactly the amount of her husband's income. While she knows approximately how much he makes, he may not tell her the precise amount of his bonuses. Similarly the wife, though generally honest and forthright to her husband, may not tell her husband precisely for what she is using money and may even overstate some of the household expenses in order to have some extra money. Especially if the husband frequently asks her for spending money, the wife may put aside a small amount telling him she is already out of money when in fact she has a little available. Many a wife feels so dependent on her husband for money and subject to his whims, that she feels it necessary to hide a little money from him. This practice makes it possible for her to get by for a short time in case of marital difficulties, or, more commonly, buy something on which her husband is reluctant to spend money.

These minor deceptions are used at times to increase the area of financial freedom, but generally the couple plans together for major purchases. They may even consult with their children and neighbors. When children are small, they may go together on Sunday to a department store shopping for pleasure items as an entire family.

Almost all salary men receive sizeable bonuses twice a year which may total as much as from two to six months of the husband's total salary. The regular smaller monthly salary serves to limit regular expenditures, and the large bonuses, in effect, constitute a forced savings which the families then use to buy larger items of equipment or put into savings. Yet planning and saving are so heavily ingrained in their outlook that one has the feeling that most of them would be saving even without the bonus system.[2]

THE LIMITS OF FRUGALITY

Although Mamachi residents look at their habits simply as customs, in comparison to America, many seem to be the epitome of frugality. For example, in the home the same room will be used both in the daytime and at night, eliminating the necessity for separate living and bedrooms. Generally the mattresses for the bedding are kept in a closet and pulled out at night. A table used in the daytime can be folded up at night to make room for the bedding. Using cushions and bedding on the floor obviously is cheaper than the beds, chairs, and davenports that Western families must buy. Since company is usually greeted only in one room, simple and less expensive materials can be used in the "family rooms" which receive the greatest wear. Fuel is conserved by heating only the immediate sitting area in only the coldest months. When bath water is heated, the same tub of water is used for the entire family (sometimes including nearby relatives), everyone having cleaned himself with a small pail of water before getting in the tub. Paint is rarely used even on the outside of wooden houses. Some kitchens still have dirt floors, no houses have basements, and all houses have very simple foundations. In the more modern homes, a kitchen containing modern electrical equipment may become a display room open to guests, but in most houses the kitchen facilities are crude and closed to guests.

By Western standards the amount and quality of food are inadequate. Rice is the main dish in a way that no dish is the main dish in the West. To overstate the case slightly, it is eaten in such quantities that all other food is used for flavoring. Fish is available in abundance and variety and is used to flavor the rice. Small fish bones are eaten, providing needed calcium. Since virtually no spices are used, soy sauce and many varieties of pickles are served at every meal to season the rice. Vegetables and meat are eaten with rice and in much smaller quantities than in the West. The Japanese slice meat very

---

[2] In Japan as in the United States, the middle class is characterized by having a very high proportion of savers. Cf. Nihon Shakai Koozoo Choosa Kai, *Howaito Karaa no Ishiki Koozoo* (The Structure of White-Collar Class Consciousness), Tokyo, March, 1962 (mimeographed), p. 232.

thin, and it is no accident that they use the word "roast" to mean simply high-quality meat, since they never cook the large cuts served in the West. Various kinds of inexpensive seaweeds are often eaten. Bean paste and bean curd are used with other relatively inexpensive items for making soups. Fruits although used daily are still considered somewhat of a luxury. Milk is drunk primarily by children or sick people although milk products are increasingly available. Imported drinks, such as coffee, which are expensive by Japanese standards are used by most salary men in limited quantity for special occasions. Daily shopping for fresh fish and vegetables is the rule. Most families own small wooden ice boxes for short-term food preservation, but freezers and once-a-week shopping expeditions are unknown.

Many services which one must pay for in the West are in Japan performed by friends without charge. A person staying overnight in another city usually will stay with a friend or a friend of a friend, unless he is traveling on an expense account. When seeking a job, getting personal counseling, or seeking a special technical connection, one is likely to get help from friends rather than to go to an official agency. Although private detectives (to provide personal information, especially regarding employment and marriage) and real estate agencies are still widespread, one feels safer and saves money if the services are performed by friends. When one wants to use a public facility, such as a meeting hall to entertain guests, it is often possible to get a big discount through friends. Some people will call upon a rich friend to help them entertain guests. A wealthy man may feel honored or at least honor-bound to assist, and the person making the request shows his appreciation by various favors. When he gives a present in return for a favor, it need not be expensive. An expensive but tasteless present would be insulting, for it would imply paying off a favor of friendship with money. Rather, it is expected that one show considerable kindness and thoughtfulness by giving a present or memento with style and grace. Photographs may be sent after a get-together as one way of showing appreciation. A favorite gift is some special product brought back from another part of Japan or from abroad. A family with an obligation to a neighbor may have their son buy famous local products for them on his school trip. The Mamachi resident feels that the trouble one goes to in bringing something back from a distant place is an indication of how appreciative one is. Indeed, almost every corner of Japan has some famous local product, and since so many children in these families go to distant places for school trips, guests are often treated to local delicacies, and houses are filled with such famous local products. In whatever way favors are returned, it will emphasize feelings of personal appreciation rather than money, and for large favors one will feel a long-term obligation.

In addition to the frugal use of double-duty household facilities and to obtaining free services from go-betweens and friends, various customs serve to conserve possessions. Shoes are not worn inside the house since they bring in dirt and mar the floors. Only stockinged feet or bare feet are permitted on the straw mats which are swept every day. These mats can be re-covered once every year or two, but even a replacement is not expensive. Covers are used for all items of furniture including the cushions one sits on. The most valuable dolls are kept in glass cases and may be preserved for more than one generation. Television sets, electric toasters, and other appliances come with covers which are carefully placed over the equipment when not in use. Machines are not discarded so long as they can be repaired. Even paperback books come with extra covers, and hardback books are sold with a protecting cardboard box as well as a thin paper cover. At home and even for neighborhood shopping, the wife wears a white apron which covers not only the skirt as in the West but her blouse and sleeves as well. The child going to nursery school wears an apron as part of the uniform so that his regular clothes will not get dirty. Children of grade school age wear shorts and long stockings even in thirty or forty degree winter weather. While the families regard this simply as a custom, the wearing of shorts does make it possible to avoid worry about patched knees. Even though the women save by doing their own sewing, it is considered embarrassing to wear in public anything that is patched. Nylon hose, however, are mended, since this mending does not show. Old clothes are worn at home, and clothes which are beyond repair are cut up and sewn to make washcloths, hot pads, and rags. Instead of buying new magazines, a Mamachi family may belong to a neighborhood club in which several members exchange magazines to split expenses, or they may buy their books or magazines at second-hand magazine and book stores. Boxes which formerly contained tea or cookies are kept for storing kitchen items. Younger children may protest about wearing hand-me-downs but the pattern is still fairly widespread, particularly in families which cannot easily afford to buy new clothes. It is perfectly permissible to wear the same clothes for several days in succession, and school uniforms make it possible for a child with only one or two suits to be well dressed throughout the school year. These frugal practices make it possible to conserve resources and live on little income, in a manner not too different from that of a few decades ago in the United States, and in Europe today.

Rich or poor, the Mamachi family will guard what it has. Often barbed wire is placed above the high fence, and many have a large dog to chase off possible burglars. There is a special word, *rusuban,* for a person who stays at home to guard the house while everybody else is away. Some houses can only be locked from the inside, and most families are unwilling to leave the house for more than a few minutes unless someone in the family or a close friend or relative stays in the house to see that nothing happens to it. Whatever the rationale surrounding the concept of *rusuban,* it does indicate the family's concern for conserving what it has.

By and large the new middle class is unable even to imitate the big businessman's conspicuous display of wealth: the chauffeur-driven car, membership in an expensive golf club, the use of several servants, and lavish entertaining. Elegant restaurants and *geisha* places in Japan are high-priced even by Western standards. Two or three hours of entertainment by geisha girls and eating out are likely to cost a hundred dollars or so for a group of only three or four, the equivalent of an average salaried person's monthly salary. Rich men display their wealth conspicuously like the nouveaux riches in America a generation or two ago when large fortunes were first accumulated.

In contrast to what William H. Whyte has called the "inconspicuous consumption" of the American organization man, the Japanese salary man and especially his wife would like to imitate the richer classes in their conspicuous display of wealth. But with their small income they can afford few flamboyant gestures. The greatest display is at a child's wedding. Although the movement to simplify

ceremonies has become stronger, it is not unusual for the parents of
the bride and groom to spend an equivalent of two or three times
the young husband's annual salary on the wedding, the renting of
expensive clothes, sizeable gifts to all the guests, and a lavish feast.

The wife's kimonos which are worn for going out socially or for
formal occasions may also cost the equivalent of several months of
the young husband's salary, and even salaried men's wives may have
several kimono outfits (including sash and shawl to match). Though
Western-style suits vary in quality, these differences are more difficult to distinguish, and suits are relatively unimportant as items of
conspicuous display. Some modern women have at least one or two
dressy Western outfits which are much less expensive than the
traditional kimono. Being modern and Western makes it possible
for them to avoid the dilemma of either buying an expensive
kimono which they cannot afford or buying an inexpensive one
that looks cheap.

Although only a few families may be able to distinguish variations of quality in most items of merchandise, they all can recognize
the major status labels of high class stores, and the purchase of an
item with a label from Mitsukoshi or Takashimaya, or the delivery
of equipment in Takashimaya or Mitsukoshi trucks, which neighbors
would be certain to notice, does have a status meaning. As one man
wryly commented, some of his friends will walk right by a small
shop on Mamachi's main street and go into Tokyo to buy an identi-
cal item costing perhaps twice as much in order to be able to show
off the Mitsukoshi label.

Since the bedding is aired outside every few days and thus is
open to the neighbors' view, a Mamachi housewife generally tries
to put her best quilt forward. Laundry too is aired outdoors in a
neighbor's range of vision but it generally is not as crucial for determining status as, for example, a kimono, and it causes somewhat
less concern.

Entertaining guests can be an important way of conspicuous
status display. Generally it is considered better to entertain guests
outside than in the home. It is thought that a person entertains in
the home because he cannot afford to go outside. If one does entertain a guest in the house, one shows more respect for the guest by

ordering the delivery of various kinds of food from a restaurant.[3] The kinds of refreshments and the dishes on which they are served all carry implications of a certain status. Having leisure and money for flower-arranging and tea-ceremony lessons and music lessons for the children is now within the reach of the average salary man's family, and still signifies the ability to enjoy the refinements of life.

The salary man often has difficulty balancing the need for frugality with the desire for high status in the eyes of his neighbors, friends, and associates. He must be frugal yet disguise his miserliness to friends by acting as if he were willing and able to spend freely, especially for guests. The expression used to mean to reveal one's weakness or inadequacy (*boro o dasu*) literally means to show one's rags. Many observers have noted that Japanese families make clear distinctions between the *omote* (what is open for outsiders to see) and the *ura* (what is not open). While there are many meanings to these expressions, one of their important functions may be to permit outward display and private frugality. One can, in a sense, have his cake and eat it too, provided one reserves the good cake for company.

THE FREEDOM TO SHOP
Families have two general alternatives in making small purchases. One is to buy as steady customers in a small local shop; the other is to buy as strangers in a large establishment like a department store. Similarly, in making larger purchases, it is possible to choose between going through personal connections to arrange discounts and going to a large department store where all people will be treated equally. The confidence of getting a good buy when shopping at a local shop or when making special arrangements for a discount derives from the steady relationship between the store and the customer or between the store and an intermediary. Minor price adjustments are still sometimes made, and regular customers may be given slightly lower prices. In buying at a department store, con-

---

[3] This is one example where the specific customs vary by region. In the Kyoto area one does not order food from the outside for a guest. For this information I am indebted to Robert J. Smith.

fidence of receiving fair treatment derives from the name and reputation of the store. Just as the large organizations have been the first to set regular salaries, so large stores have long had a fixed-price system. But now many smaller stores are gradually moving toward fixed prices, and even strangers may be given the same price as regular customers.

A customer who goes to a place where he is known is assured of many personal considerations. He is greeted by a friend, the items are tailored to suit his wishes, purchases may be made or delivered to suit his convenience. Although department stores cannot match the personal situation, most department stores make an effort to train attractive young sales ladies to be pleasant and charming to the customers and to provide the many services of an American department store, and perhaps even more.

Going through friends who have a special contact with some manufacturer, wholesaler, or retailer has the advantage of permitting savings. Many families select their electrical appliance not on the basis of brand preferences but on the basis of personal connections enabling them to get a discount. Nearly everyone who works in a store or factory is entitled to a discount for himself or friends, and a sizeable portion of purchases are made through these discount arrangements.

But at the same time, going through friends has the disadvantage of building up obligations, and though many families continue to use friends, others are willing to pay higher prices in order to avoid being in debt to friends. Unless the saving is great, the friend is close, and the discount easily arranged, many people hesitate making requests through friends. Going through friends also limits the range of selection. Of course, one can find out the general range of supplies a seller has before accepting the introduction, but once the introduction is made, there is a strong obligation to buy. If the product turns out not to be suitable or if there has been a misunderstanding, the obligation as a result of receiving a special favor in the form of reduced prices makes it virtually impossible to make adjustments wtihout creating some problems in the relationship with the friend. These situations are commonly known as *arigata meiwaku* (a favor which caused trouble). As greater discrimination in selecting items develops, these limitations on free choice are increasingly considered undesirable.

Going to an impersonal department store permits greater freedom in shopping. For example, most Mamachi families have Western-style clothes made by one tailor, since nearly all dress clothes are still tailor-made. Frequently the relationship is close, and the tailor understands what the customer wants and how to make it. But in the other cases, as the family begins to prefer styles which the tailor cannot make, their habitual loyalty declines and they begin to shop elsewhere. The same problem affects the family's relationship to other small shops. In the department stores one can look at large selections as much as one pleases with no obligation to buy, and as critical judgment grows, this is regarded as increasingly important. The old pattern of saving money by using personal relationships is still widespread, but it is slowly giving way. Even for the salaried family on a limited income it is increasingly considered worthwhile to pay a little more for the freedom to shop and avoid the obligations and possible strains resulting from purchasing through friends. Just as the salary man has come to appreciate the freedom from paternalistic restraints that come from a more contractual relationship with his place of work, so he and his wife have come to desire similar freedom from personal restraints in purchasing, a freedom that is possible on the basis of fixed prices in impersonal settings.

Chapter V

FAMILIES VIEW THEIR GOVERNMENT

THE NATIONAL IDENTITY

The Mamachi resident unquestionably has a positive, though amorphous, attachment to his country. He feels that he shares with other Japanese a race, language, and culture which, as a result of Japan's long isolation from other countries, are distinctive. He does not lack positive sentiment about Japan, but he has difficulty finding parts of his national tradition which he can be proud of. Unlike the old middle class who have more commonly responded to Western contact by chauvinistic nationalism and a revival of tradition, most salary men are convinced that Japan must adapt its traditions to the modern age. But the problem of national identity is the problem of finding in their tradition something that is both unique and worthy of the modern age.

Some Japanese have attempted to solve this problem by arguing that Japan's superior spirituality should be combined with the West's superior material development. But for Mamachi residents, who consider much of Japanese tradition as unsophisticated, superstitious, irrational, and feudalistic, this formula is clearly inadequate. The popular mythology of Japan which was officially propagated as literal truth[1] before the war is clearly unacceptable to the scientifically trained salary man. The image of Japan expressed in the fervent nationalist indoctrination in the 1930's was probably never completely internalized by most salary men, and it is certainly incongruous with their image of present-day Japan. Today, they laugh among themselves about having memorized the names of all 124

---

[1] For an account of many Japanese myths, see Mock Joya, *Things Japanese,* Tokyo: Tokyo News Service, 1958. The stories connected with the founding of the country and the succession of divine emperors were accepted as official.

emperors when they were school children. Even the story of the founding of the country, a crucial symbol for national unity in all countries, was originally promulgated as literal truth, but has now been reduced to the status of a Shinto myth.[2]

The problem for the salary man is that since he accepts the superiority of modern science and many Western values, he has difficulty taking pride in his heritage—he is not even sure what is unique to his heritage. Unlike citizens of other countries where the definition of a nation's uniqueness has undergone continual modification through close contact with other countries, the Mamachi citizen has not had an accurate definition of what is distinctly Japanese, and he has, therefore, been less prepared for the sudden massive assault of Western culture.[3]

The Mamachi salary man is in the anomalous position of loving his country but of depreciating it on the basis of Western standards, which he increasingly accepts as his own. Just as Mamachi residents are sensitive to each other's personal evaluations, so are they sensitive to a Westerner's view of Japan. Not having firm convictions of their own about which Japanese characteristics are valuable or desirable, they are seeking the evaluations of foreigners and doing everything possible to gain their respect. In 1959–1960, during our field work, Mamachi residents were already talking about things they could do in improving Japan so it will make a good impression on foreigners when the next Olympics are held in Tokyo in 1964.

Their defeat at the end of World War II came as a crushing blow to their pride and left them without a sense of national purpose. As much as Mamachi residents resented the military rule during wartime and realize in retrospect how mistaken Japan was to embark on such an ambitious program of territorial expansion, they admit that they had shared the dreams of glory about Japan's becoming a leader of Asia and a great world power. Now, like citizens of European countries which recently have divested themselves of empire, Mamachi residents must adjust themselves to seeing their

[2] According to this myth, the grandchild of the Sun Goddess descended into Kyushu with the three sacred treasures with a heavenly blessing that Japan should prosper and endure forever.

[3] See Masao Maruyama's essays for an analysis of the problem of opening the country and other problems of the Japanese political order. (English translation published by Oxford University Press, 1963.)

nation as weaker in relative power and feeling helpless in doing much about it. The Mamachi resident is left with little sense of a national goal except to be relatively more modern or rational, and this goal seems unexciting by contrast with the dreams of glory and the superpatriotism before and during the war.

Unlike totalitarian countries, Japan is not undertaking an official rewriting of history. But an analogous process is going on in Mamachi. People have discarded much of the history as taught until the end of World War II, and are emphasizing some aspects of their history and neglecting others. They de-emphasize the entire military period of the 1930's and World War II and talk more about the great cultural accomplishments of the Nara and Heian periods, about the courage of liberal leaders in the 1920's and 1930's who fought for a modern pluralistic society; and some are beginning to see the work of Emperor Meiji more for its contribution to modernization than for its contribution to absolutism, which set an example for the militarists in the late 1930's.

As with history, so with other symbols of national pride. Although they still enjoy the tea ceremony, flower arrangement, ancient temples, and traditional art, these are now less a source of national pride than Tokyo Tower, the modern Ginza area of Tokyo, the rate of economic growth, and Japan's standing in international sports contests.

New bases of national pride are beginning to emerge, not in what is unique to the Japanese tradition but in what is the most desirable combination of East and West. Unlike citizens of Western countries who enjoy only Western culture, Mamachi residents feel they can share the benefits of Western and Japanese culture. They can, for example, have Western electrical equipment along with Japanese gardens and tatami mats, Western and Japanese-style food, Western and Japanese-style clothing, Western and Japanese music, Western and Japanese-style painting. Although there are difficulties in reconciling specific traditional practices with modern ones, the over-all goal of building a superior culture by combining the best of the East and West does give a general perspective for the solution of these difficulties.

The Imperial family remains the most important single focus for patriotic sentiments. Unlike the politicians, the Emperor was not considered responsible for the war, and because he is no longer so aloof, many people have come to have even more affection for him since the war.[4] Mamachi residents recall that before the war the Emperor rarely appeared in public and that if he did, people bowed so low they did not have a chance even to look at his face. During the war, when the streetcar conductor announced the approach to the Imperial Palace, everyone bowed to the floor of the car. Since the war, however, the Emperor personally greets the crowds at the palace on the first two days of the New Year and on his birthday. Everyone can see his pictures on TV and read stories about the Imperial family in the newspapers and magazines. Although some of the most progressive youths of Mamachi raise questions about the value of the Imperial system, the overwhelming majority of these families feel devotion, affection, and enthusiasm for the Imperial family.

For popular and spontaneous excitement no event during our period of research could be compared to the wedding of the Crown Prince and the new Princess. Everyone devoured the newspapers and magazines before, during, and after the wedding, and decorations were everywhere. The only time that a request was made to interrupt an interview during our entire research period was when a family wanted to watch televised films of the Crown Prince and Princess on their honeymoon trip to the national shrine of Ise. The little girls of Mamachi idolized Princess Michiko and copied her hair styles and clothing. Though few people in Mamachi took up tennis because the Prince and Princess met on the tennis courts, many were well aware that tennis became more popular because of this fortuitous event. They were pleased and proud that the Princess was a commoner, and they avidly followed the activities of the Princess's household. The birth of a child to Princess Michiko was followed in minute detail and was a favorite topic of conversation for Mamachi residents. Similarly, although to a lesser extent, they followed the marriage of the Emperor's daughter Princess Suga, reading the newspaper and magazine stories about the house furnishings and family plans. They were delighted when one of the princesses agreed to have her own radio program, and their respon-

[4] Cf. Takeshi Ishida, "Popular Attitudes toward the Japanese Emperor," *Asian Survey*, 1962, 2:29–39.

siveness helps explain why requests for public appearances of members of the Imperial family have been far greater than can possibly be met.

Before and during World War II, because the Emperor and the government officials were linked together as representatives of the national interest, it was difficult for Mamachi residents to have a legitimate basis for criticizing government officials. Although politicians never had wide popular support, the officials who acted in the name of the Emperor were ordinarily immune from public criticism.[5] As far as political attitudes of Mamachi residents are concerned, the important change in the Emperor's status after the war was not his official renunciation of his divinity. Many Mamachi residents had not believed in his divinity before the war, and they remained devoted to him after the renunciation. The important change was the separation of the Imperial institution from governmental power. No longer can the Emperor be used to cloak and legitimize the actions of governmental leaders.

As a result, national officials have been deprived of their most important source of popular support, and political leaders who were never even cloaked by the Emperor still have no legitimate basis for winning the people's respect.[6] Although elections provide a basis for legitimizing them, even if elected they do not enjoy the high status accorded to government bureaucrats, and even government bureaucrats no longer enjoy the immunity of servants of the Emperor. From the point of view of the Mamachi resident, in order to be respected, a person should be committed to his group and should

---

[5] Cf. Robert A. Scalapino, *Democracy and the Party Movement in Prewar Japan*, Berkeley and Los Angeles: University of California Press, 1953.

[6] For example, in a 1956 *Mainichi* poll, in answer to the question, "Do you think the House of Councilors has accomplished its appointed tasks?" 78 percent of salary men said no, compared to 64 percent of merchants and industrialists, 68 percent laborers, and 60 percent of farmers and fishermen. Cited in Allan B. Cole, *Japanese Opinion Polls with Socio-political Significance, 1947–1957*. Medford, Mass.: Tufts University, 1958, p. 370.

In a 1957 *Asahi* poll, in answer to the question, "Do you think government is trying to eliminate the three evils of corruption, violence, and poverty?" 46 percent of the salary men said no, compared to 41 percent merchants and industrialists, 43 percent industrial laborers, and 25 percent farmers and fishermen. *Ibid.*, p. 372.

In a 1954 *Yomiuri* poll in Tokyo, Osaka, and Yokohama, in answer to the question of "Do you have confidence in your present congressmen?" on the average 68 percent said no, but among salary men, 77 percent replied no, 9 percent replied yes, and 21 percent said they did not know. *Ibid.*, p. 409.

not be pursuing his own self-interests. But political leaders continually are expressing individual interests or, at best, the interests of a small clique without respecting the rights of others. There is no underlying consensus whereby the supporters of the losing candidate support the person elected simply because he is elected. The loser does not form a "loyal opposition"; he expects, in return, that his wishes will not be respected by the majority. Even those who vote for the winning candidate, however, usually do not feel their candidate is looking out for their interests but for the interest of a small clique. From the view of the Mamachi resident, there is a big difference between, for example, the Meiji leaders who were devoted to their country and the opportunistic politicians who now hold office. Their vague affection toward things Japanese may be expressed through occasions like the wedding of the Crown Prince but it is not expressed by the acts of their political leaders.

In part, the problem of legitimizing political leaders stems from disagreement over the value of various aspects of the national heritage. It is difficult for a politician to find any broad basis of consensus by which he could obtain a large following, even among Mamachi residents alone.

The problem of legitimation of political leaders has been compounded by the onus laid on many groups and individuals associated with the military effort in wartime. Even the residents of Mamachi who were themselves soldiers feel a repulsion toward the military leaders. Before and during World War II, the military was extremely contemptuous of the civilian population. The residents of Mamachi still recall the fear they had of their own military and the danger of trying to oppose any of their wishes. They feel that they endured many years of suffering in vain for a military which led them to a national debacle. Many of their friends and relatives died during the war because of the military's mistaken judgment. The repulsion to the military could hardly be more extreme and more complete.[7]

---

[7] Mary Ellen Goodman, an American anthropologist, analyzed compositions of 1250 Japanese and 3750 American children in grades one to eight on "What I want to be when I grow up and why." She reports as follows: "Most striking of all Japanese/American contrasts are those having to do with the military and religious roles. . . . The Japanese child . . . totally ignores all roles related to the military or to the national defense, and discusses national welfare solely in terms of health, peace,

Military forces have been declared illegal under the new constitution, but most Mamachi residents see little distinction between the military and the new "Self-Defense Forces." Even the police are regarded with much the same fear and caution as the prewar military, and to some extent the attitudes toward the discredited military are transferred to the police. During the period of research, when the Diet debated the strengthening of the police force, many Mamachi residents agreed heartily with vigorous press warnings about the dangers of such a measure.

The same opprobrium extends to civilian leaders connected with the wartime government, thus including many of Japan's ablest political leaders and bureaucrats. Kishi, the prime minister at the time of the interviews, is one example. The residents of Mamachi felt that it was difficult to place full confidence in such a man who turned so easily from participating in a militarist campaign to representing Japan in the era of peace. Indeed many Mamachi residents could not understand why the United States would allow Eisenhower, a former World War II general, to become president in peacetime. They asked whether America's victory led America to respect the military so much. Even the Japanese flag and the national anthem were so closely associated with the discredited war effort that they have been slow to revive as national symbols. For many years after the war most residents did not use the flag, and only few are beginning to fly it again.

The wholehearted rejection of militarism by most Japanese is not sufficient to give Mamachi residents confidence that there is no danger of a return to prewar authoritarianism. Many are genuinely afraid that in time of some domestic economic or political crisis an unselfish national leader might arise with sufficient appeal as an unselfish patriot as to win the necessary following from the more selfish politicians and lead the country back to totalitarianism, and that they would be powerless to stop such a trend. It is partly this fear that makes them so adamant in their objections to the strengthening

---

and prosperity. This is distinctly not true of the American children" (p. 996). She further reports, "Americans express much patriotic sentiment and much concern for the national safety; in fact, they do a great deal of verbal flag-waving. We get absolutely nothing of the sort from the Japanese boys" (p. 983). Mary Ellen Goodman, "Values, Attitudes, and Social Concepts of Japanese and American Children," *American Anthropologist,* 1957, 59:979–999.

of the police and other measures which might provide the foundation for the return of a totalitarian regime.

The average person in Mamachi does not feel a part of the collective guilt for starting the war in the same way many Americans feel guilty for the dropping of the atomic bombs. On the one hand, Mamachi residents feel that Japan was forced to go to war, and on the other, that it was the decision of the militarists, not their own decision. They do feel, however, that Japan made an enormous mistake to launch a war she could not win, and their feelings about Hiroshima are more resentment at the devastation than moral criticism of the United States for using the atomic bombs.

In thinking about foreign affairs, Mamachi residents seem to feel strongly on three points. Firstly, they want international alignments that will be of benefit to Japan. They feel they have more to gain from close relationships with the West than with China or Russia. They are grateful for the economic help and technical advice they received during the occupation, which, they think, they would not have received had they been occupied, for example, by Russia or China. They consider the United States to be very wealthy and Americans more humanitarian than the Russians. But they also think it in their interest to have some trade and cultural relations with China and Russia within the context of keeping their strongest ties to the West.

At the same time, however, another strong consideration is their sensitivity to any situation in which Japan is placed in an inferior position. They wish Japan to be treated with respect. They resent it when the United States considers the opinion of European allies, without giving equal weight to Japanese opinion. To be in a position of economic and political dependence on the United States in which Americans can dictate the terms of economic and political arrangements reminds them of the bitter days when the United States imposed unequal treaties, excluded Orientals from migrating to the United States, and sent her troops to occupy their country. As one Mamachi man put it, "Because of Japan's mistake in starting and losing the war, we are forced to be America's samurai." In their personal relations, most salary men are happy they have been largely emancipated from "feudalistic" relationships where they, as inferiors, had their personal lives controlled by paternalistic superiors. In their identification with the nation as well, they are anxious for Japan to be freed of pressures restricting their independent action. This feeling seems to underlie the unpopularity of the Security Pact which was signed during the period of our field work.[8] The widespread objections to the Security Pact in no way affected their personal relationship to Americans, nor did it seriously damage their friendly feelings to the United States as a whole. In their view, Kishi railroaded the Security Pact through the Diet to please the United States. Eisenhower's desire to come to Japan so soon afterward was taken as evidence that the American government supported Kishi's tactics, and that Kishi had been responding to American pressure to enact a measure that was not in the best interests of Japan. Many residents of Mamachi did feel that it was necessary and even wise for Japan to accept the Security Pact in one form or another, but all were bitter about Kishi's tactics and American pressure. They do not criticize the United States for legitimately pursuing her own interests, but resent that Japan must still play the subordinate role. It is a wound to their national pride rather than a criticism of American policy as such.

Despite their feelings about the Security Pact they are inclined, on the basis of stories about American soldiers in Japan, American movies they have seen, and second-hand reports, to regard Americans as basically generous and human, albeit a bit overbearing. Most have much less knowledge about Russia, and the few stories from people repatriated by Russia or about the problems of Russian restriction on Japanese fishing have given Russians a somewhat more frightening and less humane image. Many people were in China during the period of Japanese expansion, and this tends to give them a healthy respect for and a feeling of guilt toward the Chinese peasant, which is coupled with a historic tradition of close relations in language, religion, and a wide range of customs. Although many are sympathetic with the efforts of the Chinese Communist government to improve the lot of the common man, they are happy that

---

[8] The original Security Treaty between United States and Japan was signed September 9, 1951. During our period of research in Mamachi, the Kishi government was debating the renewal of this treaty. At one point in the debate on whether the Diet term should be extended, Socialist members were carrying on a demonstration in the corridors of the Diet. The government had police remove the demonstrators and during their absence passed the renewal of the revised Security Treaty in 1960.

they do not have to live under such tight governmental regimentation. But they consider China much less frightening and dangerous than Americans do, and they would like to have somewhat closer economic and cultural relations with China than they now have.

The third consideration that dominates their thinking about foreign affairs is an intense hatred and fear of war. Having been devastated in World War II and having had two cities of their country destroyed by atomic bombs, Mamachi residents not only despise their own country's military but all countries' military. To have American soldiers on their territory seems terrible to them because it means subordination of Japan's wishes to the wishes of Americans and greater likelihood of becoming involved in war. They are annoyed at the United States for having forced them to build up their "self-defense" forces after having previously urged on Japan a constitution renouncing all military forces.[9]

Most Mamachi residents would prefer to have closer relations with the West than with the East because they think their best interests are served in this direction. But neutralism,[10] within the context of stronger ties to the West, has a great appeal both because Japan might escape the position of servitude in its alliance with the West and because they think Japan would be less likely to become involved even if war should break out between East and West.

THE ROLE OF THE CITIZEN

The ability of present-day residents of Mamachi to laugh at their fear of officialdom before 1945 indicates that they now feel greater freedom and confidence in facing government officials. Yet, in comparison with American standards, they still are very humble before officials and still regard encounters with them as trying experiences. From their view, the manner in which government bureaus operate depends in part on the whim and disposition of the officials. The applicant's strategy is to get on the official's good side and win

---

[9] Cf. the symposium, "Japan Since Recovery of Independence," *The Annals of the American Academy of Political and Social Science,* November 1956, No. 308.

[10] In answer to the question of whether they prefer a pro-American, pro-Soviet, or neutralist policy, salary men are slightly stronger in their preference for neutralism than most Japanese. In a *Shimbun Yoron Choosa Renmei* poll in 1953, 42 percent of salary men favored pro-America, 2 percent pro-Soviet, 46 percent neutralism, and the rest gave no opinion. Cited in Cole, *op. cit.,* p. 694.

his favor. The applicant will smile when angry and reply pleasantly
to brusk remarks. Unless they have introductions, Mamachi people
seem to feel it necessary to plead in order to get an official to
respond in the desired manner. They know about the bureaucratic
techniques of systematic postponement, indefinite answers, and
"passing the buck," and they expect that the least sign of annoyance
will mean a longer wait and poorer service. Most Mamachi residents
are uncertain about the rights of a citizen vis-à-vis the government
and think that it is rude or senseless to try to oppose an official on
the basis of regulations. They believe that it is not might or law
that makes right, but position. A person in a position of authority
is always right and can ensure that his wishes are carried out.
Despite attempts to define the situation differently, even government welfare assistance is viewed not as a right but as a privilege
granted at the pleasure of an official.

Because Mamachi residents, and especially women, feel helpless
before the government, they try to avoid contact with government
officials whenever possible. If a meeting cannot be avoided, they
will try to obtain a personal introduction to an official. A man who
brings letters of introduction or establishes mutual contacts can
hope for better treatment than would be accorded a stranger. With
good introductions, he is likely to be received in grand style, be
treated with efficiency, and be made to feel important. Although
the average salary man does not necessarily look up to a bureaucrat
as a person, even if he himself works in a government office he is
hesitant in applying to another government bureau without the introduction of friends or colleagues.

The Japanese are generally law-abiding but they do not equate
rules with morality. They have seen law changed drastically with
shifts in power—some laws rigidly enforced by their own military,
other laws laid down by their conquerors. Obedience to laws then,
seems to reflect prudence rather than morality.

In certain cases, cheating or deceiving the government, particularly about taxes, is not considered reprehensible. It is difficult for
a salaried employee to hide the amount he is paid, because it is
known at the company. But the independent businessman, the small
shopkeeper, or the independent professional often systematically

understates his income. Large businessmen, by their contacts and consultants, frequently can arrange their accounts so that they do not have to fear punishment by the government. But small businessmen almost inevitably worry that the tax officer will require them to pay more money and in a way lacking in grace and dignity.

Although an individual person almost never objects directly to the government about the way he is treated in a government office, groups of citizens occasionally present complaints collectively. For example, some Mamachi residents went in large numbers to complain about the sewer system in their area. Other groups protest plans for roads, noise from factories, or heavy traffic. But even large delegations do not expect to receive much consideration unless they are introduced by a person of power or position in that bureau.

As yet there are few groups devoted to securing or preserving the rights of citizens. Generally, it is felt that these functions will be served by the people in power, or by the more powerful citizens of the community, and if these functions are not served residents feel that all they can do about it is protest loudly. It is difficult to imagine organizations with a wide membership base such as the Civil Liberties Union, and since women are so removed from politics it is even more difficult to imagine an effective Japanese League of Women Voters. Despite the growing interest in public opinion, most residents of Mamachi do not expect that under ordinary circumstances public opinion and the activities of the citizenry will have a serious impact on their government's decisions.

The experience of Mamachi men as salaried employees in large organizations has served to lend support to the prevailing view of the powerlessness of the citizenry. They have found that the way to be most effective in their organizations is to work through people with whom they have a special relationship. If they have a connection with people in power, then usually it is possible for them to express their opinions, and the people in power will tend to assist them in getting what they wish. However, if they do not have such contacts, it is hopeless for them to try to affect company policy. Thus in business as in politics, a man's influence on decisions depends in large part on his position within the organization and upon his relationship with the people at the top. By their contacts and power, influential high-status salary men are more conservative politically[11] and expect to play a role in governmental processes, but ordinary salary men do not.

Even in the local community salary men take little part in political activities. Because their center of activity is in the firm or bureau which has no ties to the local community, they have much less interest in suburban politics than the old middle class of small business owners and independent professionals who control the reins of local power. Furthermore, the salary man and his family are generally among the newcomers to Mamachi and would have difficulty breaking into local politics even if they were interested, expecially since most important issues like budgets for schools and road and sewage construction are decided by the local bureaucracies rather than by local elections in which all can participate. Even participation often means only petitioning the local government.

The feeling of powerlessness of the citizen in relation to the government is unmitigated by confidence in the democratic processes. Residents value the right to vote and have a vague hope that their combined votes may have some influence, but they do not feel that voting, in fact, has much effect on government decisions. From their point of view, government decisions are made by the higher-ups in private meetings, often at geisha houses, and are completely beyond the control of the average citizen. They are not happy with the situation but they feel powerless to change it.[12] Although the average American citizen may have little more influence in governmental decisions than his Japanese counterpart, the American is taught to feel that his vote and opinions do count and that he has effective avenues for redress of grievances. The Mamachi resident,

---

[11] In a Tokyo survey in 1962, it was found that 39 percent of one group of office workers in large enterprises and 51 percent of another group supported Socialists. However, only 14 percent of the officers in these enterprises supported the Socialists. Nihon Shakai Koozoo Choosakkai, *Howaito Karaa no Ishiki Koozoo* (The Structure of White Collar Ideology), Tokyo, March, 1962, p. 265. The evidence from this and other voting studies shows that ordinary salary men are more likely to vote Socialist than are laborers.

[12] Indeed, books like the Japanese translation of C. Wright Mills, *Power Elite,* which argue that elitist cliques exist, are extremely popular among salary men, especially those who are recent graduates of universities. In Japan, the government bureaucracy has more power and political functions vis-à-vis the political parties than in America and many Western countries. Therefore, the feeling of being excluded is likely to be greater than when officials are more subject to the will of the people.

being more cynical of the government's tendency to look out for its own interests and ignore the interests of outsiders, has no such basis of optimism.[13]

SALARY AND THE MODERATION OF ALIENATION

Part of the alienation toward the government in power rests on this feeling of being looked down upon by governmental leaders. The salary man, like other Japanese, feels intense loyalty to his own groups and intense hostility to groups from which he is excluded. Because government leaders, and particularly government bureaucrats, tend to have close-knit elitist groups unresponsive to the wishes of the average person, it is difficult for the salary man to identify with governmental leaders. One of the strongest complaints against the government, that it is a "tyranny of the majority," clearly reflects the concern about exclusive government groups imposing their will without giving sufficient consideration to others. The salary man does not feel that the government leaders are "of the people," but of a series of in-groups to which he does not belong.

In part, the alienation to the government in power seems to rest on the desire to modernize government institutions. Since the government has more than its share of leaders representing rural and special-interest conservative groups, it seems far more traditional than salary men wish it to be. Many salary men connect their feeling of disillusionment with the government to what they had learned in their university days. In contrast to many of the older middle class who support conservatives and even the radical right, salary men are in favor of developing a rational approach to government just as they wish to develop rational procedures in their own firm. But even if they could respect the methods of operation of government departments, salary men cannot identify with what they see as the primary purpose of any government bureau, the perpetuation and strengthening of its own power.

For many Mamachi residents, criticism of the government gives them a feeling of remaining true to their feelings of protest and the

---

[13] Many Westerners had hoped that with the rise of the middle class, the democratic processes would be strengthened. Although the participation of the middle class in voting and in free speech and criticism undoubtedly poses certain restraints on authoritarian rule, the relatively closed nature of groups still poses formidable obstacles to the broad expansion of political participation and influence.

ideals of democracy which they had espoused so vocally during their college days. They are convinced that the militarists came to power in Japan because people did not stand up for more democratic practices. In general, as salary men grow older and rise higher in their firms, they become more conservative. Some salary men seem to feel slightly ashamed of having adjusted so well to the firm, to have lost the feeling of protest, and of doing so little to help the cause of democracy and the nation's welfare. However, many who in their own behavior have become more conservative retain much of their strong ideological opposition to the government.

Although feeling excluded from governmental processes, the salary man maintains an active interest in political affairs and keeps himself well abreast of the news, especially in national affairs.[14] Japanese are avid readers, but the salary man, being better educated than the average, is particularly well read on broader issues affecting his country. The Mamachi man commonly reads both the morning and evening editions of one of the three large dailies, as well as weekly and monthly magazines, and he often discusses politics with friends at work. Although wives are generally much less informed about national political activities than their husbands, they, too, follow at least the main trend of important political events.

Most salary men are moderate in the manner in which they express opposition to the government. They enjoy many of the virulent criticisms of the government in the newspapers and pass on their bitter criticism in conversation with friends, but they are not likely to participate in riots and demonstrations. Even if they vote for the Socialists, as many salary men do, they explain that they do not really respect the Socialists, who seem to them irresponsible in their behavior. They are not as much for the Socialists, as they are against the government; they doubt that the Socialists would be freer of corruption and mismanagement.

The moderate way in which salary men express opposition is not simply a result of the fact that companies prefer to hire college students with moderate political views—many a salary man admits

---

[14] In an *Asahi* poll in 1952, 87 percent of salary men questioned knew the Diet was in session compared to 70 percent of merchants and industrialists, 65 percent industrial laborers, and 57 percent of farmers and fishermen. Cited in Allan B. Cole, *op. cit.*, p. 392.

having been more leftist in his youth. Rather, his moderation seems to be a result of the fact that he seems sufficiently comfortable with his present position and sufficiently pessimistic as to what would be accomplished by more active political participation; thus he is reluctant to place his position in jeopardy. Mamachi men know that although firms are ordinarily loyal to their members they have been known to sacrifice a member should he become too embarrassing; and that short of dismissing an employee, the firm can exert powerful informal pressure on the deviant.

Chapter VI

THE SEPARATE COMMUNITIES OF HUSBANDS, WIVES, AND CHILDREN

For informal social life, a husband does not meet with his wife's friends, the wife does not associate with her husband's friends, and they rarely go out together as a couple.

Shortly after arriving in Mamachi, we invited six families to our house for a picnic luncheon. As soon as the invitations were issued, the wives got together and decided that husbands were not to attend, and indeed, the husbands did not attend. Despite ideology to the contrary, it is clear that husbands and wives will not easily adopt a pattern of shared social life, and that women are as little anxious as men to push for a change. A husband centers his social life on his place of work, the wife on her immediate neighborhood and relatives. Even on the rare occasions when the husband brings guests to his home, a proper wife serves the guests and smiles pleasantly, but does not interfere with the conversation and often stays in another room except when serving. With their friends, husbands generally feel constrained in the presence of a wife, and wives feel even more constrained in the presence of a husband. Most wives prefer to stay at home where they can be comfortable rather than face formalities, listen to stiff conversation, and worry about behaving properly. Even couples who told us they would like to go out together found excuses for never doing so.[1]

Paradoxically, the separation of the husband's and wife's social

---

[1] Many Americans in Japan have commented that while they can communicate with Japanese men, they find it difficult to develop meaningful relationships with women. It may be suggested that this is because they have largely seen the women in public situations or in the presence of their husbands.

lives is more complete in the modern salary man's families than in many traditional families. In farm and small-shopkeeper families, although men's and women's activities are carefully separated, a woman's closest friends are often the wives of her husband's friends. Consequently, husbands and wives have a feeling of belonging to the same social community although there may be little direct interaction between men and women. Independent professionals and businessmen have more opportunities to go out with their wives, and the women often become friendly with the wives of their husbands' friends. Not so the salary men, where the husbands' friends usually have no relationship with the wives' friends.

Sometimes, however, the Mamachi husband and wife pay visits together on formal occasions like New Year's, weddings, and funerals. Some modern couples, immediately after marriage, proudly go to movies, plays, and concerts together and sometimes attend parties with friends. Yet, in most Mamachi families this visiting stops abruptly shortly before the first child is born. While some young couples talk of going out occasionally even afterward, they rarely do, except perhaps for visits to relatives. Occasionally, husbands do visit with husbands of the wife's neighborhood friends. However, most husbands have little to do with their neighbors, not only because their own social life keeps them busy but also because they are mildly embarrassed by intruding into what is essentially the wife's domain. Although doing things as a couple is usually regarded as "modern," even in traditional homes elderly husbands and wives have been close and do many things together. Life expectancy is almost the same as in the United States, and after the salary man retires at fifty-five or sixty, the elderly couple generally spend more time together than they ever did when younger. Elderly couples go to Tokyo together for shopping or entertainment and, if they can afford it, take trips together to hot-springs resorts, famous shrines, or scenic spots.

THE FATHER AND HIS COMPANY GANG

Salary men have more time for recreation than small shopkeepers or independent professionals, and most of the recreational activities are with their friends from work. Because of the long distance from home to work, it is difficult to go home after work and then return to the city for an evening of recreation. Various polls have shown that it takes the husband an average of two to three hours to get home. While commuting may require a long time, the transportation alone could not possibly take that long. It is rather that this is the time for recreation. After work, the men stop off someplace to sit and chat, have a drink and perhaps a bite to eat.[2] Most company gangs have their own favorite hangouts: bars, coffee houses, small food-specialty shops, and the like. Here, by spending only a few cents, they can have long leisurely conversations. It is here that they talk and laugh freely about sports, national and world events or the daily happenings in the company, complain about bosses and wives, and receive the consolation of their friends and of the sympathetic girls behind the counter.

Some men, particularly the more conservative or serious, do not like the gay life of the company gang and prefer to come home at an earlier hour to be with their families. Those who do not always stop off with the boys may walk around for an hour or so seeing sights, looking at department stores, or playing *pachinko* (a popular kind of pin-ball machine), *go, shoogi* (Japanese chess), or mahjong —all easily available at public or private places on the way home.

Even those who do not participate regularly in the daily gang activities join in company-sponsored special activities such as field day, baseball, tennis, table tennis, fishing, or the overnight trip to an inn. Even government offices have special funds to cover the expenses of such excursions. At least part of the time on the trip is spent enjoying the hot bath, but there are other activities such as fishing, skiing, baseball, sight-seeing, and mountain-climbing. The camaraderie often reaches its peak in the evening with drinking and singing. Often the group is large enough to charter a bus or occupy most of a railway car, and the fun begins when they get on the train. Aside from trips paid entirely by the company, the gang can often take advantage of a company discount at special inns and restaurants, even for trips not officially sponsored by the company. In contrast to the American social hour or cocktail party, where

---

[2] In some Boston-Irish families studied by the author in 1954–1958 as part of a project directed by Dr. F. Kluckhohn and J. Spiegel, it was also common for men to stop off on the way home from work. In these families, as in the Japanese salaryman family, the wife and children have a relatively independent existence with the father less centrally participating in household activities.

one talks personally to one or two at a time, Japanese parties or trips are oriented to the whole group, except for hiking, sight-seeing, or bathing which require smaller groups and permit more intimate discussion. Although as many as twenty or thirty people may sit together listening to stories and joking, speakers are often more intimate than they are in private conversation. On such occasions men openly air their troubles and sometimes make personal confessions or tell jokes designed to correct personal problems within the group. At other times, someone in the group with special talent will tell funny stories or perform by singing or playing a musical instrument. Such group recreation is not limited to the salary man, except that he usually can enjoy recreational trips more frequently, and at company expense, and that his group is formed on the basis of place of work rather than on the basis of neighborhood, village, profession, religion, age, or kinship.

Generally those who stop off together after work are the ones who see each other most at work. Although it usually consists of the same positions sometimes people at different levels, who constitute a kind of *batsu* (clique) within the company, also go out together. Perhaps clique members have gone to the same school or have had a close leader-follower relationship for years, the leader offering guidance and help in return for loyalty and support within the company. Actually the clique may consist of a much larger membership than the small informal group which stops off on the way home, but even then the smaller informal group may be determined by membership in the bigger clique.

Because employees ordinarily expect to continue together for their entire careers and groups are so tightly integrated, maintaining smooth relationships is a much more critical problem than in the United States. Although everyone may be loyal to the group, minor differences of opinion (what Freud calls the narcissism of small differences) can create tensions upsetting to the group members. Going out together for recreation is crucial for keeping personal relationships strong enough to withstand the tensions which arise during the course of work.

Because most men belong to no group other than their work group they are sensitive to the slightest difficulties in personal relations. For example, some men are distraught about the way they are treated by superiors.[3] Others become envious of one of their group selected as a "fair-haired boy" by the superiors, especially if he begins to flaunt his favored status. But by relaxing together after work and going together on company trips, the men can maintain sufficient rapport and camaraderie that these complaints and rivalries seem minor.[4]

The problem of controlling competition also helps to explain the exclusion of wives from social activities. Because wives have less personal investment in the husband's work group, they are more prone to gossip and thus are considered to be a strain on group solidarity. Wives are likely to be jealous of other wives who have nicer clothes, homes, or more education, and may drag their husbands into their discontent. Furthermore, status differences among wives may not accord with status differences among the husbands at work. If one man has a little more money through his family, this need not influence his position at work but it would affect his wife's style of living. When asked why wives are not invited, salary men are not always sure. They all have a feeling that it would be a nuisance and interference to have them around. Some say it would cost too much money, and part of that expense would probably be in keeping up with wealthier colleagues. When wives do go out with their husbands, it is more likely to be with old school friends rather than with colleagues, and the group is likely to break into women talking with women and men talking with men. Wives are sometimes invited to formal occasions, but then there is little opportunity to gossip.[5]

---

[3] In sentence-completion items, salary men frequently referred spontaneously to difficulties they had with superiors. On items asking about troubles, their main concern was often their superior at work. Similarly they were often annoyed when their superior did not look after them or when they did not please their superior. Yet these men ordinarily have no alternative than to stay in this relationship and try to make it as good as possible. The only other possibility in most places would be transfer to another section within the company, which would not entirely end their difficulties.

[4] Following Durkheim, one can also say that this solidarity makes it possible for the group to enforce its norms on the members. It should be noted, however, that the integration into the organization accrues to all employees and is not based on occupational specialization. Cf. Emile Durkheim, *The Division of Labor in Society*, Glencoe, Ill.: The Free Press, 1947.

[5] Following this line of thought, one would expect that paternalistic companies with company housing would have serious problems because wives gossip about other women. Brief contact with one Mamachi small-company apartment project suggests that this is so. Mr. Jack Knowles, who investigated the internal dispute in the

Even though wives are reluctant to express jealousy, everyone recognizes that they are often jealous of the office girls who not only do secretarial work, but also perform many informal services such as running errands and serving tea—services performed in a way to flatter the men in the office. In spite of the fact that peer group activities tend to be exclusively male, occasionally an office girl or a bar girl becomes a regular participant. Sometimes friendships with office girls develop into sexual relationships although these still seem to be relatively infrequent.[6] Even when there is no sexual relationship, men naturally do become fond of certain girls at work. When the company has an overnight trip to the country, the girls from the office generally go along and sometimes may be particularly friendly with certain men. There is an aura of romance associated with the office girl, and it is now so common for single men to marry young girls working in the same office that this kind of marriage is given the special name, *shokuba kekkon* (literally, "work-place marriage"). Since most girls quit work on marriage, office girls are generally young, and it is not surprising that wives often feel concern about their husbands' relations with girls in the office. Japanese firms have a strict prohibition on women working in the same firm as their husbands, and require women to quit immediately if they marry someone in the firm. This tends to sharpen the separation between the firm and home and suggests to what extent the company recognizes the threats to work-group solidarity.[7]

Oji Paper Company, a company in northern Japan with company housing, reports that workers said they could get along with each other better were it not for the wives.

[6] Professor Shinichi Asayama, the Japanese counterpart to Alfred C. Kinsey, finds that in recent years the amount of organized prostitution has greatly diminished but the number of Japanese men having some kind of sexual relationship with the women at their working place had greatly increased.

[7] It may be suggested that Americans are able to permit husbands and wives to go out together because the firm is not such a tight-knit group. In Japan the range of meaningful contacts is so limited that relationships with co-workers involves such intensity of feeling that rivalries and difficulties cannot be treated in an objective way or dismissed as unimportant. However, many large American firms with a close-knit executive group are also concerned with the threat of wives to the solidarity of the work group but the solution of the problem, as noted in William H. Whyte's description of the wives of management, is to bring the wives more closely into company affairs.

In answer to a sentence completion "women are . . . ," both men and women frequently described women as home-bodies, who do not enjoy going out.

If a man carries on an affair with a girl in the office, it need not disrupt his relationship with his wife. Long-lasting affairs involving considerable expenditures may lead to divorce, but wives who know or suspect that their husbands are carrying on affairs often resign themselves as long as the husband meets his family financial duties and still expresses his affection to her and the children. Some wives even say their husbands are milder and easier to deal with if they have a sexual outlet outside the home. Other wives are jealous about the husbands' relations to office and bar girls. They know liaisons exist, and because they are excluded from their husbands' office life, they are never certain about their office relationships. Ignorance is more likely to breed suspicion than bliss, but because the wife has no opportunity to see other employees or their wives who might give her accurate information, she generally resolves her feelings by denying the suspicion or denying that it matters even if such affairs exist.

Problems of the wife's jealousy of office girls may be illustrated by the case of a wife who knew a girl working in her husband's office. The girl reported to the wife that the husband was particularly friendly with another girl in the office. The husband denied the story, and the wife could not determine whether the story was true or not. She felt there were grounds why this girl might be spreading false rumors, but she also could see signs that her husband did not love her. This worry about the husband's fidelity led to the most violent arguments in the couple's long years of marriage.

Mamachi residents usually explain that wives do not go out with husbands because it is not a traditional custom, because it requires too much money, or because the wife should be protected from undesirable influences. Yet their reluctance to permit wives to go out with husbands has a strength which goes far beyond economic considerations or mere custom. It may be suggested that the husband is reluctant to permit any possible encroachment on peer group solidarity and also reluctant to give the wife full access to his peer group because she might be able to make an independent assessment of his occupational role which would alter her image of his position at work.[8] The wife also wants to avoid any possible

---

[8] I am indebted to Ronald Dore who first called my attention to this problem. Most Mamachi wives have considerable respect for the husband and his position.

encroachment on the solidarity of her neighborhood group and because she lacks information about the husband's relations with other women, she resolves her feelings about his outside activities by considering them beyond her scope of concern and refusing to let them interfere with her marriage.

The Mother and Her Neighborhood

Because companies take in new members only once a year, the husband joins at the same time as large numbers of other men. In the welcoming activities, orientation program, and daily work, he is thrown into contact with his peers so that he has no difficulty in developing personal relationships. The wife, on the other hand, after her marriage moves into an unfamiliar and probably long-settled neighborhood where she has no friends. While she may make friends fairly quickly in some of the new housing developments in Tokyo, in Mamachi and other suburbs it still takes her many years to win personal friends. When we asked one family whether they felt lonely when they first moved to Mamachi, the husband immediately replied, "No, not at all," but the wife said with feeling, "Yes, very lonely." She went on to explain that even after several years in the community she still did not feel completely at home and that she did not have many close friends.

When a wife first moves to the neighborhood, she makes the rounds to the *mukoo sangen ryoodonari* (immediate neighbors) carrying a small carefully wrapped present of towels, post cards, or soap, along with her husband's name card. But even on this occasion, it is unusual for a neighbor to invite her into the house. While the neighborhood group collects a few cents a year to pay for street lights and local shrines, and the immediate neighbors agree to help each other in case of fire or theft, the emotional significance of the neighborhood groups is very slight, a mere vestige of the powerful neighborhood groups of rural Japan in an earlier era. A Mamachi wife cannot expect to develop close relationships simply because she lives in the neighborhood.

A young wife's only close friends usually are relatives and former

---

Yet the fact is that in the firm they are often very subservient to various superiors, a fact not entirely in harmony with the authority and power the husbands enjoy in the home.

school mates. Unless she is particularly fortunate in living near these friends or relatives she is not likely to see them often. Indeed, the young wife is expected to devote herself completely to her home, husband, and, when they are born, children. It is thought improper to spend much time away from home visiting relatives or friends, even before children are born. To avoid the intense loneliness of the first few years of marriage many wives arrange to live near relatives or friends. Many are even willing to live with or next door to in-laws in order to have somebody with whom they can have meaningful relationships.

Usually a child is conceived soon after marriage, and from then on the wife is completely occupied with the child. Since the Japanese wife considers child care a satisfying and all-encompassing occupation, the mother of a young child finds her social isolation more tolerable than a childless wife. Nevertheless, most mothers want to make friends, even though the time spent in caring for small babies leaves almost no opportunity for it.

Most deep friendships with neighbors develop slowly as a result of frequent meetings over a period of many years. Groups of women who were living in Mamachi during the war feel particularly close to each other. During air raids, food shortages, and difficult living conditions, the women often met together either voluntarily or in air-raid shelters. They took turns drawing food rations or going to the country for food, and if one had a sick child, friends would share food rations with her. Since many of the men were away during much of the war, either in the service or at their place of work, the wives became extremely close. No relationships formed since then equal the intimacy of those wartime ties. The closeness of the older inhabitants is enhanced by the fact that they consider many of the new residents to have lower social standing and especially consider recent immigrants from the country to be less refined.

Wives who have come to Mamachi more recently have developed friendships mostly through the PTA or other school groups. Through the frequent school meetings, mothers become friendly by discussing their common problems in rearing children. Besides the school meetings and introductions through friends, young women have almost no opportunities to become acquainted.

While most of the mothers enjoy the opportunity to attend PTA meetings, younger, less educated women may feel uneasy. A new PTA member is reluctant to express herself for fear that some of the older women may criticize her. Since this is typically the only group to which she will belong, a young mother attending the PTA for the first time is making her social debut, and she is concerned about making a proper impression on the teacher and other mothers.

Older women of established position in the community generally are expected to accept the honor and responsibilities of PTA office. The honor of being a PTA officer was demonstrated by a mother who reported that when she was elected an officer one of her friends who wanted a position became much less friendly. PTA officers consider their work a great responsibility, and even the higher-status mothers are afraid that something may go wrong for which they will be criticized. They are expected to attend frequent meetings, plan programs, raise money, smooth the ruffled feelings of mothers who feel their children are slighted, and take the responsibility for all children on school trips. This hard work is not regarded lightly, and many PTA officers are relieved when their turn of office is over.

Although reticent in expressing their competitive feelings, mothers are aware of the relative social status of each family. The fact that schools require parents to pay for school trips, lunches, text books, and other supplies, and that PTA's rely heavily on donations accentuates the concerns about a family's financial standing. Some poorer families have to accept charity to send their children on school trips or to buy school lunches. Because such matters often become public knowledge, it can be embarrassing for a family that has difficulty in paying. For example, when one child was reported sick on the day of the school trip, some of the other mothers suspected the family could not afford the trip and sent a representative to the child's home to offer financial help. Of course the child was delighted, but the family was ashamed to admit they had so little money. They then had to try in various ways to repay the families who had made it possible for the child to go on the school trip. Although the salary man's family usually can afford the minimum expenses, many families cannot contribute to the frequent appeals to supplement the regular school budget.

Until all children are in school, most mothers are so occupied with their care that they have little time to participate even in PTA groups; afterward the situation of the salary men's wives changes drastically. Mothers who had been looking forward to having a little free time suddenly find themselves bored. Since the salary man's wife almost never has any work of her own or any responsibilities for her husband's work, she generally looks around for more neighborhood and PTA activities. If she has lived in Mamachi for several years she probably already has a number of acquaintances with whom she has become friendly through school activities or daily shopping. She and some of her friends may decide to start a study group for cooking or sewing (either Western or Japanese style), tea ceremony, or flower arranging, and sometimes she may be invited to join a group of older ladies. These groups, like the American ladies' bridge club, offer opportunities for regular visiting and casual gossiping.

Aside from such activities, not only does a mother's life center on the children, but her friends in the community are made largely through her children's activities, and children are usually her main topic of discussion. Younger and lower-status women will listen closely to the "veterans" telling how to persuade a child to study, how to motivate the child to keep her informed of his activities, how to teach the child co-operation, how to get the child into a good school or arrange a successful marriage. After they get to know each other still better they may complain about husbands, and "veterans" will give tips to the younger ones about keeping husbands satisfied and co-operative. Younger and lower-status women tend to be properly reserved, volunteering little except an occasional nodding approval or thanks for the advice they receive from the older ladies. Although mothers' groups may meet at the homes of wealthier families, poorer women are too embarrassed to invite a group to their "small dirty" home.

When talking with us, many expressed envy of American wives who go out with husbands, and many were curious as to what it would be like. Several went so far as to try it for the first time during our stay, but reported that they were too tense to enjoy themselves. When out with husbands and their friends, they have to be so careful to behave properly that it is difficult to go beyond polite pleasantries. Moreover, they must be so retiring that they generally prefer the more relaxed times with their lady friends. One wife, upon hearing about a husband and wife going on a trip for a few days responded, "how nice," but after a moment's reflection added, "but what would they talk about for so long?"

Most of these women have no chance to become casual friends with any man aside from their husbands, and it is considered bad taste to show any sign of friendliness toward another man. On the few occasions when a husband's friends come to the home, the wife may join in the conversations but more commonly she is little more than a polite waitress. There are occasional stories of a woman becoming friendly with her child's male tutor, or with a male teacher of tea ceremony or flower arrangement, but such relationships are almost unknown in Mamachi. There are occasional jokes about the attractiveness of certain men teachers, but that is about as far as it goes. Any suggestion of special friendship with a man could seriously hurt a Mamachi woman's reputation. One woman said that before she was married she was friendly with a group of young men and young women who called each other by their first names. However, nowadays when she sees one of these men she is extremely embarrassed because her instinct is to call him by his first name and yet it would be improper to do so in her role as a housewife. All this indicates how strict are the morals restraining the wife from any kind of intimacy with other men. By and large, a married woman's life is limited to her own children, a few intimate women friends, and the PTA, but these relationships often have a depth and significance that are rare for her American counterpart who has a broader range of contacts.

THE CHILD AND HIS FRIENDS

Until he finishes grade school, the child, like his mother, finds friends within the school district. Until late adolescence, the child is a part of the mother's world. His social network is limited to the mother's contacts and does not include children of the father's friends. In contrast to the American suburban child who is chauffeured by his mother, the child rarely goes farther from home than he can walk. It is unlikely that he would know any children living outside his immediate neighborhood except for relatives. His sphere is limited to his home, the homes of neighbors or friends, the nearby streets, and the schoolyard.

For children who go into Tokyo for junior high school, the routine changes greatly when they first begin the commuting. Since they must leave home early in the morning and return home shortly before supper, they have little opportunity to play with the children in the neighborhood. At their junior high school, they develop close friends with whom they visit between classes, during lunch, and in the recreation period, but there are almost no extracurricular activities and no opportunities for meeting these children after school, or on Saturdays and Sundays. Ordinarily, evenings and weekends are spent at home with the family. Just as the mother's life centers on the children, so children center their life on her.

Because upper-class mothers often have more outside activities, and the child remains in the same school system for many years, he forms close friendships at school which ordinarily last throughout life. In poor families, the mother who goes to work, takes in work, or helps a husband in his shop cannot devote herself so completely to the children, and the child's peer group often assumes great importance by default. By contrast, the membership in the peer groups of the children of salary men are more likely to change as children are separated by the results of entrance examinations.

Although the membership may change, the child generally belongs to a single intimate group just as his father or mother belongs to a single intimate group. At the junior-high-school age this group may develop on the basis of mutual liking among students who attend the same class or commute to school together on the same train. Since students at this age generally have no opportunity to stay after school for extracurricular activities, the commuting ride usually is the key opportunity for developing friendships. Once relationships develop, friends may see each other occasionally in the evenings or on weekends. In high school or college, special activity groups often replace the informal commuting group, but the pattern of belonging to a single group, around which all one's activities center, does not change. The activity may be skiing, hiking, mountain-climbing, music, radio, literature, politics, or some special hobby, but it is more common for one group (even if formed primarily for a single activity) to perform several activities than for one child to belong to more than one activity group. A child in a ski club who wants to go mountain-climbing is more likely to urge his ski companions to go mountain-climbing than to join a separate mountain-climbing club. Although girls in high school and college are usually expected to come home directly from school, boys are given more freedom to stop off at tea or coffee houses with their friends, just as their fathers stop off on their way home from work.

Just as some of the father's most enjoyable associations are on trips with company associates, so many of the children's closest associations are formed on the special trips which all schools sponsor. Although boys and girls go on these trips, their activities are strictly segregated by sex. In addition to overnight trips, at the end of the sixth grade and at the end of junior high school and high school, there are school trips ranging from two or three days to a week, arranged by the PTA and school boards. As on their father's company trips, activities are oriented to the group as a whole. Pairing or breaking into small groups is discouraged to the extent that sleeping arrangements might be rotated each night. Much of the fun is in just traveling, eating, singing, and sightseeing together. Out of a hundred students perhaps ninety-nine will be on the school trip. The hundredth will be very sick and remember sadly the rest of his life that he missed the trip. These trips are major events in the students' lives, requiring months of planning; they are discussed and commemorative photos viewed for months and even years afterward.

Some boys of high-school and college age form private groups of classmates for excursions, especially for skiing and mountain-climbing. Sometimes girls form their own groups and very occasionally, if boys are willing and the girls' parents are satisfied with chaperone arrangements, girls may go along with the boys. Ordinarily, however, girls are excluded and because of the frequent planning meetings and the excitement of the trip, these groups tend to become the center of one's deepest friendships.

To the extent that a child's world expands beyond his neighborhood it does so largely through his relatives. Cousins of the same sex and about the same age are likely to develop close ties. If one cousin is slightly older than another of the same sex, he may become maternalistic or paternalistic to the younger, especially if the younger has no older sibling of the same sex. The younger often has a deep respect for the older, visiting as often as possible and asking advice on all kinds of questions. Overnight visiting is rare except with relatives, but during vacations children often spend a few days at the home of a cousin.

Sometimes a child will spend part of his vacation with grandparents, and if so, he may become friendly with children in the grandparents' neighborhood. Occasionally relatives do not get along well, but by and large children have positive relationships with relatives and look forward to these visits. Though parents may be reluctant to visit rural relatives because of the obligations it might pose for them, the children are more likely to regard trips to relatives in farming or fishing villages as sheer delight.

When boys leave high school and college to go to work, they quickly form new relationships with men at work, but for girls, graduation means the end of many friendships and is an occasion for weeping. They know there will be few opportunities to get together with old school friends and little opportunity to form friendships of equal closeness. They gradually become separated from each other by marriage, and once they live in different neighborhoods and have the responsibility of caring for children, they rarely have a chance to meet. After completing school many girls stay at home, perhaps taking a few special lessons in preparation for marriage. Those who work for a few years after school may develop friendships at work and feel the same kind of loneliness when they give up their jobs that others felt when they left school.

Many parents are reluctant to allow a daughter to work because they are afraid that she would lose her simplicity and perhaps even form irresponsible relationships. While, as de Tocqueville commented, the American girl may protect her virginity by her own skills based on independence and fairly broad contacts, the Japanese parent is afraid that his daughter, lacking in experience, would be unable to resist the first man who came along. Hence, although many girls work between school and marriage, it is often thought better for her to stay at home, taking lessons in cooking, flower arranging, sewing, tea ceremony, and other housewifely arts rather than to work where the family has no control over her relationships. After leaving school, the daughter may work two, three, or four years at home with her family until marriage arrangements are completed. The girl's stay at home at this age is, in a sense, preparation for the limited social world she will know after marrying, just as her brother's loyalty to groups from his own college is preparation for the loyalty he will feel later to his company.

The most important relationships until, and sometimes after, marriage are those with the same sex. While "dance parties" are not uncommon in college nowadays, dating still is not widespread, and at high-school age it is virtually unknown. One girl, when asked if there was any dating in her (coeducational) high school replied that there was a boy and girl who did ride home together on the train and that the other students kept talking about it because it was so unusual. Even college-age students who meet at "dance parties" in the course of skiing or hiking weekends, or through introductions, are awkward in relating to someone of the opposite sex. Young girls anxious to form dating relationships find it difficult to arrange opportunities, and therefore many of them in the end let their families arrange their marriage despite their professed ideology to the contrary.

THE NARROW WORLD

Perhaps the most striking characteristic of Japanese society is the existence of a series of tightly-knit groups, connected by a controlled and limited amount of movement. Although a salary man has a broader perspective than the traditional middle-class man, these differences are minor when compared to a more openly mobile society such as the United States. The contrasts between the Mamachi wife and her Western counterpart are even stronger. Some Japanese who are humanitarian or have a broader range of contacts (for example, those who have lived in Japanese overseas colonies before World War II or traveled abroad after the war) have been urging their fellow citizens to take more responsibility for the welfare of people outside their own narrow world. But neither their urging nor the growth of modern bureaucracy have succeeded in greatly weakening the Mamachi citizen's sharp distinction between friend and stranger.[9]

---

[9] Though there are folk stories in which kindness to strangers in need is rewarded, the traditional Confucian philosophy supports the view that one should

Mamachi residents do have more opportunities to encounter strangers than the middle class in rural areas and have, therefore, developed routines for dealing with them. But compared to the upper class who have self-confidence, poise, and a wider experience in greeting strangers, the Mamachi salary man is reserved and therefore relies on these routines and formalities to deal with outsiders. The formalities may be jovial and even include lavish entertainment or they may consist of curt evasion. But in either case, the effect is the same. Strangers are kept at a proper distance and not allowed to penetrate into the inner circles.

Because the Mamachi resident ordinarily belongs to only one or two intimate groups to which he is absolutely devoted, these groups tend to absorb his total personality. He has no clear conception of himself apart from the group. He rarely belongs to special-interest groups with specific and limited purposes. His intimate group may cover a wide range of functions: recreation, gossip, travel, advice, and mutual assistance in making proper placement of children or in consumer purchasing. An individual typically has so little experience with other groups that he has little critical judgment for evaluating his own group and feels there is nothing to do (*shikata ga nai*) but accept his own group's standards. Lacking the security of belonging to other groups, he ordinarily makes no attempt to withstand group pressures. Although a wide span of individual difference and free expression is permitted members who are loyal and accepted by the group, on basic issues, which affect group welfare, members are sensitive to the prevailing group sentiment.

Because of the tight-knit nature of each group, a person is reluctant to leave it and face the difficulty of entering a new one. If it is necessary to move, as when a child is placed in work or marriage or when a family moves to a new community, a family takes great care in establishing connections to the new group. The difficulty of moving is reflected in the special ceremonies at the time a member enters or leaves a group.[10] All occasions of entering and leaving a

---

feel more affection and obligation toward those in one's own social sphere than to outsiders.

The contrast between America and Japan is much like Kurt Lewin's distinction between America and Germany. Cf. Kurt Lewin, *Resolving Social Conflicts,* New York: Harper & Brothers, 1948, chapter 1.

[10] All families still react with great feeling in discussing *mura hachibu,* the practice

group are carefully ceremonialized. Even a short trip is important enough to call for farewell and welcome-back parties, and whole groups gather at train stations and airports to send off a departing member. Aside from formal ceremonies of welcoming a bride to a new neighborhood and welcoming a man to his company, the entrance into these new groups is a major event, and it may take many months or years before a new person is totally accepted.

Because of the sharp differences between friend and stranger, in considering the Mamachi community it is necessary to distinguish: (1) acquaintances, who stand outside the bond of close-knit groups, (2) benefactors, who stand on the periphery of a group or form the bridge to another group, and (3) true friends, who are firmly inside one's own group.

Acquaintances

When meeting a stranger without proper introduction, one is apt to encounter a wall of apathy covered by formal politeness. The other person need not be hostile; he can be polite, but by his reserve, impersonality, and vagueness he indicates his caution in pursuing the contact. A Mamachi resident has no feeling of obligation and little feeling of sympathy to strangers.[11] In getting on and off crowded trains and buses, for example, people push in a manner which, though impersonal, is rude even by Western standards. As the saying goes, "You can throw off your shame when traveling."

To help break down the wall of apathy and escape the role of stranger, nearly every Mamachi man carries some calling cards in his pocket. They contain his name, position, and place of work, and,

---

in which a villager who had seriously violated the norms of the community was socially ostracized and even expelled by the villagers. This was regarded as the most complete and final punishment. One might contrast this fear of being on his own with the spirit of the American frontier which glorified an individual setting out on his own. Cf. Robert J. Smith, "The Japanese Rural Community: Norms, Sanctions, and Ostracism," *American Anthropologist*, 1961, LXIII:522–533.

[11] In completing sentences such as "the neighbors are," those who have lived in a community for a long time express a more positive attitude toward the community than do newcomers. While older wives express satisfaction with their neighbors, young wives who have moved in recently make such comments as "the neighbors are very talkative," "gossipy," "critical," "unfair," and the like. Such differences seem to reflect the length of time required for acceptance in a new community. Although this tendency was more pronounced in rural areas, the same general pattern is noted in the urban groups.

unless he wishes to keep it secret, his home address and perhaps his phone number. In exchanging name cards, he tries to mention a mutual acquaintance or a well-known friend in order to establish his own social position and break through the role of stranger. In some cases he may have a mutual acquaintance write a short note on his own name card, which can then be shown to avoid any doubts about the connection. The assumption clearly is that connections are helpful in obtaining favorable treatment. Women have fewer opportunities to greet outsiders and it is regarded as pretentious and overly independent for an ordinary wife to have a name card of her own.

If a person is properly introduced by an important friend he is likely to get good treatment, and there is a vague expectation that the important friend will return the favor. High-status people are given special consideration, and many Westerners are treated kindly because they are seen to have relatively high status. This is not a generalized friendliness, for many Mamachi residents complained of rudeness from people who had welcomed my wife and me very graciously.

When a person is properly introduced, even though the situation is still formal, he is likely to be greeted warmly. If handled skillfully the contact can be pleasant, but the atmosphere is contrived, and the laughing, though real, is impersonal. Mamachi residents are more frank than Westerners in clarifying social status, but more cautious in expressing personal opinions. Although undergoing some modifications since the war, a standardized etiquette prescribing relationships between people of different degrees of familiarity and of different social status remains widespread. The less familiar the acquaintance and the higher his social position above one's own, the more one uses honorific language, deep and frequent bows, impersonal expressions, humble body gestures, and self-depreciation. Although in recent years the polite language has tended to be simplified and the most honorific terms have become less common, distinctions indicating the degree of social distance between persons remain basic to the language and to the social interaction.

Although the foreign observer is struck by the amount of protocol, it must be remembered that, when he is present, the situation is likely to be more formal than it would be otherwise. He is also impressed with the amount of skill, sensitivity, and considerateness of Mamachi residents in handling each properly introduced person and each new situation smoothly. It is not surprising that they consider foreigners brash. The skills of dealing with acquaintances are cultivated to a much higher degree of refinement by a resident of Mamachi than by a comparable member of the American middle class. The skilled person is able to find just the right level of politeness. Overly polite language or incessant bowing would create as uncomfortable a situation as would overly familiar treatment. The goal in such situations is naturalness in according the other person the respect appropriate to his age and status. There is a proper way to treat inferiors just as there is a proper way to treat superiors.

The exceptionally skilled person who feels at home in formal situations and relates easily to people whom he has just met is much admired as an aid in promoting smooth relationships between strangers.[12] Even if an ordinary person handles acquaintances adequately, underneath he usually feels a strain. The aggressive, talkative individual frequently serves a social function similar to the skilled person. Others seem to be relieved to have him take the responsibility to keep things moving even though he may be basically unpopular. On the one hand the group may give him the "go ahead"; on the other hand they dislike him as too aggressive.

Such persons are crucial in settings where people do not know each other well, for otherwise they are likely to remain reserved. Mamachi residents are undoubtedly sincere when they say it is unpleasant for them to have to put up with so many formalities, not only because of the stiffness, but because it interferes with dealing with the matters for which the group was originally called together.

Formality, when compounded with the uncertainties of relative status, can lead to difficult situations. For example, when a group is seated in a drawing room, the most honored person is placed near the *tokonoma*, a special decorative alcove on one wall of the room. If several people of about equal status enter the room, each man may insist that another take the honored position, and con-

---

[12] This is also one of the crucial functions of the geishas employed by the more successful businessmen. Salaried families generally call on children or talented friends to serve this role.

siderable time may elapse before a decision is reached and everyone can sit down. Sometimes it happens that everyone humbly refuses to take the honored seat and it is left empty. Participants in such polite bickering are likely to find the situation taxing rather than amusing, but nevertheless they hesitate to be immodest by taking the seat themselves. This problem never arises in the presence of someone of clearly higher status. The higher-status person would graciously, with a slight show of modesty, accept the honor.

If formalities cause so much discomfort, one may ask why they continue in such force in these modern suburban families. One small part of the answer is that people derive aesthetic pleasure from forms and ceremonies. Many praise an elegant style of speech or writing, and many admire formalized rituals like the tea ceremony.

At the same time, the use of respectful language carries the connotation of higher-class behavior and careful upbringing. Many lower-class people explain that they haven't learned how to be properly polite, and many upper-class children still get special training which performs the same function as a finishing school. Since many Mamachi families have come from rural areas within the last generation or so, they perhaps are more concerned than other groups about their speech, behavior, background, and the art of social intercourse and politeness. Showing the proper reserve, like using the appropriate respectful language, is considered the mark of a refined person. While at times they wish they could be more frank, Mamachi residents still have more respect for the reserved person than for the outspoken individual.

Many people, especially the women, have had little experience in meeting strangers and are unsure of how to act. Often, a person with long experience in meeting different groups has a confidence which permits him to avoid formalities and to break through the stiff barriers. Most Mamachi residents do not have the confidence or the breadth of experience to allow themselves this freedom.

Higher-status people are often as reserved as the lower classes in meeting strangers, not because of lack of confidence, but because they are afraid that too great a display of friendliness will result in difficult demands being made on them.

Part of the reason that formalities exist is that strangers exist.

Formalities make it possible to be polite but cautious. In a group of strangers, it is difficult to tell precisely what possible connections and powers the other person might have, and hence it is wise to avoid doing or saying anything that might give offense. It follows that it is prudent to avoid committing oneself to views with which the other person might disagree. If questioned directly about his opinions, it is safer to give a polite but ambiguous answer. Children, questioned by adults they do not know well, may try to charm the adult by giggling or smiling, but if unsure of themselves they may give no answer at all. If asked about their career plans when not sure they will realize their ambitions, children may say simply that they do not know or have not thought about it, even if they have discussed the same matters with their parents or intimate friends. Foreigners visiting Japan, while charmed by the gracious hospitality, often find it difficult to get their Japanese acquaintances to express true feelings. If the foreigner presses, the host probably will express some opinion. But the standard Mamachi strategy is first to try to get the foreigner to express his opinion and then to agree with it, preferably with new arguments and examples to back it up. Indeed, nearly all foreign observers, even ones of widely different persuasion, have been pleased to find that their impressions of Japan were confirmed by their polite hosts. To the Mamachi resident it is considerate rather than deceitful to agree with a guest's expressed opinion and to keep quiet about his own feelings to the contrary. The Mamachi resident finds some validity in what the other person is saying and he simply highlights this side of the truth rather than presenting contrary evidence. This is being both truthful and properly respectful, but in case of doubt, showing proper respect is probably more important.

By keeping relationships impersonal, a Mamachi resident also avoids revealing information about his own friends that might threaten the solidarity of his group. Even if a person has negative feelings toward members of his group, he carefully avoids expressing them in front of strangers. As in the traditional Japanese proverb, even brothers who quarrel within their gate are united against outsiders. As much as one may want to develop close relationships with an outsider, one does not accomplish this by revealing secrets or negative characteristics of members of his own group. To foreigners whom Mamachi residents meet casually, they may complain about Japanese in general, but not about members of their own group.

Elaborate ceremonies and politeness represent a way of maintaining contacts and ensuring courtesy to outsiders while protecting the boundaries of one's own group. The problem for the Mamachi resident is that old forms are changing, that different people follow different forms, and that in completely new situations it is not always clear which form to follow. In case of doubt, most people choose to be on the safe side, to be more rather than less formal. The risk of being considered too formal and polite is ordinarily not nearly so great as the risk of being considered rude and impolite.

Benefactors

In "traditional Japan" [13] obligations to benefactors were often life-long and in some relationships, as between the tenant and the land-lord, they were even inherited by their respective descendants. In Mamachi, most obligations are of much shorter duration and less diffuse. Because the salary man has security and is automatically entitled to welfare services through his firm, he has less need to incur personal obligations than most people. Although he does have some feeling of obligation to superiors at work, the most characteristic situation in which he incurs obligations is when a family member moves from one tightly-knit group to another: entering a school, obtaining a job, arranging marriage, or finding a house. Because urban society is more pluralistic than rural society there is more flexibility in determining which relationships will be used to obtain favors. One's relatives, classmates, former teachers, and work companions may all be used to provide the link between one group and another. Not only must the benefactor go to trouble to make the arrangements, but he must also assume some responsibility for the success of the arrangements. The recipient may not have had intimate relationships with the benefactor previously, but once he re-

---

[13] The expression is placed in quotations because recent historical research reflects many variations in tradition and because patterns were not always strictly adhered to regardless of these variations. However, the evidence suggests that obligations have been much stronger than they are at the present. For these traditional obligations see Ruth Benedict, *The Chrysanthemum and the Sword,* Boston: Houghton-Mifflin, 1946.

ceives an important favor, he feels an appreciation and obligation which is not completely discharged on a mere contractual basis.

All human relationships in all societies result in some duties, but it is only when the feeling of obligation to the other person is stronger than the feeling of affection that one is particularly conscious of the obligation.[14] In the relationships of children to parents, wives to husbands, younger siblings to older siblings, one is ordinarily not so conscious of the obligations because the feelings of affection are so strong.[15] One does favors for friends without thinking of them as obligations; but without a close personal relationship the feeling of obligation may be keen, and the relationship tense.

Often, of course, there is a very thin line between kindness and a feeling of obligation.[16] For example, one Mamachi father reported that on a fishing trip to an isolated area he became extremely thirsty and stopped to ask a farmer for a glass of water. He was promptly given the water, and since he was pleased, he gave a small coin to one of the children. It probably was not necessary for him to do so, but he was grateful and felt that the money he could easily afford would mean more to the small child than it did to him. Later, while the man was waiting for his bus at a nearby bus stop, the boy and his mother brought him several rice cakes. In this case, neither the giving of the coin nor the returning of the rice cakes were required and neither need be considered an obligation. They were probably more an expression of kind feeling than of duty. If, on the other hand, a person is given a party or a present by an acquaintance with whom he is not particularly friendly, he will probably feel an obligation to return this favor, particularly if it is clear that the other person gave the party in the hope of receiving a favor. The returning

---

[14] Cf. A. R. Radcliffe-Brown, "Introduction," *African Systems of Kinship and Marriage,* London: Oxford University Press, 1950.

In the immediate postwar period *giri* and *gimu* were the center of enormous public concern and debate. It may be suggested this concern reflected the postwar upheaval and the weakening of ties between relatives. In that period many acts which had previously been sufficiently internalized to be considered kindness came to be thought of as obligations.

[15] Cf. Ruth Benedict, *op. cit.,* for a detailed account of the traditional values connected with obligation.

[16] Cf. Takashi Koyama, *Gendai Kazoku no Kenkyuu* (An Investigation of the Contemporary Family), Tokyo: Koobundoo, 1960.

of this favor would be considered more of an obligation than a kindness.

In previous times (and even today in smaller enterprises) the most crucial and all-encompassing obligation was to the person responsible for the husband's livelihood. Even in the large bureaucratic firm, there is a diffuse personal relationship between superior and subordinate which goes beyond contractual relationships. The emotional tie with the superior is not as relaxed as that between equals, but is often very strong, and there is an air of intimacy as great or greater than in similar relationships in the West. Yet in areas of the superior's personal involvement, the subordinate is reserved and deferent. Exactly how an employee expresses his wishes or complaints depends on his relationship to his superior. If a superior makes a mistake, an inferior with a good relationship would point out the mistake directly, taking necessary precautions not to embarrass the superior. If he did not have a good relationship, he might engage in circumlocutions to avoid saying it was a mistake. As much as he might hope that the superior would discover his own mistake, he would do precisely what his superior asked him to do, regardless of how unreasonable it might appear to him. The subordinate concerned about his superior's approval asks for directions and follows them with scrupulous care, thus relieving himself of responsibility and avoiding the risk of criticism. If the superior does not specify what is to be done, as embarrassing as it may be to ask for more directions, the inferior probably would apologize for his own stupidity or indicate by vague facial expressions that he did not understand. In this way he can elicit more precise instructions and avoid even more serious embarrassment later.

A devoted employee often praises his superior, telling him how nice he looks, how capable he is, how much he knows, and the like. This flattery keeps the employee in good grace and the superior in good spirits. At times, it appears that one of the responsibilities of the inferior is to help the superior maintain his self-confidence. Often the superior seems as dependent on the praise of his subordinates as they are on his approval. Although flattery, if clearly insincere, has just as negative an effect among the residents of Mamachi as anywhere in the world, our impression is that the people of Mamachi generally compliment with skill and sincerity and that compliments usually bring favorable responses. Not having firm independent evaluations of their own behavior, superiors seem as responsive to group opinion as inferiors.

Conversely, criticism often has a devastating effect. If an employee is criticized he will be upset even if he tries to avoid blame by saying that he was not told or that someone else was responsible. If he really feels the criticism unjust or is angry with his boss, he simply may put up a wall of silence. But a person usually worries a great deal about his standing with his superior, and will apologize for his mistake and promise to do better, even though he may not think himself entirely to blame. If criticism continues, he may begin depreciating himself for his own stupidity, selfishness, inattention, lack of education, poor family background, and the like. In such a state, he would do almost anything to make amends and win back the grace of his superior.[17]

The subordinate, in his desire to obtain approval from his superior, may probe with a comment like: "Since you have a special guest, I tried to cook a special little cake. I prepared it very badly, please excuse me." If the subordinate has done his work at all well, he will be rewarded with the compliment he was fishing for. If he feels that he has been neglected by his superior, he may depreciate and criticize himself saying he is stupid and incompetent. In this way he elicits his employer's attention and response. Such statements are humbly given, but in a certain context they clearly mean that he is concerned about his being treated so badly.

While these patterns characterize many subordinate-superior relationships even in the large bureaucratic firm, it is often said that the very talented employee does not have to display such deference and demeanor. Indeed the capable and confident young man often can be very straight-forward in dealing with his superior while the one most worried about his ability to please a superior will be the most careful about his demeanor and will work hardest to fulfill his tasks to the letter of the law.

---

[17] In the sentence completion the most common response to the item, "if I am ignored," was one of extreme annoyance and anger. On the other hand, to the item, "if I am warned (about something) or criticized by my superior" the most common response was one of willingness to acknowledge mistakes or try to correct them; some even would express appreciation of their superior's calling it to their attention.

Regardless of the subordinate's behavior, the superior is usually very direct about what he wants done. Unlike some Americans who feel obliged to persuade or coax their subordinates because of their democratic ideology, the Mamachi superior does not hesitate to give specific orders. At the same time, his authority does not prevent magnanimity and kindness, and in fact he wants to be thought of as a kind man. It is true that some superiors take advantage of their subordinates, making them prostrate themselves to request every little favor, and then innocently respond as if they simply had not realized that the subordinate wanted something. Most superiors, however, though authoritarian, are interested in the welfare of their workers.

The relationship of the maid to the mistress of the house tends to be even more all-encompassing than the relationship between the salary man and his superior. Yet, with the increasing scarcity of the labor supply and the rising costs, the number of maids has greatly decreased, and only the wealthiest salary men, along with the successful independent professionals and successful business-men, can still afford household help. Nevertheless, many Mamachi families have had such household help until recently, and a few still do. The most common source of help is the country girl who comes to a household when about sixteen or seventeen and works there for a few years until she returns to the country to get married. To work in a better home is still considered good training for marriage, and formerly, as one man stated jokingly, "it was as hard for a maid to get into a really good home as for an honor student to get into Tokyo University." When one servant returns to the country, often a friend or relative takes her place at the same house and serves her turn of several years. Often there is a succession of maids from the same rural village going to work in the same household. Generally a servant works from early morning until late at night, but the actual physical work is not particularly demanding, and while always on duty she is not always working. When the maid first arrives in Mamachi, she is generally cautious and obedient, and what feelings she has she keeps to herself, taking special care not to reveal any signs of discontent. Once she becomes familiar with her surround-ings, she can be more relaxed with the lady of the house, particu-larly if she knows she is performing her work ably and pleasing her mistress. For many purposes the maid is treated as a member of the family, albeit a low-status one, and just as the housewife has no days off, so the servant works all week. She may be called upon for virtually any kind of personal service or help. Usually the lady of the house will later help find a suitable spouse, contribute money toward her dowry, give her household goods or clothing, and perhaps even help with problems which arise after her marriage. After marriage a maid might have a chance to visit the city, and if so she would certainly bring her children to show the lady of the house. Once the actual period of service is over, most obligations end, but often a closeness remains which makes it possible for the servant to return to her former mistress in time of need. The hiring process, the nature of the work, and the nature of the relationship once the period of service is over all go far beyond mere contractual relationships.

While live-in maids virtually have vanished from the ordinary salaried family, many features of that relationship are found in the position of relatives living in the same household. If, for example, a married man's sister is still single when the parents die, she may come to live with him and his wife, since it is still thought uneconomical and cruel for her to live alone. The brother and his wife usually provide board and room and help her find a suitable spouse or, in the meantime, help her find some kind of work. In return, it is expected that the sister will be obedient to the wife and will help with the household chores. In this relationship, however, the subordination of the unmarried sister is not as clearly defined as the subordination of the maid, and there is likely to be considerable conflict, especially if the single sister is older than the wife, has a close relationship with her brother, or is not particularly enthusiastic in fulfilling her household responsibilities. In one family, for example, the husband's younger sister spent much time at home and was very friendly with her brother but gave only a minimum of household help to her sister-in-law. Antagonism covered by a stiff politeness developed between the wife and the sister and became increasingly severe. Although the situation improved after the husband, at the wife's request, intervened to ask his sister to be more cooperative in the house, the tension continued until the sister's marriage, and the wife's complaints continued for some time afterward.

Although the younger sister is one of the most common additions to the nuclear family, it is also common to have one or more grandparents or a nephew (or niece) from the country while he is attending a Tokyo school. These relatives, either on the father's or the mother's side, often complain that they are being treated unfairly, much like step children, whereas the family is likely to complain of the burden imposed upon them by such a child or his parents. While at any one time most families do not have somebody living with them, at some time in the life cycle most families will have the experience of providing for relatives. How a kinsman is treated may be governed in part by comparative age, degree of closeness, and the like, but even a close relative has a diffuse obligation to his host which he repays by yielding to his wishes and assisting with work around the house. One kind grandfather, for example, very conscious of the fact that he was an economic burden on the household, refused to eat any of the more expensive food and was reluctant to complain when he thought the grandchildren were too noisy.

Although some families may have such long-term and all-encompassing relationships, every family is likely to have been benefactor or recipient of small favors. Because almost everyone has a number of friends from school, work, kinship, and neighborhood, there is considerably more room for manipulation of these contacts. If, for example, Mr. A has done you a favor and you have done Mr. B a favor, you may arrange for Mr. B to do a favor for Mr. A. Or if you have not yet done Mr. B a favor, you might still arrange for him to do a favor for Mr. A with the expectation that you would be glad to do him a good turn at some time later.

Sometimes a Mamachi resident wishes to build up a feeling of obligation on the part of a person who may be of assistance at a later time. Since it is not proper to go directly to the person and ask for a favor, one must first establish a good relationship through favors or presents. It is possible to begin such a relationship through a mutual acquaintance if one does not know the other person; once introduced, one can begin the process of building up the obligation.

Of course, there is considerable variation among individuals in their skill, sincerity, and aggressiveness in approaching others. Some people are too timid to approach a person for favors unless they are already intimate. Others think it is not honest to seek a favor unless the relationship is a sincere one, and that it is wrong to be too aggressive in approaching a superior just to get favors for one's own limited ends. Others are fairly aggressive in making the acquaintance of strategic persons, giving them presents and performing various services for them in order to get what they desire. Many people are quite considerate of a superior's feelings and perceptive in discerning what presents or favors would be truly appreciated, and many are willing to give more help to the superior than they request in return. Virtually everyone is concerned about pleasing a superior and is upset if the superior should indicate some displeasure to him.

While Americans may consider it bribery to give presents in anticipation of later favors, many people in Mamachi consider it brash and impudent to do otherwise. Yet Mamachi residents also are uncomfortable in receiving unsolicited gifts because of the expectation that they will be called on to return the favor, and their discomfort is likely to be tinged with annoyance if the giver seems particularly aggressive, persistent, or insensitive in making unreasonable demands.

Often the prospective recipient will try to prevent such gifts, especially if they are in anticipation of favors which he cannot reasonably perform. It is sometimes difficult to refuse a present gracefully, but the recipient quickly can give a return present to neutralize, or at least minimize, the obligation. Sometimes an obligation simply has to be overlooked. For example, a private-school principal who receives several presents for every vacancy in the school has no alternative but to express neutral appreciation and ignore the gifts since he cannot admit all donors.

Sometimes a person, although willing to be of assistance, is unable to fulfill a specific request. If success is doubtful, he probably would try to do what he can but would explain the difficulties beforehand so as to prevent the other party from being disappointed. Through promptness, kindness, and thoroughness, he would demonstrate the extent of his efforts so that failure would not be considered intentional. If he did not show such sincerity, his failure would be interpreted as unwillingness because the only polite way to refuse a request is to announce that there were problems and difficulties which made it impossible to fulfill.

Many people are cautious about accepting even small requests since they may entail a great deal of responsibility. One woman, for example, was asked to introduce an appropriate young man to her friend's daughter but not to go to any trouble. She refused the request, later explaining to my wife that she could not make an introduction so casually. If, for example, the young man later refused the girl, not only would it be embarrassing for both the girl and the go-between, but it could also hurt the girl's self-confidence for future introductions. This seemingly simple request had too many ramifications to be taken lightly.

There are various reasons why an introduction might not work out well, and all reflect on the services of the go-between. One introduction failed because one party arrived at an inappropriate time at the other person's house, causing embarrassment. In this case, the go-between's relations with both parties were too formal to allow her to ask when a convenient time for introductions could be arranged. Introductions often backfire if not enough care has been taken and not enough questions asked. The successful introducer must have a relationship with both parties that enables him to be frank without giving offense. But no matter how skilled the go-between may be, his work requires thought and planning, and he ordinarily takes his obligation seriously.

Even two acquaintances may negotiate through go-betweens, but they ordinarily approach each other directly, dropping hints to see if the other is willing to perform the service desired. For example, as we became more obligated to the people who were helping us with our research, many subtly began asking for favors. For one thing they wanted to learn English from us. They did not ask us directly but dropped hints by saying, for example, that their child, who was studying English in school, had difficulty with his pronunciation and had we any suggestions as to how he might improve. While we might have recommended listening to a tape recorder or a radio, we felt a certain pressure to volunteer our services since we had received favors from them. (We did volunteer, and we feel it made a significant difference in obtaining their co-operation on our project.)

It is also not usually necessary to go through go-betweens to approach a relative, but closer relatives may be used to convey a request to distant relatives. It is difficult to refuse these requests even though the demands seem unreasonable. For example, if a younger sister is pressed by her parents to help an older brother financially she may feel that she cannot refuse even if it means she must draw upon her husband's savings. Although she might be reluctant to sacrifice for a brother, she is likely to accept more readily the responsibility of contributing to the support of aging parents. But contributing to the brother's and in some cases to the father's finances and having to ask her husband to provide this help is likely to be considered an unwelcome duty and tends to stiffen relationships with the family. Such problems receive considerable attention in popular literature and on TV and radio.

If all people in Japan had the economic security that salary men have, it would rarely be necessary to rely on personal benefactors for economic aid. Indeed, salary men rarely need such assistance. But there are many other groups in Japan who do not have this security and who, because of their particularistic relations with a salary man by virtue of kinship or friendship, feel they have legitimate claims to help from them. Salary men generally prefer to avoid entanglements with relatives, but they do consider it only proper to give aid to parents and, in special cases, to brothers, sisters, or close relatives on both sides of the family.[18] Beyond the assistance given to aged parents, the most common help they give is to rural family members who come to Tokyo for school or work. In contrast to the time when the fathers or grandfathers first came to the city, rural families now look up to the migrants to the city. They see the salary man as a man of power, comfort, and leisure. The rapid rise in the urban standard of living compared to the rural has exaggerated the difference, and the desire of the rural dwellers for education and placement of children often makes them dependent on the urban kin. One man reported that when he goes back to his native village, not only does he have little in common with old acquaintances, but he is treated with such overwhelming respect that he feels uncomfortable. Most people of Mamachi have sympathy for people in the rural areas. They remember or have heard about the arduous lives which their forebears led when they lived

---

[18] Cf. Yoshiharu Scott Matsumoto, *The Individual and His Group*, Philadelphia: American Philosophical Society, 1960.

in the rural areas, and since many of them have not been to the country for many years, they are unaware of the extent of recent progress and imagine present-day rural life to be worse than it is. Some feel guilty for leading such comfortable lives while the farmer still has such hardships.

Furthermore, many Mamachi families became indebted to their rural relatives in the latter part of the war and the early postwar period when they sent their children and wives to the country to escape the air raids and to be near the source of food. Although the farm people were having trouble providing for themselves and were not always hospitable to the newcomers, they were often a considerable help. The people of Mamachi remember this with gratitude. However, the soldiers or overseas colonists who returned after the war are often bitter that their rural relatives did not give them more help. When they returned to the rural areas just after the war to set up a new life, many found that former friends or relatives ignored them. At that time farmers were commonly chary with assistance. They were in difficult straits themselves with shortages even more severe than during the wartime, but they welcomed the more affluent Mamachi evacuees more enthusiastically than the impoverished returnees from overseas who were in no position to return the favors.

Salary men are not as troubled by requests from rural areas as independent businessmen, who are frequently asked to offer employment. Nevertheless, some salary men receive similar requests, particularly if they are in companies which have openings for people lacking special technical skills. For many Mamachi families requests to find openings for rural relatives pose serious problems. Because a Mamachi family may be the only city contacts the country relatives have, the Mamachi resident feels responsibility for trying to find an opening in the city, but these openings are usually scarce, and the responsibility is a heavy burden.

Most people of Mamachi reported that they go back to the rural areas less often than they should. While they feel they ought to go back at least once a year for the traditional ceremonies honoring departed family and ancestors, many have not been to the ancestral home for years. By not returning they can avoid the presents and favors which are given in the hope of assistance in placing children in

Tokyo. If they do go back they try to stay only a short time and to see only the most intimate friends. However, the villages are small and news travels quickly, and at least some of those expecting to go to Tokyo are likely to come around with presents. In making a request the rural person entrusts everything to his city benefactor and conveys the feeling that his entire life depends on the benefactor's willingness to help. While guilty about his failure to help the needy people in the country, the Mamachi resident is caught between their dependence on him and the likelihood that he will be unable to help them. The result is often an effort to avoid the situation no matter how much one would like to see relatives or the ancestral home. If help is asked by letter, such avoidance would take the form of not answering or writing a noncommittal reply.

Success in job placements for rural friends or relatives imposes continuing burdens. One salary man, for example, has been successful in getting several village people jobs as boiler men and other laboring jobs in his organization. Since the young people are new to the city and know almost no one other than this sponsor, their parents look to him for supervision in the city. He must see that the boys do not get into trouble or marry the wrong kind of girl, and this responsibility cannot be taken lightly. When the sponsor and his wife visit the rural areas they are greeted with many presents and honored by the boys' parents and by other people hoping to place their children in the city. In this particular company, the boys worked out well, so the company is willing to use this village as one of its sources of unskilled labor. The company's view is that since the boys are known to one of the important salary men in the firm, they are likely to be more reliable and to do better and harder work than people with no such contacts. To show their appreciation these boys frequently come to the house of their sponsor and offer various kinds of help. For example, they do the annual New Year's house-cleaning. The home of their sponsor becomes their home away from home, a place to relax or to find help with their personal problems.[19]

---

[19] The problem of relatives or people from the country visiting or imposing upon urban families is a common theme in modern Japanese stories. In one television serial "home drama" during our stay in Japan, the story concerned a distant relative who came to visit an urban family posing as a close old friend even though the

Friends

Close friendships in Mamachi usually are limited to a small group of
the same sex. Within this group people are relaxed and do not worry
about formalities. They can talk and joke about their innermost
concerns. It is partly the sharp contrast between seeing a close
friend and a mere acquaintance that makes contacts with outsiders
seem so stiff. This is in contrast to the United States, where one may
be friendly with a casual acquaintance. The visitor to Japan who
does not appreciate the difference in behavior toward friends and
acquaintances is likely to consider the Japanese as more formal than
they actually are.[20]

With close friends, one can argue, criticize, and be stubborn without endangering the relationship. There is inevitably a great deal
of laughter mixed with mutual support and respect. In relationships of obligation, no matter how hard people try to relax the
atmosphere, no matter how humorous or nice they are, some tension
is inevitable. With true friends, even if small obligations develop
they generally do not cause any serious problem because it is clear
to everyone that these minor duties are only incidental to the friendship.

A few residents of Mamachi have close friends from school days
with whom they still keep contact, although their meetings tend to
be infrequent, perhaps once or twice a year. When they do meet,
they enjoy themselves immensely, catching up on past events, exchanging gossip, swapping complaints. With old classmates one can
talk about problems at work that are difficult to talk about with
friends at work.

Most of the closest friendships, however, are between people in
constant contact. The husband's friends are his co-workers, the
wife's friends are her neighbors. These relationships are remarkably
intimate. If, for example, a wife has difficulty with her husband, as
most wives do at one time or another, she may turn to her neighbor-

---

urban family could not exactly recall him. The story was filled with amusing
incidents centering on the impositions he made on his hosts. For example, the
visitor ate voraciously and was caught by the husband of the house in a midnight
raid on the icebox.

[20] While Japanese like formalities, there is a systematic overestimation of their
formality by Western observers, who see them on more formal situations.

hood friends for support and suggestions for dealing with them. She may describe an argument with her husband and ask whether it is wise to apologize or to remain firm in her wishes. Most wives say that they feel freer in talking to other wives than to their husbands, and they tell other wives many things they would not tell their husbands. The same is true for the men, who generally feel freer in talking to their close working associates about certain things than to their wives.

Even the most formal of women may be informal with her close friends. One proper middle-aged lady, for example, told my wife of an overnight trip with three or four women friends to a special hot-springs, one of the few places where both men and women can still bathe together. Although they were too modest to bathe during the day with other people, they secretly bathed there during the night when no one else was around. They laughed like schoolgirls about what they would have done if a man had come. Another lady told my wife how she and her small group of friends had come upon a fertility shrine, shaped like the male sexual organs. Although most women were too embarrassed to say anything, the most courageous member of the group asked the caretaker of the shrine many questions about the history of some displayed instruments which had been used by court ladies. The more bashful ladies listened to the discussion and laughed with amusement afterward, expressing appreciation for the courage of the one who had asked the questions and speculating about the possible satisfaction which could be derived from such instruments. These same ladies are very formal, stiff, and polite outside their group. They even tease each other about the politeness of their bowing and the stiffness of their formalities which they notice on other occasions.

Generally members of the most intimate group are of roughly the same status, but where status differences exist, they are acknowledged and do not seriously interfere with the closeness of the group. In a group of friends from work, for example, if one is treated as a "fair-haired boy" by his superior, he may be accorded more respect by his peers. Similarly among wives of the same social position, if one is slightly older or has more experience than the others, she may be listened to as an expert on certain kinds of questions. Such true friendships may take years to develop, but since there is relatively little movement of the man from company to company or of the wife from neighborhood to neighborhood, once made they are seldom broken.

TECHNIQUES OF SOCIAL CONTROL

Because most groups are so stable and because people in the same group know each other intimately over long periods of time, social control does not ordinarily require overt reward and punishment or even the direct expression of negative feeling, something most Mamachi residents consider crude and unnecessary. Because people are so limited in the number of groups to which they belong they are very responsive even to subtle changes in attitude.[21] This responsiveness and sensitivity makes the techniques of ignoring, overlooking, and postponing very effective instruments of social control. Although close friendship makes possible a wide range of behavior without creating antagonism, one is cautious not to go beyond acceptable bounds. A good group member never gossips about a friend to an outsider since it might get back to his friend, but he often gossips about outsiders to a friend.

The most effective way of dealing with a person who has caused difficulty is through the collusion of a group in rejecting him. The residents of Mamachi still use the expression *idobata kaigi* (the meeting around the well) to describe a group of women getting together to gossip about local events. Some of the suburban women jokingly comment that the new *idobata kaigi* is no longer at the well but at the playground where mothers exchange their views while watching their children's play. If a group of women together decide to ignore another woman, she can be devastated. While to my knowledge no one in Mamachi has been expelled from the community for violating the customs and morals (*mura hachibu*), the same term and method is still used socially to isolate a disliked person. People are, in effect, shut out from groups for their aggressiveness, egotism, or failure to live up to their group responsibilities. This sanction is effective in Mamachi because the mother who lacks

---

[21] In the sentence-completion test, one of the commonest answers to the item "most feared" was "rumors." Similarly, in the item, "what do you dislike most" many people responded "rumors." Judging from the frequency with which rumors were spontaneously mentioned, they are a potent force in Japanese lives; more so in rural villages, but still powerful in suburban Tokyo.

informal acceptance in her PTA group virtually has no other place to turn, and a husband rejected by his work group has no other opportunity for developing close friends. Quiet group pressures can be very effective.

The rules of politeness require very indirect ways for expressing disapproval and disagreement, and even fellow Mamachi residents sometimes have difficulty distinguishing between postponement and refusal, between exaggerated flattery connoting criticism and sincere praise, between a vague agreement meaning no and a vague agreement meaning a weak yes. Sometimes, of course, even the speaker may not be clear what his own final response will be.

But usually the general meaning, even from subtle clues, is perfectly clear. All that is unclear is the reason underlying the response. When a person complains that he cannot tell exactly what another is feeling, this almost always means that the other did not give a sufficiently positive response, but that one does not know why. Such vague replies often create anxieties greater than a direct explanation would create. Many people who are refused feel there is something wrong with them, and the diffuse nature of the rejection by postponement, avoidance, or vagueness is often felt as an attack on one's entire character. Undifferentiated emotional responses of fear, anger, or self-depreciation are common.

These subtle means of refusal are not unknown in the West but they are used much more frequently in Japan, and the implication is generally more negative than would be true in the West. If someone who has come to ask assistance begins by saying, "I am so and so. Do you remember me?" an effective refusal would be to say, "I don't think I remember" or "I am not sure" or to misunderstand purposefully the implication, then to resume talking in a friendly manner. The initial pause, the hesitation, and the refusal to acknowledge the memory is ordinarily sufficient to express the negative feelings and, in effect, constitutes a refusal to consider the request regardless of what polite conversation or formal assent is later expressed. Avoidance is also more widely used and accepted as a technique for refusal. If a man schedules an appointment with an unwilling acquaintance, the acquaintance simply may not show up. When they meet again, ordinarily it would be rude to mention the missed appointment. If the other person should be so bold as to remind him, even subtly, of the appointment, the other person would express innocent surprise as if he had not really realized that a meeting was intended or he would profess that it completely had slipped his mind, and a man is not held responsible for forgetting, even if the unconscious motivation is clear.

Even with all these indirect means of expression the Mamachi resident feels that he has more opportunity to express his wishes than did the people in "traditional Japan," without being so crude as foreigners. If, for example, a man wants to eat soon, he may say to the friend with whom he is talking, "You must be hungry since it is getting so late," or "You must be tired." After a few repetitions of these comments, the friend will usually take a hint. Some people in Mamachi have trouble giving hints or expressing disagreement without becoming aggressive. Yet many skillful residents of Mamachi, in their own quiet and indirect way, have effective ways of making their opinions felt without being impolite.

One might have expected that these opportunities for increased frankness and the new opportunities for movement created by urbanization and industrialization would have weakened the power of small groups to control their members' behavior. This has not happened, and if anything the growth of the large bureaucratic structure has created increased stability which reinforces the ability of the small group to control its members.

The effectiveness of each group in controlling its members rests partly on its success in keeping the exclusive loyalty of its members. In Mamachi, an individual rarely has divided loyalties which would make it difficult to control his behavior because generally he has only one group outside the family which is the object of his primary commitment: the work group for the man, the neighborhood group for the woman, and the school group for the child. Even for higher-status salary men, who have more responsibility in community-wide organizations, no other outside group is permitted to interfere with this primary commitment. Each individual is also committed to his family, but the demands of the family are carefully isolated from the demands of the other groups. The effective isolation of the family from contact with the husband's place of work insures that work considerations are separated from family considerations. Similarly the separation of the husband from participation in the wife's neighborhood activities ensures that he will not interfere with her group. Each group has virtually complete autonomy, and the opportunity for family loyalties to conflict with other group loyalties is minimized.

The effectiveness of the group in controlling the behavior of its members rests in part on the long-term commitment of the members to the group. But it goes beyond this, for, even in going to a new group, it is necessary to have an introduction. In some Western societies, if a person has difficulty with others in his group, he simply moves elsewhere. In Mamachi, even moving requires the support of one's group.[22] One moves from one tightly-knit group to another, by way of bridges[23] provided by the two groups. There is no promising alternative for a person except to remain sensitive to the demands of his group.

---

[22] Japanese children in explaining why they wish one occupation over another are more likely to mention the influence or connection with a relative. Even if American children learned about the occupation from someone else, they would not mention a relative as a reason for choosing another occupation. Cf. Mary Ellen Goodman, "Values, Attitudes, and Social Concepts of Japanese and American Children," *American Anthropologist,* 1957, 59:989 f.

[23] The expression "hashi watashi o suru" which is used to mean "act as a go-between" literally means to carry across a bridge.

Chapter VII
BASIC VALUES

Citizens of Communist countries may not enthusiastically approve all aspects of Marxism, yet Marxism provides an integrated system of values which expresses their basic purposes and gives meaning to their existence. Similarly, citizens of Western countries can point to democracy and individualism as principles embodying their way of life. In contrast, Mamachi residents do not have an articulated system of thought which embodies their fundamental beliefs. The recent rapid changes in society have weakened faith in statements of traditional ideology and no new system of consistent and widely accepted values has emerged. As many Japanese scholars have noted, whereas the Germans responded to defeat by reasserting their prewar values without seriously re-examining them, most Japanese responded by questioning their view of life and submitting it to an agonizing reappraisal from which it never recovered.

The formal statements of Confucian and Shinto ideology, though widely accepted before the war, are now so closely identified with the "feudalistic" past and tainted by association with the militarism and superpatriotism of World War II that today few Mamachi residents can accept them without serious modification. Few believe, for example, that the husband should sacrifice his family in order to serve his superior. On the other hand, many Mamachi residents believe that although democracy and individualism might help point the way to a new value system, they often are only a justification for selfishness and therefore not a solid basis for morality. They cannot admire, for example, a philosophy that permits an individual to look out for himself even if it means neglecting aged parents. A modified Marxism appeals to some youths and intellectually oriented residents of Mamachi, but the application of Marxism seems so cruel and absolute that it has little appeal to the vast majority of Mamachi residents. They cannot, for example, admire the manner in which the Hungarian revolt was crushed.

The lack of a clearly formulated and widely accepted value system has led to a willingness and even eagerness to question the most fundamental aspects of their traditional beliefs and to consider what elements of the Western value system are worth adopting. Many are willing to question views of those in authority that would previously have been accepted without hesitation—for example, the necessity of accepting suffering and hard work that was previously thought natural, inevitable, and even character-building. They question the necessity of keeping ceremonies and formalities which symbolize traditional values and status relationships. Not only men but women, children, and employees can be more open and direct in raising questions about traditional practices.

Although these questions are still discussed, they are not as omnipresent as they were immediately after the war. In large part, this is because, despite the lack of a clearly formulated statement of values, there is in fact a high level of consensus among Mamachi residents about what is desirable. Many of the soul-searching discussions rest on common assumptions about what is desirable, and the soul-searching is often merely an attempt to find a system of values which would make explicit and rationalize these widely accepted assumptions. The existence of this working consensus about what is desirable has made the lack of a clearly formulated system of values less of a critical problem than it might be otherwise. Many people occupy themselves with their daily activities without worrying about the problem of developing an integrated philosophy of life. Perhaps because of their disillusionment with the values they were taught until the end of World War II some are even suspicious of any formal statements of ideology, as if ideologies were by nature old-fashioned, superstitious, arbitrary, or misleading. Many prefer to think that they have no particular values and explain their behavior not as resulting from convictions or values, but from situations or customs, as if they had not internalized the customs. Many eagerly discuss various philosophies of life as if the philosophies had nothing to do with their own convictions. They will say, for example, that in old Japan the belief was such and such, but that in modern Japan it is different. They compare American democracy with European existentialism and the Japanese tradition, but as they say this, it is almost as if they were separate from what they describe as the Japanese point of view. They may say, "The Japanese view is . . ." or "Traditionally, Japanese thought . . ." or "Modern Japanese think . . ." Few say, "We (or I) believe . . ." or "We are convinced that . . ." [1]

Although the existence of an underlying consensus about what is desirable has made the lack of a formally stated and integrated consensus tolerable, this lack does pose problems for Mamachi groups in at least three different areas. One of these is the area of the socialization of new members of a group, because without clear precepts fully ordered into a system of thought there is no clear rationale to answer questions which arise. In the absence of general principles, loyalty can be taught only by precept and example. The concept is passed on from one generation to the next not by a standard creed, but by illustrations, stories, folk sayings, and proverbs. One hears, for example, the tale about the forty-seven *ronin*, who sacrificed their lives for their lord, which has a moral of loyalty to one's master or to his group. The annual Boys' Festival celebrates a hero named Benkei, a samurai who was absolutely devoted in serving his master. Similar folk tales honor people in high positions who have sacrificed themselves for the group. For example, there is the story of the rich landlord who gave up his land so a river could be rerouted in order to save his village, or the story of the man who set his hill-top house on fire to attract the people on the beach unable to see the approaching tidal wave which threatened them. Although youngsters can gradually acquire values from these stories without a formal creed, if a youth raises questions about these values, there are no well-considered answers.

Many parents are concerned that their children are not being taught moral principles, and some openly support the movement to

---

[1] This is much the same phenomenon as that noted by Dore and Matsumoto regarding religion. In answer to the question, "What is your religion?" people commonly reply that they have none. In answer to the question, "What is your family's religion?" they commonly reply "Buddhism." Cf. Ronald Dore, *City Life in Japan*, Berkeley and Los Angeles: University of California Press, 1958; Yoshiharu Scott Matsumoto, *Contemporary Japan*, Philadelphia: The American Philosophical Society, 1960.

reintroduce traditional moral teaching into the school system. Even less conservative parents are afraid that the children of today who are not receiving the kind of moral guidance, training, and discipline that the parents received will be unable to withstand the difficulties ahead. Many parents believe that they persevered under duress because strict moral training and the experience of suffering had given them a strong moral fiber. They fear that their children, however, can be blown by the winds of fad and fiction because they have no moral grounding. Some observers see in such parents' views an attempt to rationalize the harsh training which they suffered, but there is much to support the contention that youths have been more receptive to fads because they lack an over-all system of beliefs. Some youngsters, looking for explanations, go through a period of trying out Marxist thought. Others strongly espouse the cause of individualism and liberalism. Some are nihilistic, rejecting all creeds. But many more listen and talk about different points of view without really developing any kind of firm commitment for there are no satisfactory patterned answers to the kinds of questions they raise.

The second problem posed by the lack of a clearly stated value system is the difficulty a group encounters in handling a deviant. The able deviant who openly shows up the inability of some other member, or receives favors without showing sufficient appreciation, or gossips about group members, or engages in selfish manipulations, or behaves as if he has a higher position than his actual status calls for can be a serious problem for a group to deal with. In the long run most groups have effective methods of placing social pressure on such a deviant, but when he first calls into question certain assumptions of the group, the group does not have a ready answer. Not only is there no answer to the deviant, but his challenge often creates doubts in the minds of others as to whether they are justified in opposing him, and it may take considerable time before his threat can be effectively curbed.[2]

Finally, there is something inherently unsatisfying about not hav-

---

[2] Even in the legal system, interpretation of the law has often had a flexibility by mutual agreement, mediation, etc. Cf. Arthur Taylor Von Mehren, ed., *Law in Japan*, Cambridge, Mass.: Harvard University Press, 1963. Furthermore punishment has traditionally been more severe for offenses against close relations, especially to the father. Cf. Kurt Steiner, "A Japanese Cause Celebre: The Fukuoka Patricide Case," *American Journal of Comparative Law*, 1956, V:106–111.

ing an articulated value system. For people firmly attached to a group, the group can provide a sense of meaning and purpose, but those on the periphery or the outside have no sense of purpose. In modern Mamachi as more people come into contact with diverse groups and ideas, they feel dissatisfied with not having a sense of higher purpose and integrity to carry them through these different situations, but this dissatisfaction does not lead to a strong desire for a more articulated value system.

Because the informal consensus about values among residents of Mamachi provides a basic orientation for their daily lives, it is important to consider this consensus in some detail. It must be admitted that this attempt to state an unstated consensus is subject to many risks of error and cannot have the certitude an explanation of a formal creed would offer. However, by abstracting the patterns of belief that flow from the concrete expressions of evaluation of various people and their actions, the outlines of a value system do emerge. Although Mamachi residents would not consciously give the same interpretation of their values, the two general characteristics which strike a Western observer as being of fundamental importance are loyalty and competence.[3]

---

[3] Although I attempted to make these abstractions independently from other studies, I must admit that the strikingly similar findings of Bellah in his analysis of Tokugawa documents and of Matsumoto and of Caudill and Scarr in large-scale samplings of attitudes and value-orientations have sensitized me to these values. However, at a minimum, I have a number of independent observations which lend support to these findings. Bellah concluded that the fundamental societal values in the Tokugawa Period were "particularism" and "performance." The fact that these societal values correspond to "loyalty" and "competence," the qualities valued in personal behavior, would lend support to the view that there has been considerable continuity in the value system. Caudill and Scarr, using Florence Kluckhohn's value-orientation theory on large Japanese samples, found that in the activities sphere, the desired mode of behavior for Japanese is "doing," which corresponds to the individual quality I have termed "competence." Caudill and Scarr noted that collaterality was the preferred mode of relationship within the nuclear family and the work organization. Matsumoto and Ishida also noted the importance of collectivity orientation within the in-group and found that these relationships now tend to be directed more toward peers than to superiors and inferiors. Caudill and Scarr found, however, that outside the nuclear family and the immediate work group, the individualistic orientation is likely to be stronger. Cf. Robert N. Bellah, *Tokugawa Religion*, Glencoe, Ill.: The Free Press, 1957; William Caudill and Harry Scarr, "Japanese Value Orientations and Culture Change," *Ethnology*, 1961, 1:53–91; Matsumoto, *op. cit.*; Takeshi Ishida, *Gendai Soshiki Ron* (A Theory of Modern Organization), Tokyo: Iwanami Shoten, 1960.

LOYALTY

Despite changes in the nature and direction of expression, loyalty of the individual to his group remains the most important attribute of the respected person. In its extreme form, loyalty means that the individual can be counted on to place group interests above his own. Group loyalty means not only identification with group goals but a willingness to co-operate with the other members and to respond to group consensus enthusiastically. If given an assignment by his group he must accept the responsibility. He should avoid any situation that might be embarrassing to a member of his group and always maintain an interest in the welfare, comfort, and sense of honor of the others. A daughter is respected if she considers her parents' wishes in thinking of marriage, and an employee is respected if he does not leave a job to accept more money elsewhere. Even if differences of opinion are expressed within the group, members are expected to stick together vis-à-vis the outside. It is no longer required that the individual express loyalty in formal ways through ceremonies and gift-giving. Today a person is judged loyal when his total attitude shows that he whole-heartedly supports the interests of his group.

There is considerable discussion about Western concepts of individualism (*kojin-shugi*) but, in the dominant Mamachi view, individualism is opposed to loyalty. If one accepts the Kantian view that morality implies duty, Mamachi residents do not consider individualism as a kind of morality—they do not conceive of individualism as the responsibility of a person to be true to his own ideals. Individualism does not imply a sense of oughtness or responsibility, but rather it is seen as the right and privilege of an individual to look out for his own interests even against the interests of the group. To the extent that individualism brings with it any duty at all, it is simply the obligation of the person in power to permit a measure of freedom to the person lower in the hierarchy. In the common view, traditional Japanese morality meant only responsibilities and duties, no rights. One was supposed to be loyal to his master even if it meant getting little in return. What democracy and individualism mean to the Mamachi resident is that subordinates now have the right to expect something from their superiors, and some people in Mamachi now use this as grounds for insisting on their rights. Although it is now felt that a superior should grant some such privileges, it is still considered crude and selfish for a person to stand up for his rights. Few people in Mamachi consider it a higher morality to be concerned more with one's own benefit than with the welfare of one's group.

One of the characteristics of loyalty as a basic value is that no principle is more important than regard for the other members of one's own intimate group. Hence, there is no fully legitimate basis for standing against the group. Once group consensus is reached, one should abide by the decisions. Although some deviants attempt to justify their failure to follow group consensus in terms of democracy or freedom, these values have not been internalized sufficiently to justify the deviant's behavior to himself, let alone to other members of the group. It is true that there is now sufficient acceptance to cause some hesitation and tinges of ambivalence before an overly frank or pretentious deviant is put down, but not enough to counter effectively the eventual pressures toward group consensus, nor enough to turn an occasional deviant into a hero for courageously defying his group for other principles.

The lack of absolutes also facilitates the adjustment to new ideas very rapidly once the group arrives at a consensus. This has created a realism and pragmatism which makes it possible to absorb new patterns of behavior as long as they are mediated by the group. Although many Japanese decry the abandonment of principle in their easy accommodation to new power situations,[4] there is no doubt that this ability has made it easier to absorb new ideas in a period of rapid social change. This requires, however, considerable discussion, and there are continual informal get-togethers and discussions among Mamachi residents trying to achieve a consensus. This same process is used at the most general level to determine group values

---

[4] See, for example, Tadashi Fukutake, *Man and Society in Japan,* Tokyo: University of Tokyo Press, 1962. Western observers noting the existence of non-Western patterns in Japan are prone to regard them as traditional. In fact, many are not traditional but the results of considerable change, and Mamachi residents place little value on the preservation of tradition. They express a willingness, even eagerness, to sacrifice traditional practices if they seem not to fit with a realistic adjustment to the world today. This also accords with the Caudill and Scarr findings of an overwhelming preference for the "present time" value orientations as opposed to "past" and "future." Cf. Caudill and Scarr, *op. cit.*

and at the most concrete level to determine group attitudes toward specific subjects within the family or within some group in the community. In the bureaucracy, the *ringi seido* (system of joint consultation by people on the same level)[5] reflects the same pattern. In the *ringi seido* a person does not have specific responsibilities assigned to him but rather continually checks back with the group for final approval. Although one may question the efficiency of such a procedure, it does maintain close group co-operation. If a group achieves consensus, this makes it possible to absorb changes relatively easily because no old rules or principles interfere with consensus.[6]

The lack of absolute standards taking precedence over consensus also makes it difficult to decide by what rules the group should arrive at a consensus. The general consideration in reaching a consensus is the good of the group as seen by various people, but the problem of various strengths of feelings, relative status within the group, and objective considerations about group benefit can make the process of reaching a consensus extremely complex. Because people's feelings are carefully considered in reaching the consensus, there is no simple way for members to resolve disputes without considering all the subtleties of their relationship to each other and to the group.

The lack of absolute standards taking precedence over consensus creates problems for a person moving from one group to another. It takes time to be accepted in a tight-knit group. Furthermore, the newcomer cannot be sure of group standards, and he has no standards of his own which he knows he can apply to the new group. Even if the practices and standards of judgment in his new group are similar to those of his old group, in a dispute or in case he incurs the displeasure of the group, he has no way to justify his behavior. Unfamiliar with the norms of the group, he tries to be par-

---

[5] From Kazuo Noda, unpublished manuscript.
[6] Group consensus is perhaps the most widespread model for decision-making. For example, more than 90 percent of divorces are by collusion. Cf. Takeyoshi Kawashima and Kurt Steiner, "Modernization and Divorce Rate Trends in Japan," *Economic Development and Culture Change,* 1960. This model of conciliation and group decision is also a general model in Japanese law. Cf. Takeyoshi Kawashima in Arthur Taylor von Mehren, ed., *op. cit.*

ticularly careful until he understands the nature of the group consensus.

Although loyalty has been a basic Japanese value for centuries, there have been several modifications of patterns of loyalty within the last few decades. One of these is the increasing importance of the ties with equals as opposed to the tie between superiors and inferiors.[7] Traditionally, the hierarchical positions were more inclined to be ascribed in terms of age[8] or in terms of status in the community. Increasingly, hierarchical positions are subject to patterns of achievement, and if a superior is unable or unwilling to go along with group consensus he may be politely moved to a position of honor without power and, in effect, be replaced by someone who is more responsive to group consensus. Even in present-day Mamachi, however, it is often difficult for others to dislodge a person of authority without causing embarrassment and schisms in the organization. But even if he remains in his position officially, informal consensus can be used effectively to slow down his programs if he is not willing to follow the group consensus. "Feudalistic" has been an effective rallying cry in limiting the power of the superior.

There is also another sense in which the collateral dimension has replaced the hierarchical. In the traditional pattern, it was common for a boy to enter a shop at a fairly early age and for a girl to marry at a fairly early age; once in the small shop or the family, the young person was subject to the wishes of his superior. Now, with the prolongation of schooling and the postponement of the age at which work and marriage begin, the peer group takes on an importance at this stage which it previously lacked. Furthermore, in the large firm the salary man has many peers. When he joins the firm, he is inducted in a large class and receives training in the class. This peer group of newly inducted members becomes an important

---

[7] However, even in traditional times, there were variations which stressed collateral as opposed to lineal ties. Cf. John Pelzel and Florence Kluckhohn, "A Theory of Variation in Values Applied to Aspects of Japanese Social Structure," *Bulletin of the Research Institute of Comparative Education and Culture,* Kyushu University, 1957.

[8] Cf. Edward Norbeck, "Age Grading in Japan," *American Anthropologist,* 1953, 55:373–384.

source of solidarity which tends to place limitations on the extent to which they are subject to the authority of the superiors.

A second change in the pattern of loyalty is in the narrowing of the range of loyalty. The most popular epithet for criticizing traditional patterns is "feudalistic." In Mamachi, many traditional bonds have loosened or evaporated. For example, elders in the community who arbitrarily impose their will on community organizations would be considered feudalistic. Main family members in the country who make demands on the branch family in Mamachi are considered feudalistic. High status people who try to control some activities of low status people in the community are considered feudalistic. Too much interference by a work superior in the personal life of an employee would be considered feudalistic. All this means that group loyalties in contemporary Mamachi are focused on the nuclear family and the immediate work group.[9] The link between the work group and the company means on certain occasions that one is loyal to his own company vis-à-vis other companies and to his nation vis-à-vis other nations, but this wider loyalty never takes precedence over the loyalty to one's immediate group.

The narrower range of primary loyalties has minimized potential conflicts between loyalties. In comparison, for example, in the traditional Chinese or southern Italian family, which lacked a sharp limit to the loyalty required on both sides of the family, continual conflicts existed between loyalties to various relatives. In those societies, gifts or favors to certain relatives were taken as an insult to others, and lineage fission was often accompanied by family quarrels or feuds. Even in traditional Japan loyalties and obligations sometimes conflicted, and a hierarchy of primacy evolved by which conflicts were resolved. For example, in conflicting loyalties, a samurai was to neglect his family in favor of his lord. In some cases, however, as in the loyalty conflicts of friends versus relatives, it was not clear how these were to be resolved.

In contemporary Mamachi, however, because the basic loyalty is to one's immediate group, the conflicts of loyalty generally do not

---

[9] Caudill and Scarr found that responses to questions dealing with community relations and relations with relatives were very individualistic. Caudill and Scarr, *op. cit.*

create serious problems. The greatest problems today appear to be resulting from the not-yet-completed process of narrowing the range of loyalties. Although most families now consider that loyalty is limited primarily to the nuclear family and the immediate work group, a few try to take advantage of the rather weak expectation that it should extend to a wider circle. Aside from such problems, the conflict of genuine loyalties is rare. The most common conflict of loyalty between family and work group occurs when a husband is transferred from the Tokyo area to another city. Although moves to new communities are less common than in the United States, sometimes a man will be sent to another Japanese or overseas branch of his company for a year or two. The man nearly always accepts the move without protest, but often, because of the problems of setting up a temporary home and disrupting the children's education, the wife and children remain in Mamachi. This need not lead to a serious conflict of loyalties because even at a distance, the husband continues to meet the basic needs of his family. He supports the household and looks out for his children's future. To the extent that a conflict does exist between family and place of work, it is not usually the conflict between the family and the firm but between the family and the company gang, since it is the gang rather than the firm which places the heaviest demands on the husband's time and money.

For the wife, loyalty to her husband and children takes clear precedence over loyalty to other relatives or friends. The one unavoidable conflict is in the switch of allegiance from the family into which she was born to the family into which she marries. This conflict is generally resolved in favor of the family into which she marries, but in the first few years of marriage this may not accord with her feelings. The narrowness of the range of loyalty, however, has meant that the conflict at most affects her, her parents, her husband, and his parents. In personal relations, the husband's loyalty to wife and children now even takes precedence to his loyalty to his parents, but he generally tries to remain loyal to both.

The narrow range of present-day loyalties sets limits to the amount of loyalty conflict, but the increase of mobility outside these narrow groups makes it necessary to find some substitute for loyalty as a basis of trust. Although in most cases the value of honesty is thoroughly accepted, in some cases it is considered moral to deceive outsiders. Most people feel no responsibility for helping or being kind to strangers because there is no universal ethic which says that all men should be treated equally, that outsiders should be trusted and treated with kindness. This ethic poses serious problems with the increase of contacts between strangers as is evidenced by the widespread use of private detective agencies. The practice of making contacts with outsiders through mutual friends is thus very crucial in providing a basis of trust between strangers which is not provided by a more fully developed universal ethic.

A related problem is a person's difficulty in maintaining identity and focusing his sense of loyalty when he is not a member of a close-knit group. For example, there is often a gap in late adolescence when a youth has weakened his ties to his family but has not yet replaced them with loyalty to a new family or place of work. In this transition, the ties between classmates may temporarily fill the gap, but *ronin* who are studying for examinations and even college students often have no friendships strong enough to provide a stable basis of loyalty. School and university provide little dormitory life, and few fraternities or clubs exist to provide a feeling of belonging. It is at this age that some larger ideology seems especially attractive. Once a young man becomes a salary man and enters a firm, however, he has a feeling of belonging and becomes progressively less interested in an over-all ideology.[10]

A final change in the pattern of loyalty is the easing of the rigidity with which loyalty is demanded. For example, New Year visits of paying respect to one's superior are slowly losing their compelling quality among salary men. Bringing periodic presents to one's superior no longer seems so essential, and some capable young men do not bother with this custom any more. The relaxation of formalities is not, however, a dilution of regard for the essence of loyalty. Mamachi residents still are primarily oriented to the old values rather than the new. Even if critical of the old values they continue to think in terms of the traditional. Most of the attack on old values

---

[10] The fundamentalist "new sects" have a wide following among people who would otherwise lack close-knit groups: migrants to the city, women with marital difficulties, and men who lack secure employment. Mamachi salary men have little interest in these "new sects."

is not on the basis of the new values of individualism but on the basis of antifeudalism. Among groups of close friends, for example, there may be complaints about superiors, but the content of the complaint is not likely to be that the superior did not provide enough freedom but that he did not adequately look out for his followers. To the extent that democratic values have an influence it is to soften the harshness of the demands of loyalty and permit more tolerance for the group members who do not always follow automatically the dictates of the group consensus.

Although the underlying value of loyalty has remained, the patterns of loyalty have undergone sufficient change to polarize responses to these changes. If the modern values of loyalty which stress collaterality rather than hierarchy and allow a narrower range of loyalty and increased tolerance of deviation are placed at one end of the continuum, and the traditional views at the opposite end, it is possible to distinguish four general kinds of reaction: those who conform to the new pattern, those who conform to the new but do so defensively, those who defensively support the traditional, and those who conform to the traditional.[11]

The first, and perhaps the most common of the four types, consists of those who fit easily into the new patterns. These are the people who are loyal to their own group, faithful to group members, follow group consensus, do not want to take things literally, and are not interested in ritual displays of loyalty. They believe in frankness. They have ideas of their own, but are willing to permit other members freedom and variation, and they are deeply devoted to their group. They try to avoid situations where they might be called on for help by distant relatives and if called will offer a minimum of help in as kindly a manner as possible.

The second type, those who defensively conform to the new standards, hate tradition and any contemporary vestige of feudalism they can uncover. They resent any insinuation by foreigners that they accept tradition or that the Japanese in general are traditional-minded. Within their own family or immediate work group they

---

[11] These correspond essentially to Talcott Parson's deviance paradigm which includes conformity, compulsive conformity, compulsive alienation, and alienation. See his *Social System*, Glencoe, Ill.: The Free Press, 1951, chapter 7.

remain loyal and follow the group, but many project their feelings of annoyance at conformity on the ideological plane, complaining, for example, about the power of tradition, conformity, and the older generation. Many young girls who are able to contain whatever negative feelings they have toward their own mother, project onto mothers-in-law in general the negative feelings they suppress at home. Within the tight-knit group, often one must control one's negative feelings, and any alienation which one feels is projected outside the group toward any kind of traditional pressure for conformity.[12]

Some members of this category are not accepted either by groups upholding modern or those upholding traditional patterns, but their annoyance is more likely to be directed toward the traditional than the modern. Some of these people are envious of not being in the in-groups and would possibly be more moderate if included. At times these are the people who are concerned about what they consider the tyranny of the majority. They so resent the arbitrariness of the majority, that they do not fully accept the principle that the minority should abide by the decisions of the majority.

The third group, those compulsively alienated from the new values, are upset when others do not show proper respect for tradition and the traditional values of hierarchy and authority, self-discipline, and absolute obedience. Though considerably smaller in number and less vocal than those opposed to tradition, they may be just as adamant. This is the group who often promote the reintroduction of moral training in school and encourage teaching children more respect and conformity.

Finally, there are those who are completely alienated from the new values but who feel almost no conflict in their opinion. They are fully integrated in their own groups and, although unhappy with the newer values, do not necessarily express their opposition in terms of ideology. For example, when others argue that traditions must be changed, they may not offer any counterargument, but by their behavior and attitudes they continue to show high regard for

---

[12] As Dr. Takeo Doi has suggested, it is in part the psychological strain in adjusting to the consensus in their own group that makes it so difficult to accept a consensus arrived at in another group.

tradition. Often because of their age or high status in the community, they retain the admiration of other people in the community and are somewhat insulated from the pressures to change.

COMPETENCE

To be fully respected a person must not only be loyal but competent (*yoku dekiru* or *sainoo ga aru hito*). Competence is defined partly as talent or genius (*tensai*) but partly as the capacity for hard work (*kinben*) and perseverance (*gamanzuyoi*). Although Mamachi residents no longer take seriously the view that a talented person is being rewarded by *inga* (the Buddhist doctrine of cause and effect) for virtue in a previous life, there is an overtone to the word *tensai* which implies that a person is blessed by heaven. Although it can be misleading to rely too much on linguistic usage because the origin of the word does not necessarily coincide with its present meaning, it is not irrelevant to note that the *ten* of the word *tensai* is written with the character for heaven. But even if having talent does not denote a moral quality, hard work certainly does, and it is thought that competence is in large part the result of years of practice and hard work. Although competence is less crucial than loyalty, a person who has an important position and is not competent is regarded as undeserving, and, if it can be done gracefully, he may be replaced by one who is competent as well as loyal.

Performance (or in Florence Kluckhohn's value-orientation theory, "doing") is not valued for its own sake, but for the sake of the group. Competence is likewise considered important in the context of its meaning for the group, because a person's performance not only affects himself but his co-workers. Because groups are tight-knit, a member's success and satisfaction depend on the success of the entire group, and one slacker can undermine the position of all the others. In performing a task, one is not rewarded simply for giving his best efforts, but must produce the results for the group or suffer the consequences. If a school child misbehaves or is caught by the law, the teacher is held as partly responsible, regardless of what efforts he might have made to redirect the errant child. If a child is injured on a school trip, the mother who accompanied the class is considered partly responsible regardless of how the injury actually occurred. Because a person's responsibility is so total, most activities are not decided and carried out by a single individual but by the group.

Because most groups are relatively stable, a person usually is not judged on the basis of a single performance. The intimate association of group members over years makes it possible for them to know each other's abilities and weak points intimately. A person's general competence becomes, in effect, an ascriptive point of reference for respect accorded him by other group members. Even if he is not officially accorded a high position within the group, the fact that in forming group consensus other co-workers respond readily to his advice means that he is constantly receiving recognition for his general competence. For a person to be really competent, however, he must not only have technical skill but skill in human relations. Since groups operate by consensus, a person who antagonizes others is not given a chance to realize his potential competence regardless of technical competence.

Group members cannot all have an equal amount of loyalty and competence, and if one member is loyal but not competent or competent but not loyal, this poses a problem which might be called "incongruency of respect," and requires that the group develop some way of reconciling this incongruency. Usually, except for the time of movement between groups as in examinations, the value of competence is subordinated to the value of group loyalty. For example, within a business firm, a man is generally rewarded for his competence only after there is complete consensus that he deserves to be. A man's advancement is in part based on seniority, and at the lower level of the business hierarchy formal differentiation of men on the basis of competence is minimal. When, after several years, differentiation in status is finally made on the basis of competence, there is a feeling that the person who is promoted completely deserves the promotion, and, if anything, should have received it earlier.[13] Therefore, ordinarily, ability is rewarded but in such a way that group consensus is not disrupted.

However, the individual with ability who does not respond to group consensus is difficult for the group to deal with. If a person

---

[13] For this information I am indebted to Professor Kazuo Noda of Rikkyo University.

is incompetent as well as unresponsive, the group can effectively isolate him. Even the talented man whose services are needed may find himself in a less important position than he deserves if he is unco-operative, and if permitted to occupy a position of prominence, informal sanctions may be directed against him to limit his autonomy and power. Similarly, a mother whose children are successful in school but who does not subscribe to the attitudes of the community may not be given a position of prominence. Such cases are not always settled easily and gracefully, but once an effective group consensus is achieved, effective informal techniques can be used to isolate, degrade, and embarrass the deviant.

The common solution to the converse problem, the incompetent person who is loyal to the group, is to give him a position of honor and prestige which carries little responsibility and power. Since there is no clearly defined table of organization or rules of office, bureaucratic and private voluntary associations are flexible. This flexibility makes it possible on the basis of group consensus, to create special positions for such people where they will be accorded respect and yet where their lack of ability will not hinder group effectiveness. Of course, the person may be aware that he is not regarded as competent but often he appears grateful just to be treated with honor.

In women's community groups, where group productivity is less critical, competence is less important and social status more weighty. Yet the resolution of the conflict between loyalty and competence follows the same lines. A woman loyal to her group will be included in group activities and given a position of honor even if she is not particularly competent. But greater responsibility and prominence go to those who are loyal, responsive to group opinions, and able in carrying out the group activities.

A MAJOR VARIATION: AESTHETIC VALUES

Many Mamachi residents consider themselves closer spiritually to the French than to any other nation, explaining that they share the interest of the French in artistic values. Mamachi residents have a particular sensitivity to beauty, especially in spatial arrangements. Their interest in size, shape, and color pervades their entire life and finds an outlet in room arrangement, flower arrangement, decoration, and gardening. Even the preparation of food becomes an art form with the careful cutting and arranging in interesting designs and color combinations. They enjoy seeing the food arranged in such a way that it preserves the original nature of the food. Complementing their keen awareness of beauty in man-made products is their love of nature. This love enters the home and takes them outdoors; they enjoy traveling to places famous for their natural scenic beauty.

Many of their skills are designed to gain a mastery and self-control which they see as providing a kind of harmony with the spirit of nature. Such activities as tea ceremony, flower arrangement, calligraphy, gardening, or quiet meditation, practiced by men as well as women, are in part cultivated as status symbols for a higher style of life but they are respected because they provide this kind of self-control and harmony.

Many events are invested with a ceremonial elegance that is part of the Japanese love of grace and control. Though some regard certain features of these ceremonies, like low bowing and expensive weddings, as despicable remnants of feudalism, most derive enjoyment from the style of many formalities: the exchange of greetings, the giving and receiving of presents, the entertainment of guests, the sending-off and welcoming-home parties, the celebration of holidays and special events. Such acts are conducted with a style and elegance rising above the mundane routine of daily tasks.

Although such aesthetic pleasures have an important place in the lives of many Mamachi residents, generally aesthetic values are given a secondary role, and the opportunity to cultivate these arts is confined to segregated times and places. People are admired for their aesthetic qualities and criticized for slovenliness (*darashi ga nai*), but these qualities are not as essential to group life and activities as loyalty and competence. A few professions, such as entertainment, the arts, teaching, or the priesthood, specialize in aesthetic values. Aesthetic values may also assume a primacy for women of leisure or for elderly people after retirement. But for most people, the significance of aesthetic pleasures is found in the attempt to achieve peace of mind away from the routine tasks of housework and the heavy demands of loyalty placed upon them in their groups. Yet these pleasures are not simply a release from other problems, but represent a positive striving for beauty and a feeling of being at one with the universe. Unlike certain Western values that would actually be counter to group loyalty, the acceptance of aesthetic values provides individual gratification without threatening to interfere with group demands. If anything, by helping the individual to resolve his own ambivalences and achieve personal integrity, it makes it easier for him to follow the demands of his group.

THE MORAL BASIS OF THE SALARY MAN

With the heavy valuation on loyalty, concern with individual profit from economic activities has never been considered entirely legitimate. People like Goto who amassed the Toyoko fortunes or Matsushita who amassed the National Electric fortunes are considered overly selfish by many Mamachi residents, and they do not command the respect that Ford or Carnegie enjoyed in America. In the early period of Japanese modernization, the large businessmen had to justify themselves, not in terms of their own entrepreneurial skill and the preservation of free enterprise but in terms of their contribution to the nation. Present-day Mamachi residents likewise have little regard for those engaged directly in the pursuit of their own profit. The small shopkeeper may escape criticism if he keeps a stable particularistic relationship with his customers, but he is suspect if he appears to be concerned primarily with his own profit. Of course, entrepreneurs in larger concerns have a much higher status, but they have little leeway in the manner in which they pursue profit if they are to retain people's respect on moral grounds. Even many community leaders and politicians who are permitted to occupy important positions because of their power and ability, are not admired for their moral qualities if they are seen to be looking out primarily for their own interests.

The salary man, however, does not see himself as looking out primarily for his own interests. When he enters the company, he receives a low salary, much less than he deserves by straight economic calculations. Since his salary is regular and determined more by seniority than by his good work, he feels he is doing good work not out of his own interest, but out of his devotion to the firm. He receives a bonus not on the basis of his individual contribution to the firm, but on the basis of the success of the firm. By being committed to the firm for life and receiving many benefits for his long-term service, he, in fact, ordinarily feels loyal and genuinely interested in the firm's welfare. Thus the salary man has solid grounds for self-respect in his basic value system. He sees his own long-term interests as fully identified with the company's interests but because of his devoted service to the firm, he cannot be accused of putting his own interests first.[14]

The firm not only gives him a chance to feel loyal; it provides a basis for a feeling of competence. In some groups like his family, he may feel loyal, but he knows he is accepted even if he lacks ability. But in the large bureaucratic organization, a man must prove himself before he is admitted. Everyone in the organization is considered to have at least a minimum of ability so that he is not threatened with the possibility of discharge. The further training within the company and the continual rise in status on the basis of loyal service enhances the feeling that all men have a necessary minimum of competence.

The independent businessman may have plenty of ability but he may have difficulty in convincing himself and others that he is properly loyal to anyone but himself. In certain traditional inherited occupations, the son may be loyal to the family, but he often has a weak basis for the claim of competence. The practices of the large firm make it possible for the salary man to feel that he is legitimized both on the basis of loyalty and competence.

At the same time, the salary man is able to feel that his organization has made great progress toward getting rid of arbitrary feudalistic practices. In the small shops or in many of the smaller enterprises, the intense relationship between master and apprentice is such that the apprentice feels completely bound by the relationship with a single person. In a large organization, however, the loyalty is primarily to the firm and there is leeway given to the individual. He does not remain completely under any single person's authority.

---

[14] Japanese do not express surprise at the existence of a corporate ethic, nor is there a competing value system which can be used to criticize the corporate ethic as expressed, for example, by William H. Whyte, *The Organization Man*, New York: Simon and Schuster, 1957.

To my knowledge, none of these firms reward employees for individual services in the forms of commissions or sales, piecework, or special contributions to the company.

There is usually opportunity for contact with other people in the firm, and one's future does not depend entirely on some superior who may exercise his authority arbitrarily. The large organization fits well with the newer modern conception of loyalty.

The position of the salary man offers a unique opportunity to live according to the values which Mamachi residents consider most important. Not only does it provide an opportunity for legitimation on the basis of loyalty and competence, but it permits free time for aesthetic pursuits. In short, the Mamachi salary man is proud to be a salary man not only because he feels that he can acquire security and meet the practical problem of earning a living, but because he can have self-respect in terms of his most basic values.

Part Three

INTERNAL FAMILY PROCESSES

Chapter VIII

THE DECLINE OF THE *Ie* IDEAL

THE CONCEPT OF *Ie*

Until the end of World War II, the Japanese government saw that all its citizens, through school and mass media, learned in great detail about "the family system." As a whole the government was amazingly successful. Not only did everyone learn about the ideal family, but many attempted to model their family on this ideal. Even today, Mamachi residents, like other Japanese, remember clearly the main outlines of what they were taught about the ideal family and the model of the *ie*[1] still has an important impact on family behavior. At the heart of the system was the *ie*, the single unbroken family line, including both living and dead, and the concept of filial piety. The basic goal of *ie* members was to care properly for departed ancestors and to preserve the continuity and prosperity of their *ie*. Selling land, for example, was considered a grave misfortune, both because it was a disgrace to the ancestors and because it might seriously affect the family's fortune for generations to come. Family members sacrificed personal pleasures and wants for the *ie*, not only to gain respect or rewards in this life, but to attain immortality, for the idea of after life was contingent on the continuation of the *ie*.[2]

[1] The same word, *ie*, is also used to mean simply home or a family, but in this chapter it is used only in its meaning as a family line.

For a brief but authoritative account of the *ie*, see Kizaemon Ariga, "The Family in Japan," *Marriage and Family Living*, 1954, 16:362–368. The term *dozoku* is used to denote a locality kin group comprising main and branch families sharing the same work. The main and branch families were sometimes linked not by blood but by fictitious kin ties. Cf. Michio Nagai, "Dōzoku: A Preliminary Study of the Japanese 'Extended Family' Group and Its Social and Economic Functions," Report No. 7, Project 483, Ohio State University (mimeographed).

[2] Cf. Nobushige Hozumi, *Ancestor Worship and Japanese Law*, Tokyo: The Hokuseido Press, 1912.

165

Small children belonged to their parents' *ie.* When the children of a family attained maturity, one son, usually the first, was given the honor and the responsibility for preserving the *ie.* The other children had to find another *ie* or, if given permission, they could start a new branch to the main *ie* into which they were born. When a daughter married, her name was crossed off her *ie*'s register and entered into the register of her husband's family. The *ie* gave daughters sizeable dowries and assisted younger sons in starting out in life, but the bulk of the family land and treasures was given to the son who had the responsibility for looking after the family line.[3] In theory, the family head did not own the property, but was merely the trustee[4] in the present generation who looked after the property of the *ie,* past, present, and future. If the head of the household died, normally his son would inherit the headship. If no son were available, a younger brother of the deceased might become head if he had not yet gone to another *ie,* or a wife might take over the headship until an heir was selected.

When a bride entered a new family, she was expected to learn her new family's customs (*kafuu*) and by hard work, automatic obedience, and enthusiastic submission to prove that she was sufficiently loyal to deserve family membership. If she failed, she was returned to her original home.[5] An adopted son-in-law had to go through the same process.

The bride was not simply a bride of her husband but of his *ie,* and his *ie* referred to her as *uchi no yome* (our bride). In many ways she was regarded as an adopted daughter, and she referred to her parents-in-law as mother and father.[6] She was chosen not by

---

[3] It may be suggested incidentally that this practice played a crucial role in capital formation which was necessary for modernization. Many characteristics of modern developments (thrift, hard work, and even economic rationality) were often intimately associated with the attempt to develop and preserve the *ie.* Hozumi, *op. cit.,* notes that formerly rules existed against the *ie* giving too much away since this might interfere with family continuity.

[4] Cf. the works of Carle Zimmerman.

[5] Returning a bride was very common, especially in certain areas of northern Honshu, and it was this practice which made such a high divorce rate in the Meiji Period. The rate was even higher than statistics indicate because many brides were returned in the first months after the marriage before it was officially registered.

[6] In Tokugawa census registers, a young wife is often listed as daughter without being distinguished from a true daughter of the household. For this information I am indebted to Robert J. Smith.

her husband but by his *ie,* on the basis of her willingness and ability to work hard and transfer her loyalty to her new family, and of her having the health, vigor, and wisdom necessary to produce and rear a desirable heir. Similarly, an adopted son was selected on the basis of his ability to continue the family line. Often it was more important for him to have skills necessary to operate the family farm or business enterprise than the attributes necessary for a good husband.

The son or adopted son who became the family head theoretically had absolute legal authority over the other family members. Just as children were to obey their parents, so the wife was to obey her husband, and when her son became family head, she was to obey him. Younger brothers were to obey the elder brother. The Japanese government held the family head responsible for the behavior of family members, and he was expected to use his authority to ensure that all members behaved properly.

Just as his authority was the greatest, so was his responsibility greatest. In addition to supervising the family enterprise, he had the onus of deciding on marriage and work arrangements for his children or younger siblings. He was responsible for the health and welfare of *ie* members, living and dead. He provided for his parents in their retirement. If his sisters or daughters were divorced and sent back because they were not acceptable to the new *ie* or if sons or brothers lost their jobs, he provided temporary food and housing and assisted them in finding a new opening. As preserver of the *ie,* he supervised the care of family shrines and graveyards and made certain that each summer, at the O-bon festival, lanterns were lighted so that the spirits of departed ancestors could find their way from the grave to the ancestral home.

A prosperous family might boast of a family genealogy and a family graveyard dating back several hundred years, although some families candidly admit doubt about the authenticity of some of the early part of the record. Yet the living members of an *ie* were usually limited to a stem family of father, mother, unmarried children, a married son, his wife, and their children. In a certain stage of the life cycle, if the grandparents died before the eldest son married, the household might consist only of parents and children. If a family were prosperous and wanted to expand, then a second son would be allowed to form a branch family (*bunke*) which would remain within the *ie,* but be subordinated to the original family (*honke*). In a farm family, the second son might be given a small plot of land, or, in a business family, he might be given a small part of the business or a branch office to provide support for his family. One of his children would be selected as his heir and would become head of the branch line. Theoretically, a main family could have many branches, and branches could have branches. Officially, there was a clear hierarchy of power, the branch family being subordinated to the main family. In fact, except for communities in which the main and branch families had close contact, these relationships had little significance beyond two or three generations. Usually the branch family which migrated to the city obtained virtual autonomy over its own sphere. Sometimes a second son who set up a family of his own did not even go through the formal procedures of setting up a branch family. This son officially retained membership in his original *ie,* but once he had a wife and children, he was granted virtual autonomy.

THE BRANCH

The concept of *ie* continues to provide an important model for family behavior, but it is no longer imperative to sacrifice one's self for the *ie,* and some families without children are even willing to go without an heir. The desire to continue the *ie* is particularly weak in branch families, and in Mamachi, as in other urban areas, the overwhelming majority of families are branch families.[7] Because the main family (except for new main families formed by second sons who became independent) has a much longer tradition, it is natural that more effort will be put into its preservation than into the attempt to preserve the branch. The second son who migrates to the city has no responsibility to his *ie.* When he moves, he brings with him virtually no family treasures, he has no family graveyard or ancestral tablets and no family business to look after. Not only

---

[7] My survey data indicate that of 63 salary-man families, 86 percent were branch families; of 81 small shopkeeping families, 75 percent were branch families; of 172 farm families, 54 percent were branch families. Unfortunately, the designation of branch family does not indicate how many generations ago the branch split off from the main family. One may suspect that in many farm families this happened many generations ago.

does he himself have no *ie* responsibility, but when he dies, his heir has a very shallow lineage heritage since it began only a generation before.

Even if the son in the city does not leave an heir or if his heir leaves no heir, it is not considered a tragedy. The main family from which the branch split off will not only continue to look after the ancestors and the prosperity of the *ie*, but they will look after the tablets and graves of the abortive branch family. Most branch families would like to have an heir, but it is difficult to get a satisfactory heir if parents do not give birth to a male child. Some families with only daughters still adopt sons-in-law, but a family can find a more desirable husband for their daughter if they do not require him to become an adopted son-in-law. Most Mamachi branch families consider a good son-in-law more important than the continuation of their branch line. Similarly, Mamachi salary-man families with no children have no family enterprise to offer an attractive young man in return for becoming their adopted son, so many branch families, rather than accept a successor who might lower the quality of their branch line, prefer to be buried at the place of their ancestors with the knowledge that their graves will be cared for by the main family.

In some businesses and crafts, an economic bond joins the branch family to the main family. If a drug business expands, for example, a second son might be given financial support in setting up a branch shop, and the heirs of the branch family would continue to operate a branch shop of the larger shop directed by the main family. In such situations, the economic bond between the main family and the branch family would bring them close together, extending far beyond the business ties. No such economic interest binds the rural family attached to the land and the salary man in the city, nor is there any economic bond between an employee of a large corporation and his son, who is likely to be working in a different corporation or government office. In times of great need, the main and branch families may help each other and, if amiable, they may visit each other occasionally, but typically the tie between the main family in the country and the branch family in the city is little more than a sentimental attachment.

Main and branch families may disagree about how much to help each other, but the feelings of independence of each other have now become so strong that they rarely ask each other for aid, even in need. A more critical problem confronts the branch family if the head of the main family dies leaving no heir.[8] Family fortunes can be dissipated quickly in such instances, and the branch family is expected to see that family property is protected and the main family line continued. Sometimes a second son who is not yet firmly established in the city is called back to take over the family line after the death of his elder brother. However, we have heard of no cases in recent years where a man already established in the city has returned to take over the family line in the country. Life in the city is considered more attractive, and the urban wife and children are reluctant to go back to the rural areas under any circumstances. In two families in which an older brother died leaving small children in the country, the younger brother remained in Mamachi but assisted his brother's children until one could take over the duties of the heir. In one instance, a man got permission from his company to take his full vacation time during the busiest rice-harvesting seasons to return to his rural home and help with physical labor as well as finances. In effect, he temporarily shared the family headship with his deceased brother's wife until the children were in their mid-teens and old enough to carry out the farm work themselves. But in fulfilling this responsibility to his *ie* he created serious strains for his own wife and children who were reluctant for him to spend so much time, energy, and money looking after the *ie* in the country with which they did not feel identified. The husband felt caught between the pressures from the *ie* on the one hand and his wife and children on the other and unsuccessfully tried to resolve the conflict by remaining faithful to both.

In another case, in which the main family in the country owned no land and the heir to the family died, the branch family in Mamachi became the main family with all its responsibilities, but the location of the main family was shifted from the country to Mamachi. It was possible to remove the family heirlooms, tablets, and other property, and to preserve some of the family traditions in

---

[8] This problem, although not so common now, was an acute issue in families where a son died during World War II and was in general more common in the previous era when the death rate was higher.

the city, although not to the satisfaction of all the relatives. Arrangements were made so that the family grave plot in the country could remain there and be cared for. In this event, the branch family was forced to assume the responsibility of the main family, and the concept of *ie* could not be dismissed so lightly.

Many people in Mamachi not only find little positive value in the *ie*, but they object to concern with ancestors and family lines. They regard the family system, especially the arbitrary rule of the family head, the domination of the branch family by the main family, and the emphasis on family tradition as remnants from the feudalistic past which should be done away with as quickly as possible. But part of the desire to forget tradition comes especially from families of humble origin who now enjoy higher positions. A rich family with a long history still draws respect, but families which have entered the middle class only in the last generation are usually anxious to overlook their humble backgrounds. They seem to acknowledge the importance of the family line as a basis for respect, for they not uncommonly exaggerate the length of time their family has lived in the city or the status of their ancestors, and are eager to tell of a rich or famous relative of theirs. Not only do humble families have shorter family genealogies and fewer family treasures to preserve, but their family tree gives them little to point to with pride. It is not surprising that many of them show so little interest in ancestors.

THE DECLINE OF THE *Ie*
AUTHORITY AND WELFARE

In many respects, the *ie* has been like a corporation. Traditionally, it had a set of offices under the direction of a head, a definite membership with set relationships to each other, and regular rules of procedure. Some of the larger or more prominent families actually had written rules, which the *ie* followed to the letter of the law. One of the responsibilities of the head of the main family of the *ie* was to provide for the welfare of all its members. As long as the major wealth of the *ie* was held by the main family and could be allocated or at least controlled by the head, the system worked well. Quarrels or a shortage of funds may have existed, but the family head clearly had the power and responsibility to see that family members gave assistance to needy members. As the power of the *ie* has become weaker, however, the head of the main family finds it difficult to control the allocation of funds to needy members. The power of the main family has been especially weakened by the urban branch families' becoming richer than the main family. As it became harder for the family head in the rural areas to request assistance from the richer branch family in the city, it also became more difficult for the branch family to obtain help from the main family in time of need. The bitter feelings between relatives who sought or gave aid immediately after World War II is adequate testimony to the collapse of the *ie* welfare system.[9] Some, of course, still help needy relatives, but this is no longer common and is usually limited to close relatives. Furthermore, whether help is given no longer depends so much on whether a relative is an *ie* member but on whether he is liked and judged needy and worthy.[10] The decision is controlled by sentiment, not duty to the *ie*.

Under the old system the family may have been dominated by an autocratic head but there was clarity and integrity to the system. The main family inherited the major share of family property and accepted the responsibility of providing for needy members. The eldest son, the trustee of family property, naturally cared for the elderly parents. According to the postwar revisions of the Civil Code, responsibility is to be shared by all children. Precisely how the responsibility should be shared is sufficiently debatable to cause considerable ill-will between siblings. Many still feel the first son should bear most of the burden.[11] Even if inheritance is divided

---

[9] See the polls in Yoshiharu Scott Matsumoto, *Contemporary Japan: The Individual and His Group*, Philadelphia: The American Philosophical Society, 1960.

[10] Even before World War II, the old *ie* system was under severe attack by those who supported the democratic principles of family equality. The sections in the postwar Constitution dealing with family law represented a clear-cut victory for those who believed in equality of inheritance. The new law accelerated the dispersal of family wealth; among salary men, where no attempts are made to get around multiple inheritance, it has marked an end to the *ie*'s ability to control family money and provide for the assistance of needy members. Cf. Kurt Steiner, "The Revision of the Civil Code of Japan: Provisions Affecting the Family," *Far Eastern Quarterly*, 1950, 9:169–184.

[11] In a study conducted in modern Tokyo apartments as many as 20 percent feel that the eldest son should have the main responsibility in caring for the support of needy family members, and 40 percent still feel the eldest son should inherit the majority of the property. In a nearby farming area, where the idea of *ie* is still much stronger, 74 percent felt the eldest son should have the major responsi-

equally, the responsibility for caring for parents cannot be divided equally. In a family of three children, for example, it is not easy for retired parents to spend four months living with each child. It is expected that financial help from the children will be based partly on their ability to pay, but there is no standard formula for deciding how much ability each child has. Furthermore, regardless of a married daughter's desire to help out, her husband may refuse to help support her parents. Even if the children can come to an agreement about the care of elderly parents, those providing the assistance feel it as a burden which the other siblings might have lightened.[12] And even if the children provide plentifully, the parents often feel that they are imposing on the younger couple; and the spouse who is not the child of the elderly persons is likely to make them especially uncomfortable. The prevalence of this problem was made clear to us because one of the most common questions we were asked about family life in America concerned the provision made for older people. The pattern of single inheritance and care for elders was a stable system; the pattern of elderly parents having enough means to support themselves might be a stable system but the area between, where parents require support from various children, appears to lead to inevitable difficulties.

Parents in their forties face a difficult decision about what to do in their old age. Although they recognize the problems of living with children in their old age and want to avoid difficulties, many are afraid that if they live alone they will be lonely and unable to make ends meet. Some bravely assert that they will live alone trying to convince themselves that such a life may not be lonely. Others admit they would be pleased if their children asked them to live together. Despite the problems in the new system of multiple inheritance and weakened *ie*, no one expects the power of the household head to be revived. Furthermore, the problem of supporting aged parents is mitigated by the father's membership in a large organiza-

---

bility, and 84 percent felt the eldest son should receive the majority of the inheritance. Takashi Koyama, *Gendai Kazoku no Kenkyuu* (An Investigation of the Contemporary Family), Tokyo: Koobundoo, 1960.

[12] One Japanese movie which we saw centered on the theme of siblings deciding how to care for their aged widow mother. The most touching scene was when the mother overheard the children arguing that not one but the other should be responsible for her care.

tion. Because the company will provide a pension or at least a large lump sum on retirement, the elderly couple need not be such a financial burden on their children. Having parents live with the younger couple is considered as more natural and less of an imposition than in the United States, and now that the *ie* has declined, increasingly large numbers of parents are able to depart from the traditional *ie* pattern and live with a daughter where there is sufficient positive feeling between the women at home to avoid the conflicts commonly found between mothers-in-law and daughters-in-law.

As the capacity of the family head to control welfare activities has declined, and as the branch family has grown in wealth, security, and prestige, the main family's sanctions have lost their force. No longer is the threat of expulsion from formal *ie* membership so frightening. The family head is especially weak in Mamachi salary families because of the combination of loss of *ie* consciousness in the branch family and the feeling of independence which comes from the economic security offered by the husband's firm.

The power of a household head above his power as a husband and father now are so insignificant that the transfer of position of household head is virtually meaningless.[13] In the local community an elderly father will simply continue to be listed as head of household if he lives with a son. Similarly, the distinction between the heir and other sons has been lessened, not only in matters of inheritance, but with respect to the position of children within the family. In the past, the elder son, as heir apparent, was treated with considerable respect by other members of his family, even before he assumed the position. Not only did parents give preferential treatment to the child who would become the heir, but grandparents openly preferred *uchi mago* (children of their heir) to *soto mago* (children of their other children). While the oldest child still may exert considerable authority over younger siblings, especially in a large family, authority today is derived more from relative age

---

[13] Formerly, in rural areas, at a certain time the household head stepped down and passed on the position of family head to his son. From this day on the father was officially retired and the responsibility was officially in the hands of the son. In some cases the elderly couple moved on the day of retirement to a small separate dwelling on the same land or to a separate room, passing on their own home to their son. See John Embree, *Suye Mura*, Chicago, University of Chicago Press, 1939.

than from the prospect of becoming the heir. An older sister ordinarily has more authority than a younger first-born son.

Formerly the *ie* had considerable power in arranging marriages and jobs for the young. Since marriage was viewed as a change of *ie* for a girl or an adopted son-in-law, it was considered appropriate that the decision be made both by the *ie* receiving the member and the *ie* giving up the member. This attitude has not entirely disappeared, and wedding negotiations, arrangements, gift exchanges, and even the formal ceremonies still distinguish between the *ageru hoo* (the family which is "giving up" a person) and the *morau hoo* (the family which is "receiving" a person).

The investigations and negotiations leading to marriage, generally were carried out by a go-between (sometimes one for each side), who performed his services at the request of the *ie*. The view and temperament of the young man and young lady were considered, but it was expected that their wishes should be subordinated to the *ie*. This was not without some reason, for in the case of the first son, the young bride, after all, was coming to live with her husband's family, and might spend more time with her mother-in-law than with her husband. Even in the marriage of a second son, over which the family exercised less supervision, the family had to bear the responsibility for marital difficulties. Hence, the parents felt that their children (who until the time of marriage had virtually no opportunity for meeting with members of the opposite sex) required their help in selecting a spouse.

The young people of Mamachi now regard such marriage arrangements as remnants of antiquated feudalistic society whereby the *ie* imposes its will on the young people who must sacrifice themselves for the good of the *ie*. While the Mamachi young people no longer are expected to conform to the wishes of their *ie* as such, their parents still retain influence in deciding whom the children should marry. The residents of Mamachi differentiate between two kinds of marriage: the *miai* (arranged marriage) and the *renai* (love marriage). In the *miai*, typically the parents, and sometimes relatives and family friends, have more influence, and in *renai* the young people themselves have more say.[14] While only about half of the

---

[14] Regarding these two forms of marriage, see Ezra F. Vogel, "The Go-Between in a Developing Society," *Human Organization*, 1961, 20:112–120. The distinction be-

recent marriages are officially arranged, in the overwhelming majority parents take an active role, checking on details of the other family. Some families will engage friends or private detectives to investigate the other family. Families frequently argue about the degree of independence that young people should have in selecting a spouse, but the range of freedom subject to dispute is relatively narrow if one considers the overwhelming power of the family in the Japan of an earlier era or the much broader freedom given most young people in the United States.

Yet, compared to the previous age, siblings and friends increasingly are replacing parents as sources of introductions, and coeducational schools and places of work provide limited opportunities which did not exist a few decades ago for respectable middle-class children to meet on their own. Nevertheless, there are few acceptable ways for young people to meet without some kind of introduction. Too much freedom is still suspect. A girl who has had dates with more than two or three men before marriage is still considered a bit free and worldly, and some will wonder whether she will make a good wife. What is emerging to some extent is a combination of *miai* and *renai*—a combination considered desirable by most parents. Under this combination, an appropriate person whom the family already has investigated thoroughly and found acceptable is introduced to the young person. The young people are permitted a few meetings (preferably not too many) to fall in love and make a decision. Under such arrangements they feel they have the best of two worlds: responsible arrangements and romantic love. If a child were given freedom to make his own decision, few discussions with his parents would be necessary, but in Mamachi where the decision is typically shared between the child and his parents, the selection of a spouse may dominate family discussions for years. Certainly both parents and the older children will be included, and sometimes knowledgeable or thoughtful friends. These discussions (or arguments) turn on such questions as what kind of person is desirable, who can help locate a promising candidate, what are the relative assets and weak points of various candidates, how can they get a desirable candidate to agree, what kind of arrangements can

---

tween these two types of marriage will be explored more fully in a forthcoming work by Professor Robert Blood.

be worked out for the marriage and living arrangements afterward. Particularly if the child is a daughter, these items are discussed, rediscussed, investigated, and reinvestigated. A family tries to arrive at a consensus on each minor step along the way. Indeed, they must arrive at a consensus if arrangements are to proceed smoothly. These discussions give the parents, and especially the mother, a purpose and function which they do not enjoy in many Western countries.

Considering how vehemently some adolescents insist on the freedom to find their own spouses, a surprisingly large number later acquiesce to arrangements or suggestions made by their parents. Many young people, especially the overprotected, the bashful, the cautious, those with high standards, those with a proud family history, the undesirable *urenokori* (leftovers) who did not find a spouse on their own, find the *miai* their best opportunity to get married and accept this pattern even if opposed to it ideologically. The willingness of children to let parents take an active part in the decision is undoubtedly related also to the close mother-child relationship and the fact that mothers have sacrificed so much for the children.[15] Furthermore, because children have had little opportunity to meet contemporaries of the opposite sex, they have little confidence in their own ability to make a proper decision. The modern parent of Mamachi does not object in principle to a child's selecting his own spouse; nor does a parent insist that the child follow his parents' choice out of duty to them and their *ie,* but by questioning the wisdom of the child's choice or questioning what the child would do if something went wrong, they can instill sufficient doubt so that he is willing to accede to the parents' advice.

A daughter is especially responsive to her parents' feelings because she would have to turn to them for help in case of marital difficulty. A generation ago divorce was not simply a separation of man and wife, but the husband's *ie* returning her to her parents' *ie.* It was necessary for the divorced woman to have the support of her

---

[15] Evidence for this, based on projective test material given to Japanese, is presented in George De Vos, "The Relation of Guilt to Achievement and Arranged Marriage among the Japanese," *Psychiatry,* 1960, 23:287–301. Judging from De Vos's work, even in rural Japan the willingness to follow the mother's wishes has less to do with the concept of duty to *ie* than with the emotional bond between mother and child.

ie if she were to have a source of livelihood and a reasonable chance
of finding another spouse. Even today, because a widow or a divorcee has few chances for earning a living or finding a new spouse,
the wife generally is reluctant to get a divorce. The rate of divorce
among residents of Mamachi is still very low.[16] Even today a wife
with marital difficulty, in effect, puts her case before her family and
secures their approval before she decides to divorce, no matter how
serious the trouble.

The Mamachi family has less direct control over occupational
choice than over marital choice. Indeed, it has little reason to interfere with the son's occupational choice as long as it fits with the
family's standard of respectability. Farmers and members of lower
socio-economic groups placing a son in a small business concern
still have considerable responsibility for making the necessary personal contacts. In the salary-man family, because hiring is largely
determined by examinations or introductions, the child requires
parental support only for preparing him for admission to a good
academic institution. Once admitted, even if the boy does need
financial help from his parents, his career plans are essentially outside the scope of his parents' planning. An academic degree and
school contacts give a boy security so that he will not have to call
on his parents for assistance in finding a new job if something should
go wrong in his present place of work. Thus, even the first son in
the salaried family has gained considerable freedom from his parents' domination without the necessity of rebelling against his
parents, a situation in striking contrast to the first sons of farmers,
owners of small businesses, and independent professionals.

Symbolic Remnants

Despite the massive inroads into the authority and economic significance of the *ie* in salaried families, there still is a strong attachment to this concept. Even branch families have a strong desire to
continue the family line and an overwhelming hope that the family
have at least one son to continue the family name. In fact, most
families say they would like two sons and one daughter, so that if

---

[16] Though I do not have adequate survey data, my impression is that it would be
somewhat lower than the national average, which is about 10 percent.

something should happen to one son they would still have one to continue the family line. The feeling remains that an *ie* has a tradition and that the person becoming a member of the *ie* should learn the family's customs and share the feeling of belonging to a long line of ancestors.

As much as they would like to adopt a son or son-in-law, few are willing to accept the problems this raises.[17] But there is a common compromise solution in Mamachi to the problem of having no heir: a family finding someone who accepts no other family responsibility than that of taking on the family name and looking after the family ancestral plots and plaques. If a family has only a daughter, at the time of her marriage they may work out an arrangement with her husband whereby she would enter her husband's *ie* and take on his name and family line, providing that one male child of theirs be given her maiden name to continue the *ie* into which she was born. According to another arrangement, if a man has no children to continue his name, he may ask a second son of one of his brothers or other near relatives to take on his family name. In some main families with no children, a child of relatives may still be adopted, but increasingly among salaried families agreements are reached whereby someone will continue the family name without being required to change residence.

Even the branch families often have a feeling of attachment to their ancestral home, although separated from it by generations. Many modern salary men, when asked where their home (*kuni*) is, will answer not their birthplace or their father's birthplace but the rural village where their grandfather or even great-grandfather was born. They may not expect to visit there, although if necessary they usually will be willing to help look after the family graves and ancestral tablets, but they retain a feeling of sentimental attachment which helps define their place in the world for now and ages yet to come.

---

[17] This conforms to Professor Koyama's findings that only 21.8 percent of the dwellers of an urban apartment project (largely salary men) would be willing to adopt a son-in-law if they had only daughters, while as many as 90.1 percent of farmers living in a community within commuting distance of Tokyo would adopt a son-in-law. If a family had no children, 35.6 percent of the city apartment dwellers think it necessary to provide for an heir, but 89.4 percent of the farmers think so. Koyama, *op. cit.*

The Decline of Family Principles

The *ie* was not simply a companionship family as in the West. It was a set of rules about how members were to behave and how the organization was to operate regardless of the sentiment or the convenience of the family members. One person had to be chosen as family head and all other members were to relate to each other depending on their position within the *ie*. It was a set of principles that governed the relationship of family members to each other.

Family relationships are now less governed by principles than by sentiment, power, and convenience. If the branch family has more wealth and power than a main family, it no longer is obliged to subordinate itself to the main family simply because it is the branch. A young man looking for a job or a marital partner may listen to his parents because of their authority, because he is fond of them, or because he respects their judgment. He is no longer obliged to follow his father's or his elder brother's wishes simply because of an obligation to obey the head of the *ie*. A person seeking financial assistance may go to his relatives for help, but he does not necessarily go to the family head, nor is the family head necessarily responsible for looking after the welfare of all members of the *ie*. He goes to relatives for assistance, not because of their position in the *ie* but because he feels close to them or because they are in a position to offer assistance.[18] If one visits the main family, it is not because it is part of a required formality. If the oldest son has the major responsibility of looking after the parents, it is likely to be because he has the kind of job and housing situation that make him most able to bear this burden.

The power of *ie* principles has given way under the impact of new ideology: of forming branch families with a shallow sense of tradition and the growth of large firms providing security and welfare services. The weakening of *ie* principles has not led to chaos, because a new familial order has arisen based on sentiment and a sharp division of labor and authority. It is to the nature of this new order that we turn in the next chapters.

---

[18] Evidence from historical materials indicates that Japanese kinship terminology does not distinguish between relatives of one's father and one's mother. Cf. Robert Smith in Robert J. Smith and Richard K. Beardsley, eds., *Japanese Culture*, New York: The Viking Fund, 1962. With the decline of jural relationships between *ie* members, there appears to be no clear predominance of relationships with one side of the family as opposed to the other.

Chapter IX

THE DIVISION OF LABOR IN THE HOME

In Japanese coastal villages, some fishing boats are strictly for men, and the idea of a woman even boarding a ship is so abhorrent that many myths and superstitions dramatize the punishments for such a transgression. To many traditional Japanese, the idea of a man working in the home is as repulsive as the idea of a woman boarding a fishing boat, and while I know of no myths about the horrors awaiting a man who enters a kitchen, many Japanese young adults cannot recall ever having seen their fathers in a kitchen.

Even the terminology which has been passed down to today makes it clear that the wife's place has been in the home: The husband still refers to his wife as his *kanai* (literally, inside of the house), and friends and acquaintances call a housewife *okusan* (literally, the person in the back, i.e., of the house). Just as a captain stays on the ship when others leave, the wife looks after the house while others are away. In the past, the division of labor within the home was so complete that, when a husband helped in the home, it was thought peculiar and even improper.

This basic pattern of division of labor has been widely accepted even by urban branch families. Traditionally, the husband did not have to make use of his authority to maintain the division of labor because it was thoroughly accepted as just and natural by the wife as well as the husband. It was so highly internalized that many men could not prepare themselves a cup of tea in their wife's absence, and, if one did, women who heard of such incidents spontaneously responded with sympathy for the poor man left in such a predicament.

This division of labor remains strong even in contemporary Mamachi. What characterizes the salary-man family is partly that the husband is beginning to offer assistance in the home and, more important, that the wife no longer helps the husband with his work. In the farm family, in the small shopkeeper family, and sometimes even in the independent professional and the successful business family, the wife is expected to work alongside the husband and give him assistance in earning the family livelihood. She participates in his sphere even if he does not participate in hers. She shares his work load, and in this way is subjected to his authority. In the salaried family, the husband has exclusive domain over his sphere and the wife has almost exclusive domain over her sphere. In some ways, the division of labor is more symmetrical and complete in "modern" than in most other families.

CREEPING CO-OPERATION IN THE HOME

Although, in comparison to other families, salaried families are in the forefront of breaking down the pattern of the husband abstaining from household work, the amount of change has been infinitesimal. Some "modern" Mamachi husbands occasionally look after the children or put up their own bedding, and a few have swept the yard, run the electric sweeper, or run a few errands, but very few have ever assisted their wives in dusting, cleaning, preparing food, setting or clearing the table, or doing the dishes; and it is unthinkable for a husband to assist in serving guests. Many husbands are still unable to prepare their own meals in the wives' absence, and a few will still go without tea if their wives are away.

The wife even does the house repairs. If necessary, she takes care of the coal or charcoal. She does the yardwork. Usually she buys and cares for the husband's clothes, and some husbands are unable to locate their own clothes if they are not laid out for them by the wives.

Considering that most couples strongly believe in the equality of the sexes, that many young husbands resolve at the time of marriage to help their wives, that even the Crown Prince has set the example by assisting his wife with washing the dishes, and that husbands spend many evenings at home, it is surprising not only that the division of labor has remained so strong, but that wives have not wanted their husbands to help more in the home.[1]

---

[1] In a national *Mainichi* poll of the "Wife's Wishes of the Year" in 1953, in answer to the question, "What do you desire most of your husband?" wives gave the follow-

In part, the explanation lies in the forces of tradition.[2] While in principle, Mamachi couples want to be "modern" and not "traditional," attitudes associated with the division of labor have not entirely disappeared. Husbands often understate the extent to which they help their wives in order to avoid being teased by their friends, and some are angered or embarrassed when accused of doing housework. It is still a bit unseemly for a man to be caught helping his wife, and many wives are equally afraid of being thought incompetent for needing help.

A few wives feel burdened because they must work so hard in the home, but most take it for granted that husbands, like children, cannot look after their own possessions or prepare their own food. Almost every household has at least one story of a time when the husband tried to do something for himself such as prepare a meal or find his clothes, only to make a bungling mess which the wife had to resolve. Most wives genuinely sympathize with a man who is left alone at home for a day or two while she is away visiting relatives.

However, the persistence of a strict division of labor cannot be explained entirely as a result of "traditional" attitudes, because older couples, who would presumably be more influenced by tradition, often share household tasks to a greater extent than younger couples. Even a generation ago, some elderly men helped their wives, and now, because the division of labor is not considered sacred, adjustments can occur on the basis of convenience. One American study found that an important determinant of division of labor in the United States was simply convenience, based on the relative amount of time the husband and wife were home.[3] In part these same ecological forces of time and space would seem to

---

ing answers: increase of income 20 percent, abstinence from excessive drinking and smoking 15 percent, repair of house 13 percent, keeping regular time 12 percent, co-operation with stability of living 7 percent, giving up too lavish spending of money 5 percent, saving money 3 percent, and other 7 percent. Takashi Koyama, *The Changing Social Position of Women in Japan*, UNESCO, 1961, p. 63. The desire for a man to help in housework is notable by its absence.

[2] In a national sample in 1951, 31 percent of Japanese men and 34 percent of women approve of a man assisting in kitchenwork; 42 percent of men and 46 percent of women disapprove. The remainder gave no response or said it depended on the situation. Koyama, *op. cit.*, p. 63.

[3] Robert O. Blood, and Donald M. Wolfe, *Husbands and Wives*, Glencoe, Ill.: The Free Press, 1960.

account for some of the variation in the division of labor among Mamachi families; and because the over-all pattern in Mamachi is that the wife spends so much more time at home than the husband, the wife accepts the predominant burden of tasks in the home.

In part, the persistence of the division of labor is a method of keeping the husband-wife equilibrium. Even the wife who expresses the wish that her husband help around the home becomes upset when he follows her wish. As he begins to work, he often makes suggestions about how things should be done, and even if he does not, the wife feels uncomfortable because she knows her husband will be more observant and perhaps more critical of her management. Because the husband does not help much anyway, wives often consider it simpler to do a little more work and avoid the husband's interference.

While the husband and wife cannot usually consciously verbalize the reasons for their feeling of discomfort, it appears that the wife is concerned about her autonomy and that without directly discussing it, her cues of discomfort are sufficient to preserve her autonomy and, hence, the more strict division of labor.

To the extent that the division of labor is changing at all, perhaps the sharpest inroads are made when the wife is sick or away. In the stem family system, if the wife became sick, another woman was often available in the household, and if not, a female relative or friend would be called in to substitute. With the urban nuclear family relatively isolated from relatives, such substitutes are often not available. At the same time the modern salary man's wife now has occasional outside activities such as PTA meetings or, on rare occasions, trips to friends or relatives which take her from the household. If there is an elder daughter in the family not busy studying for examinations, she can help out, and with the "instant" food boom many boys are willing to try their hand in the kitchen. If the mother is sick or absent for an extended period, a female relative may still be called in. But frequently the husband acts as substitute for his wife. Once he makes the break and does the housework in his wife's absence, he becomes more eligible for co-operating with his wife after she returns to assume her old position.

As long as the mother is well, however, no one really substitutes for her and no one is delegated any major responsibility for the housework. Even a grandmother living in the home may not baby-sit for an infant when the mother goes out; the mother takes the infant with her. Boys frequently look after their own belongings, and sometimes help with home repairs or gardening, but they rarely help with cleaning and almost never in the kitchen. A girl in senior high school can typically cook a few dishes, but is unprepared to take charge of preparing a whole meal, using all electrical equipment, or taking full responsibility for supervising younger children in the mother's absence. Girls are thought to mature slowly and since they are busy with school work, the mother is slow to delegate responsibility.

Nor is the mother enthusiastic about passing on responsibilities to part-time maids or baby sitters. A home is defined as too unique and too personal to hire out part of the mother's work. Some families are willing to hire a full-time live-in maid who becomes, in effect, a member of the family, but even then she assists and does not replace the mother. The vast majority are not even interested in hiring a stranger for a few hours a week. The gap between family member and stranger is too great to be bridged by mere contractual arrangements. A mother's relationship with the children is considered so special that even other members of the family are rarely left to care for children. The mother is irreplaceable, her major responsibilities indivisible, and her daily schedule inflexible.

HOUSEWORK: THE DAILY ROUND

Because housework is so exclusively in the hands of the wife, she does not have to co-ordinate plans with others. She is free to plan her own schedule. Even if she has no schedule, she has regular daily activities like getting the family fed, cleaning the house, shopping, greeting her children when they come home, or serving her husband after his arrival in the evening. Most Mamachi housewives have sufficient time to perform their work without rushing, and because they usually have no special place to go if they work faster, they generally think of housework as an ongoing activity rather than something to be organized rationally and attacked with efficiency.

As in earlier times, one day's activities are hardly distinguished from another's. The one exception is Sunday and holidays when the children and husband are free to join in family recreation, shopping, or relaxation.[4] Most Mamachi wives perform all household tasks daily, including washing clothes, shopping for groceries, mopping and sweeping the floors. The ice box is sufficiently small, the floor where one sits sufficiently dusty, and laundry sufficiently tedious that the Mamachi wife finds it advisable to do the work daily. Only if she plans sewing, an outing, or some special activity will she skimp on other work. To give an idea of the daily activities we may take a fairly typical day of a Mrs. T:[5]

She rises at 6 A.M., a full half-hour before anyone else stirs, and opens the wooden storm doors so the house becomes light and airy. She lights the fire for cooking, and since it is winter, she lights the charcoal for the *kotatsu*. After preparing the food, she wakes up the rest of the family. Her husband eats before the children, and she eats part of her breakfast with the others while preparing their lunch. While the husband and older children are dressing, she frantically rushes to find her husband's lost sock and to prepare their shoes and outer garments at the front doorway. She helps them in their coats and sees them off. The older children will have put their own bedding into the closets, but she puts her husband's and small children's away.

After both older children are off to school, she straps her one-year-old on her back and begins cleaning up the dishes. She then washes out

---

[4] See David W. Plath, "Land of the Rising Sunday," *Japan Quarterly*, 1960, 7:357–361.

[5] A larger national sampling on the housewife's daily schedule in early 1959 shows the favorable position of the wife of the salary man in having free time to devote to herself and her family.

HOUSEWIFE'S TIME ALLOCATION (*in hours and minutes*)

Husband's occupation	Salary man	Factory worker	Retailer	Farmer	Fisherman
Sample size	42	59	53	53	44
Eating, sleeping, health needs	10:15	10:19	10:00	10:31	10:00
Occupational work	0:12	0:42	6:16	3:13	3:20
Family affairs	9:02	9:14	5:07	6:56	7:11
Self-cultivation	4:31	3:45	2:37	3:20	3:09

From *Fujin no Jiyuu Jikan ni Kansuru Ishiki: Choosa* (A Study of Opinions on Women's Free Time), Roodooshoo Fujinshoonen Kyoku, No. 28, 1959, p. 43.

the daily items of laundry and rushes to hang them out on the bamboo poles for fear the clouds might turn into rain. She even takes a few items from the closet to hang outside to prevent them from getting moldy, but she leaves the heavy quilts for a sunnier day. Although it is cool she opens the sliding glass doors to air out the house and begins her cleaning. By now her baby has fallen to sleep and she is pleased to relieve her back by laying him down for his morning nap. She fluffs the dust off the windows and sliding panels, sweeps the tatami mats and the wooden floor, gets down on hands and knees to pursue every speck of dust with concerted determination, and sweeps the path outside the house leaving fresh broom marks in the dust.

By the time she finishes her cleaning, the errand boys from the canned-goods shop and the fish store, along with the errand girl from the fruit and vegetable store will have taken her orders and delivered their goods, the milk man will have brought the half pint of milk for the morning, the ice man will have brought ice for the small ice box, and she will have turned away the errand boy from the butcher shop explaining that she didn't need anything. She catches a brief glimpse of the morning paper which the husband read so leisurely at breakfast, and by the time the baby wakes up she has only a few minutes to play with him before going down the street, baby on back, for two or three items at shops which do not send errand boys. While shopping she stops to chat with a few neighbor ladies and hear the morning gossip.

She returns home and prepares a small lunch for herself and the baby and, after cleaning up the dishes, rests and plays with the baby a few minutes while awaiting the return of the older children. She greets the youngest at the door, but as she is busy with the baby, she responds to her older child's announcement of his arrival by yelling her greeting from the kitchen. Both older children join the mother sitting around the *kotatsu* to relate their school exploits for the day, a conversation that is frequently interrupted by the baby who has awakened from his after-noon nap. By the time the older children are through with their snack and a half hour of studying they are off to play, but only after the mother extracts a solemn promise that they will complete their home-work immediately after supper. She digs a few weeds from the garden, brings in some flowers and puts them in a vase, sews a few rags into a dish rag, but postpones the other jobs like sewing her daughter's skirt, pickling radishes, pasting paper on the torn spots in the sliding panel, and running a few errands.

Her afternoon half pint of milk is delivered, but she must go out for the rest of the shopping herself. About five o'clock she rushes out, baby on back and basket under arm, to do her evening shopping for bread, crackers, seaweed, bean curd, and spices, but she resists the temptation to talk with her friends in order to get back and prepare supper before the children start nagging. By giving the children a few extra snacks she manages to keep them from starting to eat before the father's usual arrival time, but when he is late, she allows the children to eat first. While waiting for the father, she fills the bathtub and lights the gas fire to heat the water. Since the food requires no heating, she serves her husband his food as soon as he arrives and sits down to chat with the children. She eats with the father and chats with him as the children resume their studying, occasionally answering some questions which the children bring while the husband catches a few glances at the evening paper.

She interrupts washing the dishes to turn off the gas under the bath and give the bath water a few quick stirs. She announces that the bath water is ready, and the children, who by this time have completed their homework and are sitting talking with the father, in turn take their baths. After finishing the dishes, cleaning the table, and sweeping the floor, she gets out the bedding and lies down a few minutes alongside the children to wish them a good night. While the husband is reading the evening paper, playing with the baby, taking his bath, and watching TV, she lays out the children's clothes for the next day, shines the shoes, closes the wooden doors, puts the baby to bed, and takes her own bath. Unlike her country cousin who must stay up a half hour or so after everyone else retires in order to complete her work, the modern wife of the salary man retires with her husband.

The daily schedule is more demanding in the winter because of the problem of getting the fires going. Otherwise, except for the extra work at times of examination, the annual New Year's cleaning, the display and storage of various dolls for the different festivals, the more frequent airing of clothing and bedding in the damp season, and the assistance she gets from her daughters during vacation, her schedule is much the same in one season as the next.

A wife with small children usually has no time to watch TV or read magazines or books that are not connected with the children's schoolwork. Once all the children are in school, however, her work is sharply reduced, and though she then spends more time visiting with neighbors, reading, attending PTA meetings, and pursuing the housewifely arts, she often finds it difficult to adjust to the sudden increase of free time.

HOUSEWORK: INGLORIOUS AND GLORIOUS

When Americans hear about the daily life of the Japanese woman, centered so completely on the home, they are inclined to assume that the Japanese wife is discontented with her restricted life. This may accurately reflect the attitude of middle-class American women, who are "cooped up in the home," but not that of Mamachi women. Few Mamachi women are aware of any conflict between home and work or between home and personal enjoyment. The Mamachi wife is pleased that in comparison with poorer families she is able to devote herself to her home and family. She does not aspire to escape the home but to obtain a better and fuller life within the home, and the women she hopes to emulate are those who can enjoy and ably manage their activities in the home.[6]

A small percentage of Japanese women are now being trained in specialties which they hope to continue after marriage, but most Mamachi wives do not consider it possible or even desirable to find outside work after marriage. The number of girls attending college is relatively small [7] and high-school and college education of women is primarily focused on training which would not be useful for a vocation. Even those who attend college frequently attend private junior colleges for girls only, and even those who attend more famous universities often major in household management. In contrast to American women who feel frustrated in not being able to continue activities for which they were prepared in college, the young Japanese wife does not have to experience a discontinuity between a

[6] In a national sampling of 1863 Japanese women in 1959 only 38 percent go out for anything beyond neighborhood-shopping more than twice a month, and the most common activity for going beyond the neighborhood is still shopping. Yet in answer to the question of what you would like to do if you had more free time, 32 percent said there was nothing that they particularly hoped to do, 26 percent said sewing, 8 percent would take in work, 7 percent reading, 4 percent children's education, 4 percent flower-arranging or tea ceremony, 3 percent cooking, 2 percent rest, 2 percent movies, 1 percent newspapers, 1 percent women's club activities; 16 percent gave other replies, but virtually none said go out to work. While these percentages were not confined to salary-men's wives, they reflect the fact that the desire to find other activities within the home are far greater than the desire to find activities outside the home. *Ibid.*, p. 27.

[7] While nearly as many girls attend high school as boys (in 1957, 1,275,931 girls were in attendance compared to 1,621,718 boys), fewer girls attend universities. The ratio of girls to boys attending colleges in 1957 was 1 to 4.5 (115,600 to 521,991 but the ratio is 1 to 7 when junior colleges are excluded from the calculation of colleges (71,152 to 493,302) *Fujin no Genjoo* (The Status of Women), Roodooshoo Fujinshoonen Kyoku, No. 44, 1959.

broad range of social activities before marriage and a limited range of social activities after marriage and the birth of children. While most American parents make little effort to limit their daughter's range of social activities before marriage for fear it might make them discontented after marriage, Mamachi mothers are aware of this problem, and try to restrict their daughters' activities so they will not be disappointed after marriage. A young man and his parents want a girl who has not had too broad experiences for precisely this reason. Even well-educated men attending the best coeducational universities often do not want to marry girls who attend the same university or who have traveled abroad because they might be discontented with the life of a mother and housewife.

Despite increased opportunities for girls to move freely on their own, social circles in Japan are sufficiently restricted so that most Mamachi parents have been able, with effort, to meet the challenge of restricting their daughters' freedom. The young Japanese wife is faced, not with contraction of her social activities upon marriage, but with a move from one narrow group to another narrow group. While this change causes her to feel lonely, it does not make her dissatisfied with her new role but rather encourages her to devote herself to her home and the rearing of a family.

To the extent that Mamachi women are satisfied with their lot in life, it is partly because of the romanticization of the horrors of the life of the Japanese woman in the past. If an old lady is asked about her experience as a wife or the life of her mother, one hears a story of difficulties, often mitigated with special qualifications: in her case, the husband was kind and it was not so bad; or in her case, the mother-in-law was kind; or she herself was strong-willed. Yet when one asks a general question, such as how was the life of a young wife a generation or two ago, one almost invariably hears a stereotyped story filled with suffering. For example, when the family sat around the hearth to eat, the young housewife sat on the side where the smoke blew, but often she was too busy waiting on the family to sit at all. She ate in snatches or when others were through, and then immediately set to work again, cleaning up and preparing for the next meal. She was the first up in the morning, the last to bed at night, and always at the service of her family. Not only did she wait on the men, but on her mother-in-law and sisters-in-law.[8] Stories of a young wife proving herself or suffering abuse if she failed are filled with pathos. The image of the newly married house-wife in a strange home, exhausted from long hours of work, fighting to keep herself awake while lying in bed in the early hours of the morning to make sure she would be awake when it was time to prepare breakfast, is an image which still pulls the heart strings of the Mamachi resident.

On the basis of present stories it is difficult to hazard a guess as to how bad conditions actually were, except that the discrepancy between concrete stories and the generally romanticized stereotype suggests that at a minimum the stereotype is overstated. But regard-less of the truth of the past, the image of the horrors of yesteryear is used by Mamachi wives as a basis of comparing their lot and in considering themselves fortunate.

Yet most of them do not consider their life a bed of roses. Some even resent their husbands having such good times, spending so much of the family money, or not providing more for the home and the children. But the path to better their position is not seen as going outside the home, but getting the husband to provide more for the home. While most Mamachi wives are not dissatisfied with staying at home, they are dissatisfied with laborious and dirty tasks of housework and do want to have more time free to enjoy their children and their own pleasures. Although traditionally a wife was supposed to take pride in her sacrifice and hard work, the Mamachi wife no longer considers it admirable or even necessary to carry coal to build wooden fires by hand, to cook rice in tradi-tional pots, or to wash laundry by hand outside in cold weather. She would much rather use new electrical equipment and have time to spend reading, caring for the children, sewing, or cultivating the housewifely arts.

Electric machines are desired for their utility and because their newness imparts elegance to the housewife's life. Yet there is an

---

[8] Westerners usually think of traditional Japan as a land of female servitude. To the extent that the image is correct at all, it would be more accurate to say that it was a land of servitude of the young wife. An older wife, particularly the traditional mother-in-law, could hardly be described as servile.

even more important kind of elegance which is based on the art, not the mechanics, of the housewife's role. Housewifely arts like flower-arranging and tea ceremony originally required so much time and training to perform properly that only the wealthiest wives could aspire to such heights. Now such arts are within the reach of the average salary-man's wife, and it is to this elegance that Mamachi women aspire.

Nearly all Mamachi wives have had lessons in some housewifely arts. If they have not learned the tea ceremony and flower arrangement, they have learned knitting, Western- and Japanese-style sewing, crocheting, food-cutting and -arranging, or, more recently, Western-style cooking. They sometimes learn calligraphy, painting, or sketching. These talents are intimately connected with the housewife's role, and many girls spend two or three years after high school learning them rather than attending college, somewhat like the more limited number of American girls who attend finishing school. It is difficult for a young housewife to continue these lessons with small children but, once the children are in school, many form groups to attend special classes. There is an almost limitless variety in techniques of such skills as tea ceremony and flower arrangement. Many wives who have studied such arts for years will say modestly but sincerely that they are mere beginners. The acquisition and improvement of these skills is often a life-long goal which never ceases to be a source of inspiration.

The housewifely arts have had an enormous influence, not only on how the specific acts are performed, but on many other household activities. Those who have learned tea ceremony often serve guests with the grace and care of the tea ceremony, and those who have learned flower arrangement not only arrange their flowers and branches, but prepare and arrange food and dishes with the same eye to aesthetics. Those who have not had formal lessons are influenced by the style of those who have. It is this style which lends a touch of dignity to the housewife's role which is rarely found, for example, in the United States. The housewife's aspirations are found by perfecting the housewife role, not by escaping it.

The wife's aspirations are contained by the sharp division of labor just as the husband's aspirations are contained by membership in the large firm. Just as the man has a limited optimism about the opportunities within his firm but does not expect to leave the firm, so the wife has a limited optimism that she can expect somewhat greater comforts for self-fulfillment within her role as housewife.

Chapter X

AUTHORITY IN THE FAMILY

THE TRADITION OF "MALE DOMINANCE"

In the official ideology of "traditional Japan," the wife not only obeyed her husband, but showed that she enjoyed obeying him. According to traditional guidebooks on women's behavior, a woman's pleasure and freedom came not from asserting her independence, but from learning to want to do what she was required to do. She had no conception of rights, only of duties, and the only way to change her life was by attuning her character to the position she was expected to occupy.

However, when one asks concrete questions in Mamachi about a person's own parents and grandparents, one is often told that in their case the stereotype was not nearly so absolute, that the woman in fact had considerable say in how the house was run. In practice as well as in theory, the woman did show respect to her husband in public, but not necessarily at home. Even in traditional Japan, the husband often took little part in directing household affairs, and if the wife was supervised, it was usually by the mother-in-law rather than the husband. Even a generation ago, there was often a sizeable gap between the "beautiful virtue" of absolute obedience and actual practice.

Although the male dominance never approached the ideal, unquestionably male dominance has declined. As the popular saying goes, "since the war, stockings and women have grown stronger." Even the traditional saying, "fushoo fuzui," ("when the husband calls out, the wife jumps," the same pronunciation "fu" meaning either man or woman) is now sometimes interpreted by punsters as meaning "The wife sings out and the husband jumps." Others jokingly comment that even husbands who give orders to their wives

194

in public now apologize to their wives when they return home. While the power of the Japanese woman within the family has unquestionably increased with the growth of democratic ideology and women's political rights, these jokes, like wartime American cartoons showing rich ladies rushing to obey their maids, should not be taken to mean that the power balance has completely changed.

The contemporary Mamachi wife does have more freedom and power than the wife a generation ago. Because she receives the largest portion of the husband's regular salary without daily pleading, she controls the family budget. With new electrical equipment she has free time to use as she wishes. The increased possibilities open to her in shopping, in outside activities, and in friendships have broadened her range of personal choice. Because the Mamachi wife has no commitments outside the household, and is usually free of direction from her mother-in-law and other relatives, she has effective control over her own sphere of activities.

MAINTENANCE OF DECENTRALIZED AUTHORITY
Farmers, small shopkeepers, and even independent professionals do not have a sharp separation between family activities and business activities. Since the father conducts his business in the home and the wife helps him in his work, she is constantly subjected to his authority. In those homes the father's centralized authority remains effective even though it is increasingly resented.

In the Mamachi salaried family, however, authority is decentralized, with the wife managing the home and the husband managing his work and recreation. In general, this principle of separate spheres of authority has been highly successful in maintaining harmony and satisfying the desires of both husband and wife.

The husband's sphere presents no problem. The wife knows little about the husband's work and therefore has virtually no opportunity to exert influence over his activities, nor does she have to help him with his work.

There is, however, a problem in the wife's maintaining authority over her sphere. As the husband has more free time to spend at home, and as the relative isolation of the nuclear family from relatives permits a closer relationship between husband and wife, the wife has more difficulty retaining exclusive power over the household. The impact of democratic ideals has raised her status in relation to her husband's, but, paradoxically, by encouraging the husband's participation in the home, she restricts her own sphere of free activity. The husband still has more authority than the wife, and while he must also be sensitive to her wishes and may try to refrain from giving her orders at home, he finds it hard to avoid it entirely. And as much as the wife wants to please her husband by being gentle and obedient, she resents her husband's interference. The Mamachi wife's real concern about power is not about women's rights in political and economic affairs, or even equality within the home, but about protecting her right to manage the household without the husband's interference.

Major family issues, like the children's schooling and choice of marital partner, usually pose no jurisdictional difficulties. Such issues are considered legitimate concerns of both husband and wife, and discussions begin before either has a firm opinion and continue until a consensus is achieved. A couple may passionately disagree on the content of these issues, but there is no disagreement about the process of reaching a decision.

Often the minor issues lead to serious marital disagreements because they most clearly raise the question of who has the authority to make household decisions. Even minor queries from the husband about the method of food preparation or about the allocation of money for children's clothes can arouse a wife to a vigorous defense of her autonomy.

Eventually, if the trend toward husband-wife closeness and mutual understanding increases, it might be possible to arrive at a new principle of allocation of authority: the co-operative sharing of decisions on issues now resolved separately by either husband or wife. Such a principle, however, would require much more intimacy and mutual discussion than now exists in most Mamachi families, and a conviction on the part of the wives that they can achieve as much by open expressions of opinion as they can by subtle manipulations. This seems unlikely in the near future because Mamachi families solidly dislike extended mutual exploration of emotion, particularly the more primitive sentiments of love and hate, and consider it best for each to control his feelings and to limit his expression of personal demands. The principle of shared authority may be possible at some time in the future, but, at present, the families' efforts are directed at maintaining the principle of decentralized authority. The wife in particular has developed subtle means of preserving her autonomy. If, for example, the husband raises questions about her household methods, she is likely to act so surprised by his intrusion that she must pause and think for a minute. Then she gives either a noncommital answer that indicates she does not quite understand the question, or a brief factual answer. In either case her reply is polite but rather stiff so that the husband does not feel comfortable in probing further. She prefers to avoid questions altogether, and to this end she practises concealment and evasion. Just as the husband does not inform his wife about his work, so she omits many details of household events in their conversations. She values preserving a desired type of relationship with her husband more than reporting carefully on household affairs. Most wives would even prefer that their husbands not give any help, rather than risk raising questions that might threaten their autonomy.

A good illustration of wifely technique of putting aside *hesokurigane* (literally navel money, i.e., secret savings) to preserve independent management of household finances is the case of one clever wife who decided that sizeable house repairs were necessary and in due time broached the subject to her husband. When he learned the estimated cost, he said it was too high and they could not afford the repairs. When the wife wondered what he would consider a reasonable price, he announced his estimate. A few days later the wife happily reported that she had found a place which would do the repairs for slightly lower than the husband's estimate, and he consented to the work. In fact, the wife had not found a cheaper firm, but she had been saving regularly in a private account and used her own money to make up the difference between her husband's figures and the cost of repairs.

The husband's increasing participation in home life does constitute a threat to decentralization of authority and requires the wife to use such clever techniques to prevent interference. The wife's eternal vigilance in preventing the husband's intrusions and his conscious restraint in expressing views about problems of household management are the price of her autonomy in the home.

The Nature and Exercise
of the Husband's Authority

The fact that the husband's status is superior to his wife's is reflected in a variety of ways. Although he may call her by her first name, it is not proper for her to reciprocate but she may call him *anata* (a term used between spouses), or a term indicating parenthood, like *otoochan* (father).[1] A group of Mamachi mothers went into gales of laughter when talking about an American wife calling her husband's name from across the room and the husband calmly responding to her call. They explained that a Japanese wife would neither use her husband's first name nor call across a room to him, although a Japanese man could do both. When the husband arrives home, he expects and receives the family's attention. His wife and children hustle about getting his pipe and paper and if he wants anything else they are prepared to fetch and carry for him. If he wants an evening in town at the movies or at a bar, this is his privilege. But it is not a privilege which extends to the wife. Today both husband and wife laugh at the old tradition of a woman walking three paces behind the man, but in public women still defer to men. In mixed gatherings a woman speaks when spoken to, and then she often simply agrees with others rather than adding ideas or opinions of her own. When guests visit, the wife is more of a servant than a hostess. Of course the wife's deference and demeanor do not mean that she submits to all her husband's whims, but in a showdown, if the husband is insistent, the wife yields.

The average husband is most likely to express his arbitrary authority on matters of his personal pleasure or his wife's handling of the children. He is quick to anger if his comforts are not properly attended to at home and, lacking a clear conception of the work involved in housekeeping, he may become furious if the wife seems to spend more time cleaning or caring for the small children than attending to his pleasures. At the same time he wants the children to receive adequate maternal attention, and if a favorite child complains to the father that the mother has been harsh or that she was

---

[1] Cf. Takashi Koyama, *Gendai Kazoku no Kenkyuu* (An Investigation of the Contemporary Family), Tokyo: Koobundoo, 1960. The fact that differences in kinship terminology continue to reflect differences in relationships is indicated by the fact that more modern than traditional couples use first names and Western terms like "papa" and "mama."

not home when the child returned from school, the father is likely
to explode and demand that the wife provide proper care for the
children. Often he lays down the rules which the mother must
enforce concerning the children's discipline, their friends, and their
social functions. On such matters, and sometimes even on various
idiosyncratic matters, he can express his rights even if the rest of
the family considers him arbitrary. Although they may not be
aware of how much he must yield to his superiors at work, some
wives have suspected that the husband's arbitrary outbursts might
have more to do with problems in the office than with problems at
home.

Since the husband's superior authority is no longer supported by
the democratic ideals espoused by many husbands and wives, it is
noteworthy that she accords him so much prestige and so many
privileges. What most wives fear in their husband is not some kind
of ultimate sanction like cruelty or divorce but his more immediate
flashes of anger. Few wives have experienced physical violence,
but since men are considered by nature more volatile, more explo-
sive, and less able to endure hardships and sacrifices than women,
wives feel they must be cautious not to arouse this anger. Aside from
the fear of the husband's explosions, the continued subservience of
the wife is undoubtedly related to the lack of alternatives for her in
case of divorce or separation. But it is not simply the economic
dependence of the woman on her husband, as emphasized by Marx
and Engels, that gives the husband superior authority; it is the
lack of socially acceptable alternatives that makes her more dependent on him than vice versa. Even if the wife is not consciously
aware of these ultimate sanctions, they do serve to support the customs which give the husband his superior authority.

Despite his occasional explosions and more frequent dogmatic
pronouncements, the typical husband thinks of himself as considerate and most of the time he is. While he wants to be sufficiently
forceful to command the respect of his family, generally he is
genuinely fond of his wife and children and wants to enjoy their
love and admiration. He feels unhappy if his children regard him
as frightening and he tries, not always successfully, to overcome
their fears. Not only does the husband want to behave as a kindly
father and husband, but he also feels sympathetic and sometimes

even guilty about the sacrifices they make for his pleasures. It is precisely his sympathetic human feeling toward his wife and children and his desire to be liked by them which constitute the most effective curbs on the arbitrary exercise of his authority. Many a salary man is slow to demand what he considers his rights, out of consideration for the family's conveniences.

The Art of Husband Management

Because the husband is accorded a superior position, he can be direct in stating his wishes. Wives can be direct in stating their children's needs and basic household requirements, but most are reluctant in stating their own personal desires. However, some modern young wives enjoy frank discourse with their husbands, and in some older families the woman runs the household either because she has higher social status or stronger temperament.

Still, most Mamachi wives attain their wishes by subtle strategy rather than open request. The strategy is not always conscious, for in many ways a woman deals with her husband as she deals with anyone: by keeping a harmonious relationship and avoiding any show of unpleasantness. But this often requires such planning that it takes on the quality of an art—the art of husband management.

The Mamachi wife's arts for managing the husband are similar to those of an experienced American secretary in dealing with her boss. She studies his character and knows his moods. She knows when he must be left alone, when he can be humored, when she can take advantage of his "good days." She knows what issues she can decide on her own, what issues she can discuss openly, what issues she can discuss providing she hides certain facts and exaggenerates others. In face of his anger, she knows how to plead innocence or misunderstanding and how to lighten the anger by criticizing her own stupidity, ignorance, or inattentiveness, or by simply waiting until the anger has dissipated.

But the Mamachi wife works much harder to please her husband than a secretary does to please her superior, and in some ways she treats her husband as her eldest child. As in dealing with her child, she tries to keep him continuously happy and satisfied, because then he will respond automatically to her wishes.

A young bride searches out every little indication and listens carefully to every phrase to discover what things please her husband. She tries to avoid any direct criticism of his behavior and any assaults on his masculine ego. At most, within the hearing of her own husband she might give him a hint indirectly by complimenting another wife on something that wife's husband had done. If the husband presents a view as fact, she will not offer contrary evidence even if she is convinced he is wrong. When she wants something, she makes vague suggestions that appeal to his desires rather than to logic or her own desires. If she wants an item for the home, she is not likely to talk about its use or cost, but about how beautiful it would look or how magnificent an important friend thought it was. These hints and vague suggestions do not require the disapproving husband to make a definite refusal, a refusal that might be embarrassing for him to change later.

Yet, many a wife who is reserved and self-effacing is amazingly persistent over time, continuing to find new examples, or new authorities, or new ways to point up the advantage of her plan. Some husbands yield not because they have been sold on the advantages or have been taken in by the cleverness of the wife's strategy but because they are not strongly enough convinced of the disadvantages to be able to withstand the wife's persistent efforts.

A persistent campaign may be illustrated by the woman who decided that it was time for their family to have a television set. One day she commented to her husband that a neighbor had just bought a nice-looking Hitachi television set through a dealer friend for only 48,000 yen. A few days later she incidentally told her husband that she had heard of another family who bought a television set at a different place for even less money, but that it did not look quite as nice as the first set. Since the husband still showed no interest, she dropped the topic. But a few nights later she called his attention to an article about a special educational television program being run and she openly wondered whether such programs really helped the children's studying. In the meantime, she and the children talked about how nice it would be if the father would buy a television set and the children began asking him for one. It was not long before the father announced that he had decided it was time to buy a television set.

It is usually difficult for the father to refuse his children directly, and it is not unusual for a mother to coach a child on how and when to make a request of the father or to stimulate the child's desire so much that he will ask the father for it without the mother's urging.

Not all husband management is positive, for there are times when the wife must cope with ill temper and anger. When a man is critical of his wife she suggests, but does not openly state, her self-sacrifice to the husband by working harder, paying more attention to the husband's desires than usual, heaving an extra sigh or two, or by looking haggard, tired, and harrassed. Other wives respond to anger or criticism with somber quiet, or great surprise and innocence at the husband's criticism, or with self-accusations of inadequacy. Rarely does a Mamachi wife stand up directly against her husband to defend herself.

Some housewives are so skilled at husband management that the household runs smoothly. The husband feels flattered by his wife's hard work and devotion, retains his superior status, and yet the wife is, with proper subtlety, able to manage the household. In other cases, the wife, unable to charm him, deal with his rages, or get permission to buy things she wants, will run to her friends for help in interpreting her husband's behavior or in devising a more suitable strategy.

To some extent the skill is acquired as she gets to know her husband. Although some modern couples try to have frank discussions in their meetings before marriage, these discussions are often theoretical and do not fully cover all the aspects of the couple's actual attitudes. Even today, newly wedded couples often meet only three or four times before their wedding. Some brides try to follow their modern beliefs and express their views openly, but many are still reserved for the first months or even years of marriage until they feel it safe to begin expressing opinions or making personal requests. Some cautiously test their husbands' attitudes by dropping hints or talking about a neighbor family in which the wife has certain privileges or possessions. Many wives, after several years of marriage, recall how frightened and pitiful they were shortly after their wedding, afraid to make any requests, worried that they would not be able to satisfy their husbands. As they become more familiar with their husbands, prove their faithfulness, and produce a child (particularly a male), they acquire more confidence in their wifely ability.

The art of husband management is essentially an adjustment of the wife to the superior position of the husband. Because household affairs are more important to her and she has less authority than her husband, she spends more time trying to understand him than he does trying to understand her. She acquires more information relevant to the management of the household and spends more time devising plans to achieve her aims. The art of husband management, which is the outgrowth of these efforts, increases the likelihood that her wishes will be realized. It is an art which helps equalize the power of husband and wife without upsetting the superior position of the husband. In some ways, despite her lower status, she has more power over the activities of the home than the middle-class American wife who consults more closely with her husband.

THE MOTHER-IN-LAW AND DAUGHTER-IN-LAW

Most homes in Mamachi do not include a mother-in-law and a daughter-in-law, but if they do, the difficulties between them are almost certain to dominate the family scene. In private conversations and in newspaper columns, the relationship between mother-in-law and daughter-in-law is commonly recognized as the most serious problem facing the modern family.[2] Some girls agree to marriage on the condition that the husband make arrangements for his mother to live elsewhere. Some wives have pleaded with their husbands to prevent the mother-in-law from moving in. Some wives and mothers-in-law have tried to adjust to each other, but the arguments have been so vicious that they have been forced to separate. Some wives, who might otherwise be unhappy, console themselves with the thought that at least they do not live with their mothers-in-law. Yet, as much as they both try to avoid living together, the cost of setting up separate households combined with the limited financial resources, the filial feeling toward parents, and the lack of

---

[2] The common American stereotype is that the Japanese wife is rebelling against her husband, but it would be more accurate to say that the focus of rebellion, if present at all, is not the husband but the mother-in-law.

other satisfactory arrangements for elderly people sometimes leaves no acceptable alternative, especially when the young couple is just getting started or after the mother-in-law is widowed.[3]

In traditional Japan, the only hope of the daughter-in-law for success was to prove her loyalty to the mother-in-law by learning how to satisfy her every wish. Not only was it virtuous for a young bride to obey her mother-in-law, but it paid off in the long run. Only after proving her devotion could she hope to have the freedom to do things on her own. If she failed badly, she was sent back to her original home in disgrace. Divorces were commonly initiated not by the husband but by the mother-in-law. Some Japanese have observed that in America relations with the mother-in-law are a *kigeki* (comedy), in Japan a *higeki* (tragedy).

Compared to the problem of the mother-in-law, the problem of the father-in-law seems almost inconsequential. Because the salary man has no business connection with his father-in-law, there is no serious authority problem between them. The daughter-in-law generally has little problem with her father-in-law because he takes little interest in the home. Often there is a positive attraction between daughter-in-law and father-in-law, which is not entirely dissipated even though it is often dealt with by avoiding any situation where the two of them would be alone. Even when the father-in-law is harsh and demands that the daughter-in-law cater to his wishes, she generally finds this much easier to adjust to than the harassment of the mother-in-law.

Although the wife would prefer to live with her mother than with her mother-in-law, if they live together the husband may have a power struggle with her mother, especially if the wife and mother give each other mutual support in resisting the husband's wishes or in making demands on him.[4] But the fact that he spends so little time at home restricts the scope of this conflict. Although the wife's mother usually has considerable authority and the wife sometimes

---

[3] On the average, husbands are about three or four years older than their wives, and women live about five years longer than men. Hence, in the average family, a woman lives about eight or nine years as a widow. During this time she is likely to live at the home of one of her children.

[4] In two or three families where the mother-in-law and daughter-in-law got along relatively well, they likewise gave each other mutual support and sympathy in trying to get the husband to be more diligent in fulfilling family responsibilities.

resents being dominated, the positive feelings between mother and daughter are strong enough to bind their negative feelings. Especially if the wife has never lived apart from her mother, she feels dependent on the mother for advice and therefore readily follows her suggestions.

But there is no such positive bond to control the wife's feeling of annoyance with her mother-in-law. If the daughter-in-law does make a serious effort to serve the mother-in-law and is able and loyal, she may at times be treated almost as if she were a daughter instead of a daughter-in-law. But if she is not very competent or comes from a family of lower status than the husband, she may still be treated more like a servant. But even the best relationships are strained, and the strain is likely to be especially severe if the mother-in-law is a widow and lives with her only son.

Unlike the situation in traditional Japan, the critical problem in present-day Mamachi is not the harsh work load required of the daughter-in-law, but the lack of clarity of lines of authority. The mother-in-law has legitimate bases for arguing that the daughter-in-law obey, and the daughter-in-law has legitimate bases for expecting certain privileges. The ideal daughter-in-law is supposed to yield to the mother-in-law, but the ideal mother-in-law should not be harsh with the wife. In contrast to the situation in the United States, where the wife has primary authority, or to the situation in traditional Japan, where the mother-in-law had primary authority, there is no clear guiding principle. The object of the husband's primary loyalty is equally unclear. The answer to the traditional question, "Whom should a husband save if his wife and mother were drowning?" was "His mother" because he could always get another wife. Now the wife and mother are much more on equal grounds in competing for the husband's loyalty, and since there is no clear solution, the situation is one of continuing competition.

Although the mother-in-law occasionally goes out, most of the day both she and the daughter-in-law are at home. The latter generally does the heavy work and the mother-in-law often performs the more complicated tasks of cooking and sewing. But there is no such clear way for dividing up authority. If, for example, the mother-in-law has no income of her own, it is not clear who should decide how much spending money the mother-in-law should have. Since each typically has few interests outside the home, it is hard for the mother-in-law to refrain completely from supervising her daughter-in-law. The latter, in order to avoid the mother-in-law's disapproval, is cautious about going out of the home, buying things for the home, preparing food, and cleaning the house. Even a mere question from the mother-in-law sometimes makes the wife anxious. It is not only the actual commands of the mother-in-law which create the difficulties but the daughter-in-law's feeling of being unable to run the house as she wishes. As some wives put it, they feel as if they are forced to live with an enemy in their home.

The mother-in-law sometimes acts out her annoyance by being more critical and less willing to let the wife go out to visit friends, attend PTA meetings, or buy clothes for herself. The daughter-in-law may act out her annoyance by following the letter of the law laid down by the mother-in-law while defeating the spirit of the mother-in-law's wishes.

The battleground for the dispute is often the children. The grandmother tries to enforce her wishes on the children and to encourage them to resist their mother. The mother tries to win the children to her side and subtly encourages them to disobey their grandmother.

The wife fortifies herself for the struggle by keeping up with the latest information from newspapers, magazines, and books. She tries to keep up with the modern advice, and in discussions with the grandmother she relies heavily on "modern scientific information" to support her point of view and show that the grandmother is old-fashioned and superstitious. The grandmother typically respects scientific information, but sometimes suspects the daughter-in-law of manufacturing the things which she "read in a recent magazine." The mother-in-law relies on her superior experience and her moral conviction that because the daughter-in-law is joining her family, she should learn the family's custom (*kafuu*). The mother-in-law, after all, knows her son's likes and knows what it means to rear children. Many a daughter-in-law, not confident of her own ability to please her husband or handle the children's problems, reluctantly yields to the mother-in-law's experience.

If the husband supports either his mother or his wife against the other, his opinion is decisive, and in one way or another, the wife and mother frequently appeal to him for his support against the other. The husband, however, ordinarily tries to stay out of the dispute. He tries to play down the seriousness of the dispute, and to encourage each to be more sympathetic to the other. Only when the husband regards the situation as unbearable or judges one side as being particularly unreasonable does he take the initiative in settling the dispute by encouraging his mother to accept modern ways or the wife to be kind to the aged.

The most commonly suggested solution to the conflict between the two women is for both to show reserve, and to contain themselves even when angry. Many advice columns include hints for how the two could adjust to each other, but the crux of the advice is usually another way for humoring the other one or a way for containing one's own feelings of annoyance.

But the problem involves fundamental attitudes and status relationships. Like the Negro in the American South, the daughter-in-law no longer feels compelled to accept a subservient position. But the price of her emerging freedom is a breakdown of the old social order and an uncontrolled competition between her and her mother-in-law. The Mamachi daughter-in-law has not yet been granted complete freedom even in the most modern family, and a stable new order of relationships has not yet been established except for avoidance, a solution which is not always possible.

Chapter XI

FAMILY SOLIDARITY

THE HOUSEHOLD UNIT

Although the nuclear family has replaced the *ie* as the basic social unit in Mamachi, loyalty to the family remains strong. One rarely hears of sacrificing for ancestors or descendants, but nothing is more virtuous than sacrificing for parents or children.[1] It is true that family loyalty is not sentimentalized in talk about "our happy home" or "home sweet home," but this reflects a lack of sentimentality, not an absence of sentiment. Family altars and treasures have declined in importance, but the modern family's photo albums, souvenirs from trips, festival dolls, and the family *kotatsu* are probably equally meaningful symbols of family solidarity.

Just as the Mamachi resident makes a sharp distinction between friend and stranger, so a large barrier separates family members from outsiders. Outside the home, one must be more formally dressed, more polite, more cautious, and more suspicious. In accord with the well-known proverbs, "If you meet a stranger, regard him as a robber," and "Outside your gate, there are seven enemies," a person is on his guard outside. In the annual bean-sowing ceremony each family scatters beans in its house and yard while repeating the traditional phrase, *Fuku wa uchi, oni wa soto* (May good fortune stay in and misfortune get out).[2]

---

[1] It would be possible to argue that the husband's loyalty to the firm is at least as important as his loyalty to the family. But ordinarily these loyalties do not conflict, and there is certainly no clear-cut primacy of outside loyalty to compare with the samurai ethic which placed loyalty to the lord before loyalty to the family.

[2] In a study of festival practices in Nagano-ken, David Plath noted that while many annual celebrations have declined, the bean-sowing ceremony remains almost universally practiced. While we did not survey the frequency of this ceremony in Mamachi, it is our impression that it is still widespread. One may speculate that in

The home is a haven from the outside world. Aside from relatives and the wife's intimate friends, guests are rarely invited to a home, and if invited they are usually confined to the guest room. Other rooms are reserved for the family, and a spontaneous tour of the house is almost inconceivable. Mamachi residents prefer that their home be unknown to outsiders, and some take comfort in the fact that their house number is difficult to locate without precise directions from the family or the police substation (*kooban*). (Houses are not numbered consecutively, and the numbering is based on an area, not on a street. Because numbers were assigned to a plot of land years ago and further divisions have taken place, it is possible for several homes to have the same house number!) Nearly all homes have high fences and many have a watch dog. The gate (*mon*) to this outside fence is locked during much of the day and can be opened only from the inside. The gate is left open for errand boys, but they do not enter the house, and visitors remain at the door of the house (*genkan*) with their shoes on, until invited to come in.

Within the home, a family member takes his shoes off, stretches out on the tatami mats, and changes to more comfortable robes. In the winter time, everyone sits in the *kotatsu*, enjoying the warmth of the family circle, both literally and figuratively. Here, under the same quilt, family members eat, read, talk, and watch television. Older children may study while others in the same *kotatsu* are talking or watching TV, and younger children may lie back and fall asleep with their feet hanging in the *kotatsu*. Generally, a family with two or three children will sleep in one or two rooms. Though many people explain that this is because Japan is such a poor and crowded country, even families that have more rooms generally have the whole family sleeping in one, two, or at most three rooms, their mats lined up close together, everyone enjoying the comfort of being close together.[3]

Japan, with tightly-knit groups, there is more of a tendency for splitting objects into good and bad. This would help account for some of the strong in-group feeling and the suspicion of the outside. It would also help explain the great difference in the attitude of a wife toward her mother and her mother-in-law. An analysis of psychological aspects of object-splitting can be found in the work of Melanie Klein.

[3] In answer to a sentence-completion question which read, "When the family gets together . . . ," the most common response was that it was *yukai* (a lot of fun) and *nigiyaka* (bustling with activity). Both replies have positive connotations indicating that people think of the family as a pleasant and comfortable place.

In relation to the outside, the family feels like, and is viewed as, a single unit. Family members do not ordinarily air their quarrels to any but the most intimate friends who can be relied on not to repeat secrets.[4] Indeed some caution about inviting guests springs from the fear that family weaknesses might be revealed.[5] While family members often politely derogate their family to outsiders,[6] they carefully avoid saying anything that would reveal their family's true weaknesses. After many months of close contact with us, two or three people mentioned some item of disparaging information about a relative; until that time all members had been vague when discussing topics that might have revealed this family weakness. When the family is worried that a child may not get into a specific school, even the other children will try not to reveal to what school he is hoping to be admitted.

Gifts to a family member are regarded as a gift to the entire family. When, for example, my wife gave a gift to a child his mother did not tell him to thank us for the gift. She thanked us directly herself, and later my wife and I were thanked by the husband and the grandfather who lived in the same home. The thank you was not in the form of "Our child enjoyed your present," but "We thank your family for your kindness." Similarly, a child may bring back a memento from a school trip for a family which had done a favor for his parents.

Families rarely go out together, except for occasional Sunday outings to visit relatives, a park, or a department store, but the fact that almost all inns now have a family bath indicates some increase in families visiting inn houses. Perhaps one reason why families do not travel together more frequently is the lack of money and a

---

[4] One exception is the case of third parties who were informed of internal family problems with the hope of bringing outside pressure on another family member to behave properly. The most common example is the wife who tells a close friend or relative about the husband's failure to meet his responsibilities to his family, hoping that they will try to encourage the husband to mend his ways. Conditions must be bad, however, to warrant such a step.

[5] One lady explained that it was unwise to give maids a day off, not because they would get used to too much leisure, but because they might spread family secrets or rumors in talking with others in the community.

[6] For example, a family routinely calls its house its "small dirty house" and among friends a husband may refer to his wife as his *gusai* (foolish wife). It is even permissible for a husband to illustrate how foolish his wife is, providing this is not really likely to affect the listener's estimate of his family's status.

convenient means of family transportation, that is, the automobile, for wealthy families who have cars do more traveling together. Probably, however, the more important deterrents to family travel are the feeling that someone in the family must always be left as *rusuban* to protect the house and the feeling that it is easier for a family to relax at home than in public.

As united and relaxed as the family feels at home, it is considered improper for family members, especially husband and wife, to display affection in public. Husbands and wives holding hands or walking arm in arm are still regarded as a bit unseemly. In public, a husband carefully avoids saying anything complimentary to his wife about her cooking, appearance, or cleverness and it is equally inappropriate for the wife to compliment her husband in public. Nor is it polite for husband and wife to talk privately in the presence of guests unless they obviously discuss the care and comfort of the guests. Family solidarity is thus beyond the purview of outsiders. Some young husbands are known by their friends to be madly in love with their wives since they spend most of their free time with them, but even a man's close friends often have only very indirect clues of how fond he is of his wife. This is not because family solidarity is weak, but because in contacts with outside groups, the family wants to display its loyalty to the larger group. Just as whispering is sometimes considered impolite in Western societies because of its exclusiveness, so family members displaying mutual fondness in public are regarded as impolite. It is neither desirable nor necessary to display the inner family solidarity in public.[7] Like an eagle who hides his claws, the family hides its reserve of solidarity from public scrutiny.

THE BASIC ALIGNMENT: MOTHER AND CHILDREN VS. FATHER

Within the family, various coalitions unite or divide the members. However, before considering the diadic relationships of husband-wife, grandparent-grandchild, and parent-child (the latter discussed

---

[7] One may speculate that because of the tight in-group feelings, people are especially sensitive to being excluded. With such sensitivity to feelings of exclusiveness, a cardinal principle of true consideration is to avoid arousing the feeling that another person is an outsider.

in the next chapter), it is necessary to consider a basic pattern of emotional alignments. Internal cleavages are not unique to the Japanese family. To turn the traditional Japanese proverb around, even though brothers are united against the outside, they do quarrel within their gates. It is not always the person of low status who has difficulty gaining acceptance within the group. In the office clique, for example, the boss who senses that his men strain to be polite to him and stop their joking when he arrives, also feels left out. This is precisely the problem of the typical Mamachi father in relation to his family. He is treated in many ways as a high-status guest in the home, a welcome, friendly, and even jovial guest, but one who stands on the periphery of the intimate circle of mother and children.

The linkage of the children and mother and the exclusion of the father is not an entirely fixed and stable pattern. Sometimes family coalition patterns change from day-to-day or year-to-year. At times the father may have a particularly strong relationship with one of the children, and at other times the mother and father may be united against the children. A teen-age daughter may unite with her father to complain about the mother's strictness at the same time she unites with her mother to plot how to get the father to buy more things for the home. But in almost all families we saw or heard about in some detail, the most common emotional cleavage was between the father on the one hand and the mother and children on the other.

One woman, for example, explained that she dislikes Sundays because her husband is home the whole day and consequently she and the children cannot relax. Another woman confessed that it is better for the father to come home a little late and eat supper separately because when he is home the children must be more restrained. They cannot talk, bustle around, and enjoy the supper hour when the father is at home. Another lady who suffers from psychosomatic difficulties has a husband who does some traveling as part of his work; her difficulties become worse when he is stationed at the home office and comes home early every night, and improve when he is away.

The coalition of mother and child is not necessarily hostile to the father. It may mean only that the mother and children share things which are not shared with the father and that they see themselves as united for common objectives which are different from those of the father. The basic alignment is manifested in many ways: the reserve of the wife and children in the presence of the father, the secrets they keep from him, the plots of the mother and children for dealing with him. The children and the wife are to some extent on perpetual good behavior when the father is present. Like American students with their professor, they may joke and talk freely with their father about many topics, but they may relax more freely and tell other kinds of jokes in his absence.

The cleavage with the father is further reflected in the discussions of allocation of family resources. Since the budget is divided between the husband and the home and the salary is limited and regular, everyone is aware of how much he spends and how much everyone else spends. The consciousness of which expenses are "for father" and "for the rest of the family" is perhaps heightened by the fact that the father's recreational activities are completely separate, and neither the wife nor the children share his pleasures. Among friends, a man is expected to spend freely, as if he had no concerns about money, and membership in a company gang inevitably involves expenses. From the point of view of the wife and children, the important fact is not whether he spends to satisfy his own pleasures or to meet social pressure, but that the more he spends the less they have for their use. The mother spends virtually nothing on herself, but she wants to maximize the amount of money available for the children and home. The cleavage may be smaller if the husband goes out rarely and spends little but larger if he drinks a great deal, frequents company hang-outs, and maintains a girl friend. In either case, however, the mother and children are interested in minimizing the husband's outside expenditures, and children tend to feel that the mother is on their side in wanting to buy them more toys, clothes, or candy if only the father would bring home a larger portion of his pay check.

The cleavage between father and family is accentuated by the amount of time the mother and children spend together without the father. In comparison with the American middle-class mother, the Japanese mother spends more time with the children, the father less time. As one would expect, following Homans, this time dif-

ferential alone would make the children and mother more attached
to each other than to the father.[8] Indeed, the intensity of the father's
attachment to his work group makes it difficult for him to have the
reserve of energy required for an equally intense involvement in
internal family affairs. Because the wife and children center virtually
their entire world in the home, they have an intensely close relationship which it is virtually impossible for the father to share.

The father's power also contributes to the emotional distance
between him and the rest of the family. Because the wife and children know that the father may become firm or demanding, they are
cautious, reserved, and rarely completely at ease in his presence.
It is true that the salary man's authority is not so great as the
authority of small shopkeepers or others whose wives and children
work alongside them. But compared to the United States his power
is a compelling force in family life.

Some fathers at times try to break into the mother-daughter coalition. When the children are in bed the father may talk with the
mother about her problems and lend a sympathetic ear to her difficulties in dealing with the children. Or he may try to upset the
coalition by telling the mother to stop babying the children so much
and to make them do things on their own. Or he may respond
sympathetically to the children's wishes or their complaints about
their mother's treatment of them, thus getting one or more of them
aligned with him against the mother. Such solutions are generally
temporary. More commonly the father accepts the coalition of
mother and children as a fact of life, treats them kindly while keeping his distance, and satisfies himself that they are considerate and
look after him. Although the father is sometimes sorry to feel left
out and would like to feel closer, at other times he prefers to keep
some distance and is pleased that the family does not try to encroach
on his life.

Although this coalition of father versus the rest of the family involves strains, it almost never leads to an open rupture for there are

---

[8] The argument would be consistent with the work of Homans that more inter-
action increases liking but that authority inhibits liking. See, for example, Henry W.
Riecken and George C. Homans, "Psychological Aspects of Social Structure," in
Gardner Lindzey, ed., *Handbook of Social Psychology*, Cambridge, Mass.: Addison-
Wesley Publishing Company, 1954, pp. 786–832; George C. Homans and David M.
Schneider, *Marriage, Authority, and Final Causes*, Glencoe, Ill.: The Free Press, 1955.

many satisfactions in the familial system as well as social restraints preventing an open break. Without the family, the father would be lonely. At the barest minimum, it provides him a group where he belongs and can turn to in time of sickness, trouble, and retirement. The family looks after his welfare, sees that he is properly fed and clothed, and properly cares for his belongings. Children run to look after his comfort. He derives stable emotional support from his wife which is not equaled by any of his shorter-term contacts with women outside the home. He derives pleasure from having children and he takes pride in their accomplishments.

The wife and children are less likely to turn to him for emotional support, although they do rely on him for economic support. Furthermore, wives do turn to their husbands for help in making difficult decisions regarding the children, and young children do enjoy their relationship with their father. Older boys commonly look to their father for guidance, and older girls respond to the flirtatious joking with the father and enjoy listening to his exploits as a way of finding out about the outside world.

Part of the reason that the relationship between the father and the rest of the family is so stable despite the distance is that difficulties can be contained without disrupting the basic pattern of relationships. If, as in many modern young couples, the husband and wife desire to be closer, this is possible. But if there are difficulties and the father is disappointed with the mother and the children, he can simply enjoy more of the pleasures of the bars and the company gang and spend less time at home. Similarly, because the wife ordinarily expects to get much of her emotional comfort and support from her children and her intimate friends, she is not so disappointed if she and her husband do not have an intimate relationship.

Because the mother and children are not very dependent on the father for emotional support, they can more easily tolerate separation from him as long as he provides the family with money and assistance in placing the children. In a number of families, the husband's work separated him from his family for several months or even a year or two. Although the husband's absence did cause problems of adjustment for the family, the fact that the emotional mutual dependency was not so great as in the United States made separation easier to tolerate. The mother and children remained together and the father simply relied more heavily on work associates and visits to the local entertainment quarters.

Even if the wife and children are annoyed at the father for avoiding his family responsibility, they still have enough sympathy for him to contain their feelings. Even if the father is authoritative he generally reveals enough of his need for emotional support that the wife and children genuinely sympathize with him and recognize that he needs humoring, support, and attention.

One important consequence of the mother-child coalition is that it serves to minimize the differences between generations. In many societies with rapid social change, the difference between generations is so great that there is a sharp cleavage between the parents and the children. The common cleavages between father and the rest of the family militate against this generational break because it closely links the children with the mother, a member of the older generation, making them more receptive to her teachings.[9] Even though Mamachi youth complain about the older generation in general, they are almost invariably sympathetic with their mothers. This close tie to the mother puts an effective damper on what might otherwise lead to more serious ruptures between generations as found, for example, in the cleavages between parents and children of many immigrant groups in American cities.

HUSBAND AND WIFE: INCREASING PRIVACY AND INTIMACY

When the ideals of *ie* were still strong and the bride belonged to the *ie* and not to her husband, no great value was placed on the privacy of the married couple. In the evenings, if free time were left after the bride finished her work, while others were awake, it was thought improper for the young couple to leave the family circle and retire to their own room, if, indeed, they had a room of their own. This does not mean that husbands and wives had no affectionate relationship; on the contrary, almost like illicit lovers

---

[9] It may be argued that the same is true of many business organizations. While peer groups have in recent years increased in power, cliques combining older and younger people still remain important. To the extent that such cliques exist, cleavages based strictly on age differences are less likely to become disruptive. It may be said that cliques linking older and younger members are important for maintaining integration in a society of extremely rapid change.

they sometimes took advantage of moments of privacy. Yet on the whole, although emotional distance between husband and wife remains greater than between couples in America, opportunities for closeness have increased. They have more free time to be home alone now than a generation ago, and even if relatives live in the home, it is accepted as perfectly proper for a couple to have a chance to be alone together. The growth of opportunity for privacy is reflected in the courtship period as well as later during the marriage.

The common pattern of courtship in the previous era was for the families to investigate each other and then introduce the couple at a formal meeting (*miai*). If the *miai* went well, the families would proceed with the arrangements for engagement and marriage, but all arrangements would be handled by the family and go-betweens. The young couple would have no further opportunity to meet until the marriage. When people recount their own family's history, however, a sizeable minority of cases do not fit this pattern, either because there was no official *miai*, or because the couple or their families had known each other before serious arrangement began, or because the couple was given some opportunity to meet alone before marriage. However, even couples which did not have a *miai* usually had little opportunity to meet before marriage.

In recent years young people's freedom to meet before marriage has increased. It is now considered proper for a girl to have several dates with a boy between the *miai* and marriage,[10] but it is still rare to date without an introduction by a close friend or relative who can provide assurance that the other person comes from a respectable family.

Although Mamachi residents believe that love marriages (*renai*) are getting to be the same in Japan as in the United States, the amount of freedom given to young people for dating in Mamachi is still very limited. Not only is high-school age considered too young for dating, but too young for any heterosexual interests. Many private high schools prohibit girls from wearing make-up, having permanents, or being on streets with boys. In psychoanalytic terms,

---

[10] For some statistical information on the frequence of *miai* (arranged marriage) as opposed to *renai* (love marriages), cf. Ezra F. Vogel, "The Go-Between in a Developing Society: The Case of the Japanese Marriage Arranger," *Human Organization*, 1961, 20:112–120.

the Mamachi adolescent in his late teens has not yet resolved his Oedipal attachment to his parents and does not have a reservoir of unattached emotional energy available for falling in love with the first object he sees. As one girl put it, as much as she wants to date and form love relationships, she simply could not imagine the pleasure of suddenly just throwing herself into some boy's arms.

Parents implicitly encourage this caution because they feel it dangerous to give young people the opportunity to form love relationships without a solid objective basis in terms of social position, family background, education, and expected future life. Once there is this solid basis, however, it is considered desirable for love to proceed rapidly and for the marriage to be concluded within a few months, because a long courtship can lead to doubts and fault-finding which would interfere with eventual happiness. Besides, the extent of involvement would make it difficult to form a new relationship if the present one were terminated.

In their dating, young people now look for qualities compatible with personal companionship as well as objective qualities of family status, earning capacity of the husband, general good character, reliability, and health. Ambitious girls bent on a career are suspect by most young men. As one young college man said: "We want wives who are smart so that they can understand us, but not too smart." In a previous era, it was considered desirable for a man to marry a naïve, innocent, eighteen- or nineteen-year-old girl. It was thought that by taking such a bride, it would be much easier for the wife to adjust to marriage because she would not have developed hopes which would later lead to disappointment.[11] Young men nowadays complain that such a bride would be too limiting because she would know so little about the world that it would be impossible to talk with her. The new ideal bride should know enough to converse intelligently with her husband, but not enough to have ambitions for herself that might interfere with marital happiness.

Before marriage, young couples make a determined effort to sound

---

[11] A girl is expected to be more receptive to her family's wishes than a boy, and evidence from projective tests given in rural Japan bears this out. Hiroshi Wagatsuma and George De Vos, "Attitudes toward Arranged Marriage in Rural Japan," *Human Organization*, 1962, 21:187–200.

out the views of the partner. Because opportunities for dating are limited, each date takes on great significance. Casual dating with no consideration of marriage is almost unthinkable for a respectable young lady. On dates, most young people try earnestly to set forth their entire philosophy of life, their views about family relations in the modern age, their ambitions and goals, their interests in reading and music. These talks are usually held apart from the families, at a restaurant, a movie, play, or concert.

In the first year of marriage, before children are born, the newly married couple typically continues to go out occasionally. Many girls, however, in dating or early marriage still feel it wise to be reserved in expressing their opinions because they expect to learn and acquire their husband's opinions. Traditionally, the new bride never expressed her own views, fearing that they might not agree with the opinions of her husband's family. She listened to the conversations at her new home and, if she expressed an opinion at all, it would be in agreement with the family. Even today, the Mamachi wife does not feel as well-informed as her husband, and she is reluctant to state her opinion. Between her ignorance of the outside world and the husband's disinterest in the details of her daily life, there are not as many topics of conversation as in many American families.

Paradoxically, although discussion of children is one of the topics about which man and wife talk most enthusiastically, the arrival of children in some ways creates a greater distance in husband-wife relations.[12] After the baby arrives, the mother devotes herself so completely to the child, that she sometimes neglects the husband. The husband often begins devoting himself more completely to his firm and the company gang. If he comes home late, the Mamachi wife, tired from caring for the baby and more independent than the traditional wife, does not feel she must wait up to talk with the husband. Small children generally take naps in the afternoon and then stay up until almost the time when the parents go to bed so

---

[12] Although this same tendency is found in American families, it seems more pronounced in Mamachi where the mother devotes herself so completely to the children. Cf. Robert O. Blood and Donald Wolfe, *Husbands and Wife*, Glencoe, Ill.: The Free Press, 1960.

that even if the husband comes home early, the couple has only a few minutes to talk privately in the evening.

The interference of the small child in the privacy of the parents is perhaps best symbolized by the sleeping arrangements and the difficulty this creates for sexual relations between husband and wife. A small baby commonly sleeps between the father and the mother, on the same mat as the mother, while the father sleeps on the next mat. If children are born with no more than two or three years between them, the chances are that at least one child will be sleeping immediately next to the parents from the time the oldest was born until the youngest is several years of age. Compared to American couples, Mamachi couples have intercourse less frequently, and have less fore play and after play. The smaller role of sexual activity in the Mamachi marriage, and the fact that many couples have sexual relations after sleeping for a short period of time, would appear related to the couple's relative lack of privacy and intimacy.[13]

---

[13] A comparison of Shinozaki's Japanese sample of 635 persons in and near Tokyo in 1950 with the data from Kinsey's studies, completed in 1949, point up some of these contrasts in sexual behavior. Nobuo Shinozaki, "Report on Sexual Life of Japanese," No. 11, The Institute of Population Problems, Welfare Ministry, Tokyo, Japan, July 1957. Alfred C. Kinsey, Wardell B. Pomeroy, Clyde E. Martin, Paul H. Gebhard, *Sexual Behavior in the Human Female*, Philadelphia: W. B. Saunders Company, 1953. In the Japanese sample, 29 percent have intercourse after a brief period of sleep. Although the age groupings on frequency of sexual intercourse of married couples are not precisely the same, the following chart indicates the trend of the difference (Shinozaki, p. 16; Kinsey, p. 77):

AVERAGE NUMBER OF TIMES OF SEXUAL INTERCOURSE
PER WEEK BY AGE OF WIFE

		20–24	25–29	30–34	35–39	40–44	45–49
Japan	Age	20–24	25–29	30–34	35–39	40–44	45–49
	Frequency	2.2	1.8	1.4	1.1	0.8	0.5
United States	Age	21–25	26–30	31–35	36–40	41–45	46–50
	Frequency	2.5	2.1	1.9	1.5	1.2	0.9

In the Japanese sample, 39.9 percent reported no fore play and after play connected with intercourse. In sharp contrast, all of the American sample reported fore play. In the American sample, 99.4 percent reported kissing, and more than 90 percent reported genital stimulation of male and female and breast stimulation of the

The deep repressions of sexual desire before marriage make it difficult for most young wives to enjoy sexual activity soon after marriage.[14] Most middle-aged ladies say they were completely ignorant about sex until the day of marriage when their mother or the marriage go-between gave them a brief explanation, and perhaps a picture or two illustrating sexual activity. Many recall vividly the rude shock they felt the first time they experienced sexual relations, and they remember having regarded sexual activity as an unpleasant part of their duties in satisfying the wishes of their husband. Before prostitution was abolished in 1958, a sizeable number of wives favored the continuance of legalized prostitution, on the grounds that their husbands needed some outlets and that they would be less demanding at home if they had an outside outlet. Some of the middle-aged women who feared sexual relations in their earlier days of marriage, now admit enjoying it. Younger wives have the benefit of sex education in schools, have much more opportunity to become affectionate with their husbands either before or shortly after marriage, and have begun to enjoy sexual activity earlier in their marriage. But newly wedded women still do have difficulty overcoming their repression of sexual interests, and it is still con-

---

female. Even the 60 percent of Japanese who did engage in fore play averaged less time than the American sample (Kinsey, p. 364; Shinozaki, pp. 20 f.):

LENGTH OF FORE PLAY (*in percent*)

	0–3 min.	4–10 min.	11–20 min.	20 min. and longer
Japan	14	56	23	7
United States	11	36	31	22

[14] The following is the stage at which wives first had feelings of satisfaction in intercourse (Shinozaki, *op. cit.*, p. 23; in percent):

First night of marriage	within 1 month	within 6 months	within 1 year	within 3 years	within 10 years	within 20 years
0.4	8.3	38.0	13.0	24.1	10.2	7.0

sidered somewhat embarrassing for a young wife to admit to her friends that she enjoys sexual activity.

The Mamachi salary-man's wife, being tied to the home and the children, has neither the interest nor the opportunity to engage in extramarital affairs.[15] Traditionally, it was expected that before marriage a young man would visit a house of prostitution so he would know how to take the lead in sexual relations with his wife. The man, being older, more worldly, and more experienced at the time of marriage, did not suffer from the same sexual inhibitions as his wife. Although increasingly the young salary man's first sexual experience is with his wife, he still tends to be less inhibited toward sexual pleasures than she.

Although the problems of overcoming the wife's reluctance and of having privacy once children are born inhibit sexual intimacy between husband and wife, fear of pregnancy does not. Couples are increasingly using contraceptives,[16] and others have no compunctions about using abortion should the wife become impregnated. Because of the widespread acceptance of contraceptives and abortion, there is no need to resort to abstinence as a means of birth control.

Despite the wife's inhibitions and the distance created by the birth of a child, the husband-wife relationship has attained a degree of privacy and intimacy unequaled by any relationship between the husband and other women. Even if the husband has friends among bar girls or office girls, they supplement the husband-wife relationship instead of replacing it. The relationship with the wife is viewed as permanent, and relationships with other women as temporary. The man ordinarily expects that a girl at the office will work there only a few years and will then leave to get married herself; and the relationship with bar girls is generally not an exclusive one. The bar girl is expected to wait on many people and carry on conversations with many men. Although she tries to encourage

---

[15] This accords with Shinozaki's findings. "As regards wives, almost no one has the experience of intercourse with men other than their consorts except women who have remarried." Shinozaki, *op. cit.*, p. 26.

[16] A *Mainichi* survey found that 48.8 percent of salary men now use contraceptives, compared to 31 percent of farmers or fishermen, 34.7 percent of laborers, 37.1 percent of workers in factories and business establishments, and 48.9 percent of independent entrepreneurs.

steady customers, she must avoid getting so preoccupied with any one person that this interferes with taking care of other customers. The man also often regularly visits several bar girls, and even if he does not have several at one time, he changes from one to another. In some ways the bar girl's relationship with a man is hardly even a personal relationship. She takes little interest in him personally, and the pressures of her job set sharp limits on the intimacy she can have with any one person.

Although at times the husband may prefer the bar girl's worldliness, charm, and flattery to his wife's pressures and demands, the bar girl, typically, has a lower-class background and neither understands nor shares his fundamental attitudes in the same way his wife does. Although the husband may turn to a bar girl for entertainment and sympathy after his daily work, in any real difficulty he turns to his wife because her loyalty to him is much deeper than any bar girl's.

What a husband looks for from a bar girl or office girl is the attention, the charm, and the pleasure, the fun without the responsibility. Though the wife can provide some charm and attention, she is so concerned about the home and so preoccupied with the children, that she cannot give her husband the relaxed joking that permits him to escape his worries. To the contrary, the typical wife is always using her techniques to get the husband to bring home more money for her and the children. Because the wife can do little to increase the income of the home except by coaxing the husband, she tends to concentrate her pressure on him. Finally she has difficulty completely relaxing with her husband because he has superior authority, and because he does not fully share the intricacies of her world. For this reason and because the wife often exerts subtle pressures to get him to accept more responsibilities at home and because he is aware of the inconveniences he causes her, the husband is not always completely comfortable at home. If a man wants fun without responsibilities, he can get it from bar girls, but he ordinarily does not expect it from his wife.

The search for fun without responsibility may at times lead to intensive even though temporary attachments. Because these affect the relationship with the wife, and because they may affect how completely the husband fulfills his responsibilities to her, the wife is usually upset by strong outside attachments. The husband-wife relationship is sufficiently close so that the wife is sensitive to slight changes in the husband's moods, and, to some extent, she feels she has failed if the husband's relationship with an outside woman becomes too close. Yet the husband's and wife's spheres are sufficiently separate that the husband may derive some pleasures from relationships with outside women without fearing their interference. The husband's relationship with other women need not have any effect on the wife's limited social sphere. Because they rarely go out together and because their friends are separate, it is possible for the husband to have affairs with bar girls or office girls without this having a direct effect on the wife's social activities. As long as the husband is meeting his responsibilities at home, the wife usually tries to overlook his activities away from home.

COALITIONS WITH GRANDPARENTS

Although most salaried households include only parents and children, many homes did at one time, or will later, include relatives, and many other families have relatives next door or within the immediate neighborhood.[17]

Perhaps the most common coalition pattern in homes with grandparents is for grandparents to have close positive affectional ties with grandchildren. They commonly spend a lot of time playing with children and are sympathetic with them against the strictures of the parents. But this relationship tends to be limited to the affectional sphere. The grandchild often bathes with the grandparent,

---

[17] The rate of doubling is still much higher than, for example, in the United States. According to Japanese national statistics, in large cities 73.3 percent of the households are either single-person households or nuclear families, compared to 56.7 percent of the households in villages and towns, and 64.3 percent in small and middle-sized cities; 20.0 percent of large city households included lineal relatives (three generations or married children and their spouse); and 6.7 percent more included nonlineal relatives: Takashi Koyama in Robert J. Smith and Richard K. Beardsley, eds., *Japanese Culture*, New York: The Viking Fund, 1962. In a survey of a Tokyo apartment-house area largely inhabited by salary men, Koyama found that 79.3 percent of the households included no relative beyond the nuclear family. Takashi Koyama, *Gendai Kazoku no Kenkyuu* (An Investigation of the Contemporary Family), Tokyo: Koobundoo, 1960, p. 59. Unfortunately, there are no data that would make it possible to estimate precisely how many families will at some time live with relatives. Estimates based on the past would not be conclusive since during and immediately after the war the housing shortage caused a large amount of doubling which continued for many years, but which is unlikely to recur.

rubs his back, sits on his knees, receives little presents, and in return does little favors. But in areas of task performance, the grandparents generally take an inactive role. Generally it is the parents who see to it that children do their work around the house and their homework. If the children want comfort they may go to their grandparents, but if they want assistance in solving difficult problems, they are more likely to go to their parents. The affectionate relationship between grandparent and grandchild does not represent a simple pursuit of pleasure, but also includes obligations. Many a grandparent, exhausted from playing with a child, feels obligated to continue, and many a child, bustling with energy, remains quiet so as not to disturb his grandparents.

If there is only one child, grandmother and mother may compete for the attention of the child, and the child may waver from trying to please one to trying to please the other. In this conflict over the child, the mother usually has a head start during the first year or so because she is nursing the child, and hence sleeps with the child and cares for him when he cries. During this period the grandmother may comfort the child at times, but to the extent that she participates in child-rearing it is largely in guiding and directing the mother in dealing with the child. Later the grandmother often has the advantage because the mother may be busy doing the housework but the grandmother is almost always free to look after the child.

If there is more than one child, it is common for one of the children to be assigned to the grandmother and one to the mother. While the process of assignment is not necessarily conscious, the fact of the assignment is recognized by everyone. If there are three children and a grandfather also lives with the family, one of the children may be assigned to him. A child assigned to his grandmother is actually called and referred to as *Baasan ko* (grandmother's child). He (or she) sleeps and bathes with the grandmother and perhaps massages the grandmother's back and runs errands for her. If the grandmother is sick or bed-ridden, the child will look after her, tend to her needs. In any kind of family dispute, the grandmother can be counted on to look after the interests of "her" child.

The common method of dividing up children is for the oldest to be the grandmother's and the younger to be the mother's child. This assignment does not resolve the battle over the children's loyalty completely, because sometimes the grandmother will be away from home visiting or shopping and both children will be cared for by the mother. At other times if the mother is busy working, both children may be cared for by the grandmother. Furthermore, since the mother had an extremely close attachment to the older child during the period of nursing, she often finds it hard to give up the eldest child to the grandmother even after a younger child is born. Even when the coalition of mother and youngest child and of grandmother and eldest child is clear, there are often disputes between the children which inevitably affect the mother and grandmother on their respective sides, and disputes between mother and grandmother may later affect the children.

Another problem with this coalition pattern is the probability that the grandparent will die before the child is fully grown. A child who has been assigned to a grandparent often feels lonely after the grandparent's death, because he misses him and also because he then lacks a protector in family discussions; it is hard for him to break back into the close relationships from which he had been excluded. We knew of several cases where a child was especially sad and withdrawn for several years after the grandparent's death. Many children who were assigned the role of grandmother's (or grandfather's) child have difficulty finding any relationship that will ever replace the intimate devotion which they received before their grandparent died.

Chapter XII

CHILD-REARING

Until the end of World War II, standard guides like Kaibara Ekken's classic on the proper conduct of women set forth precisely the moral duties of wives to husbands, and of children to parents. But the government leaders and Confucian moralists who sponsored the guidebooks, did not offer advice to the parents on how to handle children. As a result, there is no formal tradition, setting forth the ideal parent behavior comparable to the set of injunctions regarding filial piety. Advice on child-rearing[1] was left for older women to pass down to younger women informally by word of mouth, and even the consensus about child-rearing which did exist in many communities was never standardized or rationalized. When one asks a Mamachi mother about "traditional" patterns of family relations, she cites a well-ordered stereotype of the ideal patterns she was taught, but when one asks about "traditional" patterns of child-rearing she has no such rationalized overview and is more likely to cite her own experiences.

Nor is the Mamachi mother clearer about what the new pattern is, for despite the plethora of printed advice now available on child-rearing and the attempt by many mothers to develop an integrated rationalized approach, there is no clear consensus on desirable practices that compares to the consensus in America represented by the wide acceptance of Spock. There is not even a single integrated set of practices which can be called the "new way."

---

[1] Child-rearing is here understood not as a body of specific techniques to train children but as the sum total of familial relationships of all kinds as they impinge upon the child and affect his development.

The Mamachi mother, lacking a single standard guide and confronting the difficult problem of providing her child with proper training for a constantly changing society far different from the society of her childhood, must seek advice from a variety of sources and then reconcile the conflicting advice with her own intuitive sense of what is proper. Most Mamachi mothers have worked out relatively consistent patterns of dealing with their children, but they are filled with doubts about whether their methods are the best.

Mamachi mothers approach the task of selecting proper methods every bit as seriously as husbands approach their work. Their attitude is expressed by a mother who explained that her task is more important than her husband's because he merely deals with things while she is responsible for moulding lives. Because this is the main work for salary men's wives and because of the limitless range of suggested methods, no topic evoked more lively discussion among Mamachi women or more close questioning of us about practices in America than child-rearing. On no topic do they read more avidly. They read advice columns in the daily papers and weekly magazines, information bulletins on nutrition or psychological problems issued by various branches of the government, accounts of mothers who have traveled abroad, "scientific investigations" of experts, and some even read the Japanese translation of Spock. But the amount of reading material is so overwhelming, the suggestions so numerous, and the possible solutions so different, that mothers look to intimate friends or meetings with other mothers and teachers at school for specific answers to concrete problems. These discussions with friends and other mothers are earnest, serious, and full of lively interchange of experiences and opinions.

Many conventional practices are questioned by the more modern mothers. Some question whether it is good for the small child to sleep on the same *futon* (mattress) with his mother. Some argue that the practice of carrying a child on the back is old-fashioned, and refuse to follow the custom. While almost no mother defends outright the desirability of bottle-feeding over breast-feeding, most no longer think it right to criticize the small but increasing number of mothers who find that they do not have enough milk and must use bottles. Others think it is not good to scare children with stories of ghosts, and many modern mothers are adamantly against teaching the child anything that smacks of superstition. Some are even experimenting with leaving grade-school-age children at home alone while the mother goes out shopping. Others argue that it is sometimes best to allow a small child to cry and believe this principle so firmly that they are willing to endure the disapproval of neighbors who still think that a baby's crying is a sign of inadequate maternal attention. But many just as staunchly, though perhaps more quietly, defend more traditional patterns, and many who advocate new ideas find it difficult to put their views into practice. Some mothers who see nothing wrong with crying find themselves so upset by their own child's tears that they cannot permit the crying to continue. Others resolve not to carry their baby on their back but later find themselves doing so because of the convenience.

THE BASIC RELATIONSHIP: MUTUAL DEPENDENCY OF MOTHER AND CHILD

Despite the wide divergence of opinion and practice among women of different ages and social classes about child-rearing, Mamachi women consistently approach the task of child-rearing in a way which contrasts with the modal patterns in the American middle-class suburbs. This difference is illustrated by a Mamachi mother who prided herself in being modern and rearing independent children even to the point of incurring the disapproval of some of her relatives but was shocked when a three-year-old American child took such an active interest in playing in the home of a stranger that he did not even notice when his mother went into another room. After this mother heard in detail some of the freedom granted to American children, she concluded that by comparison the freedoms she granted her children were minor. Indeed, the typical mother-child relationship in Mamachi is very close, both physically[2] and

---

[2] As part of my investigation of child-rearing practices, I arranged to have questionnaires distributed to about sixty families each in seven different communities—five in rural areas, one a salary-man neighborhood in a Tokyo suburb, and another a small-shopkeeper neighborhood in a Tokyo suburb. The results presented in the

psychologically.[3] It may seem paradoxical that even though the salaried family represents the most radical departure from tradition in many ways, the opportunity of the wife of the salary man to be home and devoted to the children has made the mutual dependency of the mother and child even stronger in the salary-man families than in other occupational groups. Because of the relative isolation of the mother and child from other maternal relatives, the mother-child relationship of the Mamachi salary mother is perhaps even more intense and less subject to outside interference than in traditional rural families. The father is occupied away from home long hours of the day, the mother's opportunity of seeing friends is usually limited, and once the children are born the mother turns her affection to them. She provides them with continuous attention, and, because her social sphere is so limited, she relies on them

table below are the mean age (in months) at which certain steps in child-rearing were reported to have taken place.

Activity	Miyagi farm area	Miyagi deep-sea fishing village	Miyagi off-shore fishing village	Yamagata farm village	Yamagata small town	Tokyo suburb salary men	Tokyo suburb small shop-keepers
	Month at which activity began or ended						
Began weaning	14	22	12	18	9	8	8
Stop weaning	21	32	21	30	17	16	12
Stop carrying on back	29	44	30	32	28	23	18
Stop sleeping next to child	45	130	56	102	45	45	35
Stop taking bath with child	75	80	63	87	70	72	81

[3] This observation and its implications for psychoanalytic theory are discussed by Dr. Takeo Doi, the only practicing Japanese psychiatrist with Western psychoanalytic training, and by Dr. William Caudill, who is currently carrying out large-scale research on mother-infant relationships in Japan. William Caudill and Takeo Doi, "Interrelations of Psychiatry, Culture, and Emotion in Japan," in *Medicine and Anthropology*, New York: Werner Gren Foundation, 1962. See also Takeo Doi's analysis of the passive dependency of the model Japanese personality. Takeo Doi, "Amae—A Key Concept for Understanding Japanese Personality Structure," *Psychologia*, 1962, 5:1–7. Dr. Doi has noted that mothers foster this passive dependency, and the techniques of child-rearing elaborated above can be thought of as a further specification of the techniques giving rise to this type of personality.

for companionship just as completely as they rely on her for care.

When a second child is born, and the mother must sleep with the baby, the eldest child ordinarily stops sleeping with the mother and begins sleeping with the father or a grandparent. While elementary-school-age children often sleep in a separate room, and certainly have their own mattresses and covers, it is not unusual for grown children to sleep next to their parents. Mamachi mothers may be embarrassed that this practice may not conform to how the modern mother is supposed to behave. They argue that sleeping with small children is convenient and comfortable. The baby and mother can go right to sleep after nursing; the mother can comfort the child without getting out of her quilt; in the winter, they can keep each other warm and the mother need not worry about the child getting out from under the quilt. One mother after seeing an American movie expressed her pity for the "poor foreign babies" who were forced to sleep alone. Even putting a baby to sleep is not done by rocking or sitting beside a crib and singing a song, but by close physical contact, by nursing him or later carrying him on her back until he dozes off. If the child is too heavy to carry, the mother may lie down beside the child, singing or telling a story until he falls asleep.

Breast-feeding generally continues slightly longer than one year. Many advice columns and even some government publications advise that it is wise to begin weaning at a fairly early age, and a few mothers are even using bottles. But there are also some at the other extreme, like the mother who weaned her two-year-old the day a younger child was born, or the mother of an emotionally disturbed child, who complained of the pain of waiting with full breasts for her six-year-old son to return home each day from school. Most mothers, however, begin weaning their children shortly after their first birthday while introducing supplementary food. The actual weaning may be abrupt but often, even up to the time the child enters elementary school, the mother's disapproval may not always be strong enough to stop him from teasingly fondling her breasts occasionally. Most mothers feel it unnecessary and even cruel to deprive the child of close physical contact.

Bathing is another opportunity for close physical contact between mother and child. While poorer families go to the public bath, virtually all salaried families now have their own wooden tubs, which are shorter but deeper than the average American bath. One washes before entering the tub and sits in the tub for relaxing and getting warm. While older children and adults bathe alone, the mother usually bathes with small children until they are old enough to enter elementary school. Even after the child is in elementary school, on special occasions when the mother wants to have a particularly close talk, she may have the talk while she and the child bathe together in the tub. One Mamachi parent suggested that the expression *hadaka de hanasu* (figuratively, talking frankly; literally, talking nakedly) probably derived from the practice of informal talks in the bathtubs.

Until the child is one or two, the mother carries the child on her back in a special strap when she works around the house or goes out shopping. When she goes out in the winter, she straps the child on her back, then puts on a loose fitting coat which covers both her and the infant, and the infant's head can be seen peering out of the coat. To mothers and children alike, the idea of a child on his parent's back is a pleasing one, with connotations of pleasant intimacy. In advertisements, happy children peer over their mothers' shoulders; in children's books, monkeys or bunny rabbits gayly climb around the necks of giraffes; in their play, girls strap their dolls on their backs.

Sexual feelings between parent and child tend to be deeply repressed, and the close physical contact between mother and child during the day and night are not thought of in sexual terms. Rather physical contact is seen as a natural expression of affection, which is desirable and necessary for the proper rearing of children.[4]

Even when the Mamachi mother and child are not in actual physical contact, the child is seldom out of his mother's sight or earshot. No one is considered a substitute for the mother, and rarely does a mother think of leaving her children with a baby sitter. Even if a grandmother is at home to care for the children, many mothers try to avoid leaving her with children younger than two or three.

----

[4] Cf. Drs. Doi and Caudill, *op. cit.* See also their articles in Robert J. Smith and Richard K. Beardsley, eds., *Japanese Culture*, New York: The Viking Fund, 1962. This more complete repression of sexual feelings also helps explain the great length of time it takes a Japanese couple to begin enjoying sexual relationships after marriage.

Usually the mother stays at home, or, if she goes out, she takes the child with her. If some difficulty should arise while the mother is out, the mother is blamed for leaving, and she probably would not go out again for a long time. The reaction of many Mamachi mothers upon hearing that American children are often left with baby sitters was to ask if the children would not be lonely, clearly implying that if their child was lonely or cried, they would not leave him.

Even within the home, the child is likely to be within his mother's view. Most mothers do not use cribs and while play pens or *beebi saakuru* (baby circles) are sometimes found in upper-class or independent professional homes, they are still virtually unknown among Mamachi salary men. Because of the dangers of bumping against the *hibachi* or of falling off the porch next to the sliding glass doors, the mother generally works close to a small child if she is not carrying him on her back.

It is assumed that the child will naturally want to be close to his mother and will be afraid to be alone. The mother deals with such fears not by assuring the child that there is nothing to be afraid of, but by remaining with him. The implicit attitude seems to be that the mother agrees that the outside is frightening, but that while she is there she will protect the child against all outside dangers. The mother's attitude that one must be careful in the presence of strangers is also communicated to the child well before nursery-school age. All three-year-old children know about *o-bake* (ghosts) and often playfully threaten each other acting as if they were the ghosts. Sometimes an adult, with fingers outstretched, jokingly menaces a child saying *o-bake*. If the child then becomes frightened and cries, the adult cuddles the child, promising to protect him from the ghosts. Many children who have heard stories of ghosts in the hole under the toilet ask their mothers to accompany them to the toilet even when they are old enough to manage the basic functions themselves.

Even though the mother is not consciously aware of using such techniques, her attitudes and approach tend to arouse in the child a fear of making independent decisions and to create anxiety about being isolated from family or friends. One mother, for example, had explained to her daughter that she could choose her own grade school if she were fully prepared to pay the consequences. The con-

sequence was that when the girl later wanted to change schools
between junior and senior high school, the mother reminded the
daughter that she herself had chosen the school and therefore
would have to stay there. The moral was clear: it is risky to make
decisions on one's own.[5] The threat to isolate a child can be illustrated by an explanation of a school principal. He said that on a
school trip which he supervised, the children were remarkably well-
behaved because he had warned them before that any child who
misbehaved would be left at the destination by himself until his
parents would come and get him. The combination of provoking
anxiety about the outside and rewarding intimacy serves to keep
the child dependent on his mother.

The process of encouraging this dependency begins in earliest
infancy. While the American baby who cries learns that at times he
himself must deal with his internal tensions, the Japanese infant
learns that whatever tensions he has will be relieved by the nearby
mother who offers physical comfort and, at a later age, candy or
some other sweet.[6] It is not surprising that so many children are so
anxious about the mother's leaving and that so many mothers are
frightened of the child's reaction if they were to go out and leave
the child with someone else.

While curious, the Mamachi child is frightened of the strange
outside world. We never heard of a child talking about running
away from home, and the Mamachi mother has little worry about
a child not sticking close by in public. While in America one sees
mothers chasing down the street after a child, in Mamachi one is
more apt to see a child frantically chasing after a mother who is
encouraging her child to hurry by running slightly ahead. We have
never heard of a mother punishing a child by forbidding him to go

----

[5] Mary Ellen Goodman reports that Japanese children are more responsive to adults'
wishes and less determined in making up their own minds about what they wish to
be when they grow up. Mary Ellen Goodman, "Values, Attitudes and Social Concepts of Japanese and American Children," *American Anthropologist,* 1957, 59:979–
999.

[6] In a questionnaire gathered from 92 Tokyo mothers, 85 percent reported giving
food between meals as a reward for good behavior. Damaris Pease, "Some Child
Rearing Practices in Japanese Families," Journal Paper No. J-3872, Iowa Agricultural
and Home Economics Station, Ames, Iowa.

outside,[7] but we have on several occasions heard children frantically yelling for their mother because they had been placed out of the house and not permitted to come in again until they repented their misbehavior.

Even joking can lead to effective results. One mother suggested to her daughter that she might be able to go to America with the interviewers when they returned home. Although the daughter protested, the mother began teasing more, pointing out how wonderful America was, what a good experience it would be, how proud she could be, all of which served to make the child cling even more closely to the mother.

The Mamachi child is usually polite in public or in new situations and is slow in adjusting to outsiders, including school friends and teachers. He is likely to be reserved to his teacher, and some children who are noisy at home are quiet and reserved in school. Indeed, this pattern is so common as to be known as *uchi benkei* (a child as ferocious as the warrior Benkei at home, but as gentle as a lamb elsewhere). But once children have been thoroughly accepted into the new group they can display the same noisy playful behavior as at home.

There is a continuity and compatibility between the child's dependence on his immediate family and the dependence which he later feels toward his school and work groups. Compared to the American firm, where the man is expected to make decisions within the scope of his position, the Mamachi salary man is expected to go along automatically with the group, and often he is not even aware of any decision-making process.[8] Most Mamachi residents would prefer to have things already arranged for them *o-zen date* (literally, the tray already arranged with food on it) rather than to carve out their own situations. For instance, the Japanese concept of hospitality is to have everything arranged ahead of time, including lodging, food, transportation, and detailed itinerary, rather than waiting to consult with the guest.

In Mamachi, as in communities in other societies, children grad-

---

[7] Even the punishment of locking the child in the closet (*oshiire*) which is used occasionally has the feeling of shutting the child off from the rest of the family.

[8] More joint discussion and approval is required than in American firms. Cf. Kazuo Noda's discussion of *ringi seidoo* in "Traditionalism in Japanese Management" (mimeographed).

ually become more independent. But whereas in the United States the push seems to come from the child himself, in Mamachi the push often comes from the mother. Many mothers of Mamachi, while implicitly encouraging their children to be dependent, complain about their difficulty in getting their children to be independent and feel it necessary to give them an occasional shove so they will do things on their own. In contrast, many American mothers who complain that their children are too independent implicitly encourage independence by making it sound so attractive and by accepting it as natural that the child would want to revolt and become more independent.

In the United States, many children and even adults who have strong ties to their parents, try to act brave, strong, and independent because it is considered so child-like to admit one's feelings of dependency. In Mamachi, in contrast, feelings of dependency are accepted as much more natural, and while some children resent being tied to their parents, they generally do not have to strain to prove that they are independent even when they are not.

Although this pattern of mutual dependency between mother and child remains strong in Mamachi, even through adolescence, there is a feeling that the new way, while not yet clearly defined, is toward having less dependence. Mamachi mothers, who had an opportunity to hear about American child-rearing practices and to see American children during our period of research, agreed that their children were more dependent, yet many were displeased when we first explained that American children were usually more independent. This displeasure in part seems to reflect their belief that keeping children close is gratifying for the mothers, but that allowing more independence is better for the child. Many recent advice columns have encouraged mothers not to be selfish in wanting to keep the children so dependent on them. Many mothers, who reported how long they nursed the baby or took baths or slept with him, added that they were bad to take so long or that they continued these practices so long only because their child was unusually lonely, delicate, or prone to catch colds.

At the time of adolescence, the mother's problem is especially complicated. Most Mamachi mothers feel that their children, especially their daughters, do not have the range of experience nor the soundness of judgment to make wise decisions about marriage and employment. Yet it is not entirely clear how much responsibility the mother will have for making the decisions and how much the child will demand to make the decisions on his own. Commonly the child decides at an early age that he wishes to make his own decisions, yet continues to lean on his mother for assistance even though resisting many of her suggestions. The mother's task is further complicated by the fact that she does not sufficiently understand the child's outside world to be confident of her ability to offer the right kind of assistance. In traditional rural communities, where the range of social relationships was narrower, it was easier for the mother to assist her child. True, she might not have been able to find as good an opening, but the limited range of possibilities available to her for exploration made her task simpler. The suburban wife now has so many possibilities open to her which she cannot possibly explore that she can never feel that she has completed her task. The situation is so complex, the amount of potentially relevant information virtually unlimited, the mother's feeling of responsibility so strong, and the child's ambivalence about getting parental advice so taxing that many openly envy Western countries where children have sufficient experience at a younger age to make decisions themselves. It is only through narrowing down her range of possibilities through conversation with friends and the cultivation of her child's co-operation that she can hope to achieve her task.

Perhaps some of the difficulty a mother has in planning her children's marriage, especially that of the youngest, is the result of her ambivalence about concluding an arrangement whose success means that she will then be deprived of her role as mother. The problem of the empty nest is crucial for mothers in any society, but in Mamachi where the pattern of elderly parents living apart from all married children is relatively new and the mother-child relationship is so intense, the departure of children necessitates the most painful adjustment that most women will have to make in their lifetimes. Having devoted their lives so completely to their children, many have no interests which can really take their place. Golden-age clubs are virtually unknown, and going to a *yoorooin* (old people's home) seems as bad to old people as being sent to an orphanage would seem to children.

Many are never required to separate completely but are able to live within the same neighborhood, and often even next door, and this appears to be the most ideal solution. For a mother who has devoted her entire life to her home and children, living apart seems sad. The Mamachis residents' deepest criticism of the American family is that young married couples are heartless in letting old people live by themselves. Japanese young couples are more apt to keep closer to their parents, but even being made aware that they are an economic burden or feeling relatively neglected by the children is often a crushing blow to parents. A large number of elderly ladies lived with and served their mothers-in-law when they were young and feel that it is a bitter fate that they now have to live alone without the attention from their children.

Such is the price that the salary-man's wife must pay for the pleasure of devoting herself to her children and for enjoying the freedom of living only in a nuclear family when at a younger age. The workings of the Japanese social structure make the tie between her and her child even more intense and more exclusive than the mother-child tie in most societies. When children are small this creates no serious problem. When children leave home, some speak nostalgically of their romanticized view of the earlier times when old people were happily welcomed into the family, when they were not treated as a burden, and when the younger couple followed the wishes of the elders without hesitation. Yet they know that times have changed and that their own attitudes have changed with the times.

VARIATIONS ON A THEME:
BIRTH ORDER, SEX, AND PARENTAGE

The mother's relationship with her children varies according to their birth order as well as according to their age. Everyone calls oldest children *Niisan* (older brother) or *Neesan* (older sister), but younger boys and girls are usually called by their first name or by some nickname. When a mother thinks her child is acting babyish, she does not tell him to "act his age," but to "act like a *Niisan*." Older children often are given the responsibilities of looking after younger children, and when older children reach adolescence, the mother is likely to consult with them about plans for the younger children since the older children know more about the outside world. If the father spends little time at home, the mother may share her problems with the older children and treat them like adults, even in their early teens. The mother is particularly dependent on the oldest son, and may have deeper emotional ties toward him, yet she commonly treats him with more respect and less light-hearted affection than she does a younger son. She looks to him for advice and help with younger children and for financial help in her later years.

Younger children often, in fact, fit the stereotype of being less responsible and more mischievous, but more spontaneous and charming. Many mothers delight in affectionately telling funny stories about the youngest child's exploits, tricks, and insatiable quest for attention. A mother is likely to make allowances for his "misbehavior" since he is the youngest and hence not so responsible. The youngest often is treated as a family pet and granted a certain amount of license by the older children and the father as well as by the mother. Small children call their mothers and fathers *okaachan* and *otoochan* (affectionate terms corresponding roughly to mommy and daddy). As they get older, they use more formal terms of respect, *okaasan* and *otoosan* (mother and father), but the youngest children usually continue calling their parents by the affectionate childish name much longer than their older siblings.

The youngest child is pampered and babied by his siblings as well as his mother. The mother weans him at a later age and sleeps and bathes with him for a longer period of time. Until he is three or four, he is given virtually anything he asks for. In quarrels between older siblings and children under three or four, the mother does not investigate who started the fight, but asks the older to yield. By the time the youngest is in grade school, more demands are placed on him, but often the pressure for him to act like an older sibling comes not from the mother but from the older siblings. Even then, however, the younger sibling is permitted more freedom than the elders received when they were his age.

The biggest change in the relationship of a child with his mother occurs when a younger sibling is born. The age at which a child is weaned, or required to sleep or bathe alone, or to assume responsibilities for his own behavior is determined more by the time his next younger sibling is born than by any other single factor. The youngest, having no such pressure, is permitted to remain childish to a much later age.

While most couples are anxious for their first child to be a boy, some wives argue, perhaps partly to protect themselves against possible disappointment, that it is better to have a girl first because a boy is more *wagamama* (determined to get what he wants). Mothers tend to feel that boys are more difficult to manage. They are afraid that unless they gratify a boy's demands quickly he may become uncontrollable, and some mothers become panicky if their sons do not do precisely as they wish them to. Girls, on the other hand, are thought to be patient and able to endure it (*gamanzuyoi*) if their wishes are not satisfied immediately. While many girls complain that their brothers are required to do less work and are criticized less, girls win their mothers' respect because they have stronger characters than their more impulsive brothers. Since mothers consistently treat boys as if they are impulsive and girls as if they have greater abilities to endure, it is not surprising that boys often do turn out to be less capable of tolerating frustration.[9]

This combination of birth order and sex roles tends to make the relationship between mother and youngest son especially affectionate. However, as much as she is devoted to her youngest son, the mother is sometimes concerned that he does not give her a chance to get her work done or to visit friends or attend PTA meetings because he is always following her around wanting to play. And the youngest son, accustomed to his mother's constant attention, is sometimes upset when his mother has other things to do.

While the youngest son enjoys the most pampering from the mother, the stepchild or the adopted child suffers most from neglect and discrimination. The number of these cases in Japan is large because of the number of war orphans and because parentless children are more likely to be cared for by relatives than placed in new homes where they might be fully accepted as family members. Furthermore, the housing shortages after World War II and the problem of caring for children who were finishing schooling has required relatives to care for children apart from their parents for

---

[9] This points up the inaccuracy of one wartime interpretation of the Japanese. It was thought that Japanese were aggressive in the war because they were controlled and kept all their feelings inside. If this were true, one would expect that since women were ordinarily much more controlled they would become much more aggressive under stress. Such is not the case.

extended periods, taking on a role much like that of step-parents. A number of Mamachi families have cared for rural nieces or nephews who came to the Tokyo area to attend high school or college. In case of divorce, the custody of the children in Japan frequently goes to the father's family so the child would be cared for by a stepmother or by the father's mother or sister who might have the same psychological relationship to the child as a stepmother.[10] Because the mother-child relationship is so intense, the stepchild is likely to feel particularly deprived. No matter how much the stepmother tries to be fair, it is someone else's child whom she is caring for, and feelings of fondness are not ordinarily as deep as those between the mother and her true children. The actual number of stepmothers is relatively small, but the public wrath against them expressed occasionally in newspapers, TV "home dramas," and "movies" suggests the extent to which everyone has strong feelings about the evils of inadequate mothering.

THE FATHER

In the daily work of child-rearing, the Mamachi father plays a minor role. Occasionally he plays with small children or takes older ones for a walk, but he does not share the responsibility of caring for and training the children. He does not serve as a mother substitute or as mother's helper in performing the routine aspects of child care when the mother is busy. It is true that a few modern fathers, albeit a bit awkwardly and gingerly, are attempting to help their wives, but this pattern is scarcely common enough to constitute a trend. Nor does the father often consult with the mother about questions on the daily handling of the child.

In his day-to-day contact with the children, the father is ordinarily incredibly mild. He almost never gives orders to the children, and he leaves the disciplining of the children entirely to the wife. He plays on the floor with small children, almost as if he himself

---

[10] In one study of 3754 divorce custody cases in 1953 in Japan, in 42.1 percent the custody of the children was awarded to the fathers, in 44.5 percent to the mothers. Eiichi Isomura, Takeyoshi Kawashima, and Takashi Koyama, eds., *Gendai Kazoku Kooza* (The Structure of the Contemporary Family), Tokyo: Kawade Shoboo, 1958, Vol. 5, *Rikon* (Divorce), p. 208. In contrast, in a Detroit sample of 425 cases, mothers were awarded custody in 94.8 percent of the cases, fathers in 2.4 percent. William J. Goode, *After Divorce*, Glencoe, Ill.: The Free Press, 1956, p. 311.

were a child or, perhaps, more accurately, as a number of mothers phrased it, a child with a toy, the toy being the small child. He may be very affectionate to the children, and when the second child is born he may sleep and bathe with the eldest. Fathers see themselves as very kindly in relation to their children and try to avoid telling them what to do. They often side with their children when the mothers are too strict, and sometimes give them little presents without the mothers knowing about it. Children respond to this attention and are usually delighted to have a chance to go out with their fathers for walking or shopping.

Yet children are aware that this pleasantry has limits and at times are afraid their father may explode if not treated with proper caution.[11] Children can have raucous good times with their father, but they must catch him in the right mood, and even then they may not feel free to talk to him about their own concerns. The positive bonds of affection which Mamachi children feel toward their father are not always strong enough to overcome their feeling of restraint because of the potential authority which he can exercise. In part, the respect for the father's authority derives from his expression of opinions which he does not even think of as restraining. Sometimes, as for example when the father wants the children to bring him something or to be quiet, he is so simple and direct that he does not think of himself as invoking authority; yet the children feel constrained to obey. In part respect derives from the few but memorable occasions when the father lost his temper and suddenly demanded something in a tone of voice that caused everyone to scurry to obey. In large part, however, the child's respect for the father's authority is learned from the mother. At times, she warns the children that if they do not perform properly in school or if their behavior brings shame to the family, the father will punish them. At other times the mother conveys the image of the father as an authority by more subtle means. In the father's absence, for

---

[11] In sentence-completion tests, children making critical comments about their parents most often describe their mother as *urusai* (bothersome, noisy, or strict) and their father as *kowai* (frightening or scary). This supports the view that while the mother takes care of the day-to-day discipline problems and is continually after the children to behave properly, the father is more readily obeyed on the few occasions when he does say something. Children can take their mother's criticisms and comments more lightly than their father's.

example, she may talk with the children about how to get something from the father without getting him angry. The impact of such discussions is to make the children cautious in approaching their father. Some fathers are uncomfortable about the reserve which the children feel in their presence, but even with their mild manner, playful behavior, and frequent presents, fathers have difficulty breaking through this wall of silence. Although kind and gentle to his children, the father nonetheless represents and enforces community standards to the children. It is he who loves and respects the child who does well on entrance examinations, the child who is admitted to a good school or job and makes a good marriage. Because he is a representative of the outside world to his children he cannot entirely escape being seen by them as they see the outside: aloof and frightening. And they feel they must observe some of the caution they do on the outside. As much as the father may try to avoid being cast as an authority and to win the children's friendship by considerateness, mildness, and good humor, his position as authority and representative of the outside always remain in the background.

Being home even a few hours a week is sufficient for the father to serve as role model for the boy, when reinforced by the mother's encouraging her son to behave in accord with the male role. The mother's expectations are usually sufficiently unconflicted as to obviate any problem in the boy's learning male roles. Sex roles and the attitudes associated with Oedipal ties between father and daughter on the one hand and mother and son on the other hand are also learned primarily from the mother.

Oedipal relationships are especially pronounced in late adolescence. At that time the daughter, like a person fond of someone she rarely sees, often feels more positive affect for the father even though she is in many ways more intimate with the mother. Similarly, the constellation of family roles and in particular the mother's relationship to her sons is sufficient to produce the father's rivalry with his sons, particularly his eldest son, even if the father spends relatively little time at home.

GETTING THE CHILD TO UNDERSTAND

Most Mamachi parents, fathers and mothers, are lenient with their children, especially when they are small. By Western standards grandparents are so uncritical that, as the Japanese saying goes, they "wouldn't even feel pain if the children got stuck in their eye," i.e., nothing the children do could possibly be bad or painful. Small children are permitted to run, climb, yell, stay up late, eat large amounts of sweets, keep their mothers occupied away from company, hit bigger children, and climb on their parents' laps or backs with almost no limit. Yet somehow, Mamachi mothers must train their children to become properly behaved adults.

So little do parents even think of punishing their children that mothers rarely if ever use techniques of discipline commonly used in the West. They rarely yell at, criticize, hit, spank a child, or mete out a specific punishment for a wrongdoing. Several Japanese mothers, visiting the United States, have expressed their shock at the cruelty and crudity of American mothers who spank or yell at their children in public places such as supermarkets. Yet Mamachi children do learn how to mind, are well-behaved in most public situations, polite to teachers,[12] and considerate of others. Some Western observers who have attempted to explain the paradox of Japanese permissiveness toward children alongside the children's carefully controlled public behavior have argued that mothers suddenly become strict with children when they are about five or six years old.[13] It is true that mothers become stricter as children grow older, particularly when a younger child is born and when the child enters school, but it is no sudden application of strictness that did not exist before. And even a typical three-year-old child has already learned to stay away from danger, to bow to guests, to take off his shoes as he enters the house, to treat adults with courtesy, and to be quiet in public.

The explanation of the Mamachi mother's success in training without discipline is that she teaches only when the child is in a co-operative mood. She ordinarily does not think in terms of using techniques to get the child to obey her or of punishments if the child does not obey her. Her aim is to establish a close relationship

---

[12] Miss Kazuko Yoshinaga who taught middle-class kindergarten children in the United States and Japan expressed surprise at the rudeness of the children in the United States who sometimes call teachers by their first name, sometimes accidentally bump into the teachers, and contradict them.

[13] See especially Ruth Benedict, *The Chrysanthemum and the Sword*, Boston: Houghton Mifflin, 1946.

with the child so he will automatically go along with her suggestions. To the extent that she thinks of techniques for dealing with the child, they are methods for keeping the child happy and building their relationship so that he will want to do what she says. Because her interest is in their relationship, she is less interested in getting the child to behave properly than in getting him to understand. With a good relationship, she need only indicate the desired behavior and add with a tone of encouragement, *wakaru ne?* (You understand, don't you?). If the child co-operates, he is said to understand.[14]

One of the principles implicit in the attempt to get the child to understand is that one should never go against the child. There is no distinction in the Japanese language between "let a child do something" and "make a child do something" (both use *saseru*), and the Mamachi mother avoids any situation where she is "making the child do something" against his will. In effect she limits the child's opportunity to develop a will of his own. By responding immediately to a child's needs, by going along with what he says, she makes it unnecessary for the child to develop a strong will of his own. By anticipating problems and offering ready-made solutions but few choices, she maximizes the chance that the child will go along automatically with her suggestions. She seldom gives an outright refusal to a small child's request. She is more likely to say "later" than "no." On some occasions she will give in because she feels it better to have a co-operative child in the long run than to risk a child becoming stubborn merely for the sake of getting temporary compliance.

That the average Mamachi mother is highly successful in training her children attests in part to her genuine liking for her children and her patient attempts to understand them and respond to their wishes. While she is not as sophisticated in the use of psychological terminology as her American counterpart, she is sensitive to her child's feelings and desires.[15] She carefully watches each child so as to learn his wishes, and she spends considerable time thinking

---

[14] Betty Lanham also notes the interest of the mother in *wakaraseru* (getting the child to understand). Betty Baily Lanham, "Aspects of Child-rearing in Japan," doctoral dissertation, Syracuse University, 1962.

[15] Cf. Betty Lanham, *ibid.*

about his particular nature. One of the first things a Mamachi mother attempts to do after a child is born is to find out under what circumstances he cries and to learn to satisfy him so quickly that he will never cry for more than a few seconds. She continues to be sensitive to his moods and tries to catch any difficulties before they develop. She uses a large amount of goodies of all kinds to keep him happy and *sunao* (gentle). Indeed, almost any mother setting out for a shopping trip with a child, especially on public transportation, is likely to carry along an ample supply of candy to dispense in case her child begins to show some sign of discomfort. She knows an almost infinite variety of little hand exercises, peek-a-boo games, animal imitations, songs with gestures, games to play with a child's arms or legs or face which can be used to distract or entertain a child. At home, she uses physical contact to comfort the child. She does not hesitate to crawl on the floor, hold, rock, or bounce a child or to let him climb on her back. With a larger child, she is likely to tell amusing stories or play little games. She may also use such games, many made up spontaneously to fit the situation at home, to motivate a child to perform necessary tasks such as putting away toys. So devoted is the mother to keeping her child happy that from the eyes of a Westerner the Mamachi child appears pampered. To the Mamachi mother, who has an intimate relationship with her child and depends on this relationship for getting the child to follow her wishes, this devotion appears natural and necessary.

In the context of positive feeling the mother's teaching and guidance take place so automatically, that she herself is scarcely aware of it. She consciously thinks about and plans how to get the child into a good mood, but she rarely plans how to teach a small child to be neat, to assume the proper posture, or to avoid dangerous places, even though her child learns these things as early or earlier than the middle-class American child. A mother does not explain these things to a small child or reason with him. She simply puts his body in the proper position until he is able to make the movements on his own. If the child gets near a fire or starts to climb up on a high place, she does not lecture him on the danger of fire or high places. She simply says *abunai* (dangerous), which is more of a warning signal than a command, and pulls him away before he gets there. The child soon acquires a fear of going near such places and stays away. To offer extended explanations is contrary to the spirit of child-rearing practice. It is inconsistent with the feeling that the child should respond immediately and without question and that rational explanations are less important than preserving the basic relationship. The Mamachi mother is often vague in her reasons for postponing a child's request, and this vagueness serves to emphasize further the importance of the basic relationship. Some conscious planning enters with older children, however, as explanations become necessary to make a school-child "understand."

When a child reaches the age of three or four, he is taught to withhold his aggression. When a child below that age hits an older sibling the mother may regard this simply as a form of play, but she may say that it will not do (*ikenai*) for the older child to hit the younger one. If she hears that her child has been in a fight with a neighbor, she will tell him that will not do, regardless of whether he started the fight or not. To hit in self-defense is considered about as bad as to start a fight. While the mother may sympathize with her child when he has been wronged by others, there is virtually no situation in which returning aggression is condoned. She wants the child to learn this thoroughly because in many ways any aggressive sign from the child is regarded as a result of the failure of the mother to make the child understand, just as a child crying for candy in public is regarded as a sign that the mother does not feed the child enough.

In its early stages, toilet-training is in large part mother-training. When the child is six or eight months old the mother begins to watch how often and at what time he urinates and defecates, and then tries to catch him shortly before his usual time. Many mothers watch the child at night as well as during the day. In the summer time this poses no great difficulty as the child can go without diapers, and the mother will allow him to urinate in the yard. In the winter time, however, the baby is always dressed warmly, even in the house, and because the bathroom is quite cold the child cannot be left unclothed for long. Hence the mothers concentrate their energies for training in the warmer weather. They place the child on a potty shaped like the adult toilet, or they hold the child over the edge of the porch at the proper time. Often by the age of one and certainly by the age of two, by some combination of child-signaling and mother-training, the child is dry. Toilet-training is accomplished with a minimum of struggle. Children are not expected to resist training, nor do Mamachi mothers speak of a "no" stage around ages two or three, where negativism is taken for granted as it is by many American mothers. Toilet-training is not viewed as a struggle by which the mother imposes her will. Rather, the mother simply is helping the child to prevent the discomfort that comes from being wet or soiled.

While many aspects of child-training take place automatically, there are certain things which the mother consciously sets out to teach the child. This is not thought of as discipline or an attempt to force the child, but the mother shows the child how to do something, and then the child is expected to practice. With a successful relationship with the child, the mother can expect that the child will co-operate with long hours of training. Even small children have the patience to sit for long periods of time for tasks of memorization.[16] They are taught, for example, how to recite poems or sing songs, how to draw, how to color, how to make the letters of the Japanese syllabary—all well before grade-school age. Once in grade school, the child is expected to practice his lessons at home in much the same way. But even for these periods of practice, most mothers feel they cannot teach the child if he is not in the proper mood to co-operate. Even in an earlier era when school children were disciplined with a whip (*ai no muchi,* literally, the love whip), it was thought that if the child did not feel the whip as an expression of the love and devotion of the teacher, it would do no good. If the Mamachi mother is unable to create the proper spirit of co-operation, she will try to pass on the responsibility for training to someone else—the father, an elder sibling, a relative, or even an outside tutor.

If the relationship goes smoothly, few sanctions except a vague feeling of approval or disapproval are required to get the child to

---

[16] Mary Ellen Goodman who has carried on extensive interviews with young Japanese children reported that the children showed an amazing ability to persist working on various projects and that when working on such projects they were not easily distracted by outside interference.

behave. If the mother uses. any sanctions at all, she tries to use positive ones and to ally herself with the child rather than to create any breach between them.

Flattery is used freely in front of family members although parents try to refrain from undue praise of their children in front of strangers. The mother frequently uses such phrases as *o-rikoo* (nice child) and *joozu* (skillful) in talking to the child or in talking to a third party within the hearing of a child. These expressions are used not only to describe behavior but also to mean "Mommy's good little girl will do this, won't she" or "so and so is wonderfully skillful; won't it be nice when you become so skillful?"

The widespread use of fear or ridicule, noted by virtually all observers of the Japanese scene, also serves to ally the mother and child on the same side without creating any obstinacy or feeling of opposition. Mamachi children show an amazing sensitivity to what people might think of them, and the standard device for getting them to behave properly in front of company is the fear of what outsiders might say or think. The mother, in getting the child to behave so that neighbors will not laugh, is not seen by the child as an authority-enforcing discipline but as an ally in avoiding the negative sanctions of an outside authority. Instilling fear of fathers, ghosts, or supernatural forces (*bachi ga ataru*) has a similar function. It is a way for the mother to get the child to behave without making it necessary for her to assume the position of an authority.

In simple matters where the child is not ego-involved, the mother may merely say that the child should not do something, or if he has done something wrong, she may scold him for his improper conduct. However, when the child becomes adamant in wishing something, the mother is not likely to start a hassle, but to say that something will be done later (*ato de ne*) or that it is impossible (*dekinai*) without giving much of an explanation. Even if she is refusing the child because he has done something wrong, she does not usually make this explicit. Indeed, the vagueness of her refusal and the lack of explanation make it difficult for the child to rebel directly yet make it clear that it would be wise to try to get on the mother's good side the next time.

If the child is uncooperative the mother may make vague threats of abandoning the child, of leaving him home, or throwing the

child outside until he learns to show the proper attitude.[17] By showing disinterest or by not quite understanding or remaining impas-
sive, she makes it clear that the child does not have the proper
attitude, and the usual response of the child is to try to gain back
his mother's good graces. Even her techniques of refusal have the
effect not of setting up a battle line between the two but of getting
the child motivated to try to restore the understanding between
mother and child.

Mothers who do not have the relationship with their child that
leads to automatic compliance are often frantic, being caught between their inability to control the child on the one hand and their
feeling that they should not punish the child on the other hand.
Once the magic of the close relationship is broken, there is no
legitimate way of getting the child to behave without starting all
over again by building up the positive relationship. Indeed a few
Mamachi children, usually in homes with a conflict between mother-
in-law and daughter-in-law, are virtually uncontrollable despite
constant pampering because the child does not feel close enough
to the mother to go along automatically with what she suggests.[18]
Mothers do sometimes become angry at their children and do sometimes spank them, but they never consider their indignation right-
eous, and are more likely to feel that their anger represents failure
on their part than that it teaches the child a lesson.

In some ways, the mother's position is precarious. She is held
responsible for the child's behavior and yet she does not have clear
authority for laying down rules. If the father or mother-in-law dis-
agrees with the mother, she must yield to their authority. Her only
hope is that her relationship with the child is sufficiently close that
the child will follow her wishes. Her authority position is not suffi-

---

[17] In a study in a smaller city in central Honshu, Betty Lanham found that of 255
mothers using a threat, the most common kind was that someone would laugh at
them (162 cases) or at their family (47). Many threatened that the child might become sick (116), that the mother would leave home (53), send the child to another
house (49), or lock the child outside the house (42). Betty Lanham, *op. cit.*

[18] Clinicians at the Japanese National Institute of Mental Health have noted a
regular syndrome centered on a pampered yet uncontrollable child caught between
mother-in-law and daughter-in-law who both undercut the child's close relationship
with the other. Neither is able to develop the kind of relationship with the child that
leads to automatic compliance.

cient to produce compliance otherwise, and it is always possible for the children to complain to the father that the mother has been too strict. Even in the modern salaried families where the mother is given considerable freedom at home during the day, the husband may overrule some of her decisions. The techniques by which the mother builds a close relationship with the children may be viewed as a brilliant adaptation to the problem of managing the children without a clear mandate of authority that would permit her to exercise more direct sanctions.

GETTING THE CHILD'S CO-OPERATION IN STUDY

Since the mother must get the child to do an enormous amount of work in preparation for entrance examinations, during the grade-school years she is in many ways like an assistant teacher and in the summer vacation like a regular teacher. Even when the child is in high school and the mother is unable to help with the content of the study, she must continue to bear the responsibility for seeing that the child puts in a sufficient number of hours of study. And even if she does not understand the content, she may hold the answer book and drill or quiz the child about his lesson. She does virtually everything the teacher does except give a grade for the course. The situation here is an intensification of the Mamachi mother's basic problem in dealing with her children: she must get the child to co-operate in doing his work without having the clear-cut authority to enforce it. It is a problem so serious that some mother-child relationships crack under the strain.

Yet many do succeed, and one of the basic means by which they obtain co-operation is to convince the child of the importance of the examination. So all-pervasive is the spirit of the infernal entrance examinations that she rarely needs to use special techniques to get the child motivated to achieve. The continual talk about report cards, school preparation, and examinations, along with specific concern about the child's performance is adequate to create an impression on the mind of the child, but the mother often consciously tries further to increase the motivation. She does not hesitate to play up the status distance between her family and a higher-status family in order to indicate the advantages of studying hard.[19] Because the Mamachi standard of living is low enough that minor differences in income determine which electric machines a family owns and how nice a toy a child can have, the Mamachi child is taught that the job he attains will make a crucial difference in the style of life he can lead and in the security which he can have later in life. The Mamachi mother does not hesitate to connect the importance of examination success, and hence examination study, with success in later life. Not only does she typically do little to ease the child's anxiety about examination success, but she even encourages the child's uneasiness. By creating this uneasiness about success, the mother encourages the child to respond to her direction. She need not force the child to study because the child himself is so anxious about his success that he "understands" and wants to co-operate with the mother. She passes on to the child the demands of the outside world not as an agent of the arbitrary outside authority but as an ally who will assist him in meeting these demands.

Creating anxiety about possible difficulties in making the wrong marital choice has similar functions. It increases the probability that the child will voluntarily want to co-operate with the mother.[20] Most mothers do not consciously plan to make their children more anxious. But being anxious about their children's success and desirous of motivating the child to co-operate mothers create these anxieties almost instinctively.

---

[19] I am indebted to Tadashi Fukutake who first alerted me to this problem.

[20] Evidence from psychological testing reveals how deeply children have internalized the feeling that they should follow the mother's wishes in studying and in finding a spouse. Cf. George De Vos, "The Relation of Guilt Toward Parents to Achievement and Arranged Marriage among the Japanese," *Psychiatry*, 1960, 23:287–301.

Part Four

MAMACHI IN PERSPECTIVE

Chapter XIII

ORDER AMIDST RAPID SOCIAL CHANGE

Having examined Mamachi families in some detail, we may now be able to understand how certain features found in Mamachi contributed to the amazing success of Japan in the modernizing process.

Although the contemporary Japanese social structure is in many ways different from the social structures of Europe and America, it is not simply a holdover from traditional patterns. The closed and legalized class system of the Tokugawa period has become an open class system. A predominantly rural nation has, in the last few decades, changed to an urban nation in which less than one-fourth of the male population earn their living from farming, fishing, and forestry. The landowner-tenant relationship has been weakened or destroyed by land reform.[1] The *ie* is being replaced by the nuclear family. In the city, small firms have been giving way to large organizations and government bureaus, and the old paternalism is fast weakening.

In spite of all this change, the picture that emerges from this study of Mamachi, as of other studies of Japanese society, presents a relatively orderly and controlled life. This is particularly striking when compared to the massive disorganization in Europe and America during the industrial revolution and to the revolutionary disruptions in the Chinese family.[2] Although Japanese themselves have been conscious of the strains of adjusting to rapid change, they have not experienced the massive social disorganization so characteristic of many Western cities and of developing countries during the rapid

---

[1] For a fuller description of the changes in rural Japan see Tadashi Fukutake, *Man and Society in Japan*, Tokyo: Tokyo University Press, 1962.

[2] Cf. Marion J. Levy, *Family Revolution in Modern China*, Cambridge, Mass.: Harvard University Press, 1949.

migrations to the cities. The divorce rate in the United States is now five times as high as in 1885, but in Japan it is one-third as high as in 1885.[3] Although the crime rate has gone up slightly, it has not risen sharply enough to indicate any process of widespread disorganization.[4] The process of migration to the cities has been amazingly steady,[5] and the amount of job-changing has been relatively moderate. Unquestionably such rapid change has caused considerable strain in every Japanese individual and group, yet the disruption has remained within bounds, and a high degree of social order has been maintained throughout the transition to a modern society. It is important to consider features of Japanese social structure which have helped to maintain order at the time of the transition to urban industrial society and at the present time when the society has already achieved a high level of modernization.

THE TRANSITIONAL ORDER
In other studies, a number of features of Japanese society have already been shown to be important for the ease of Japan's modernization: a high degree of common national culture on the eve of modernization, political unity and stability, the high valuation placed on hard work and productivity, and the planning and organization of the Meiji leaders. Other features have emerged from the present study which are important to consider in the light of their contribution to this orderly process.

The Kinship System
The Japanese stem-family system, whereby one son received the inheritance and continued living with his parents while other sons went elsewhere, facilitated a smooth transition from rural to urban society. The Japanese family lines have had a continuity over generations which perhaps is unsurpassed by any other country. Even under European feudalism, land worked by a family without an heir might revert to the crown to be reassigned, but in Japan the

---

[3] Cf. Takeyoshi Kawashima and Kurt Steiner, "Modernization and Divorce Rate Trends in Japan," *Economic Development and Cultural Change*, 1960, 9:213–239.

[4] This evidence is analyzed in detail in the forthcoming work by De Vos and Mizushima.

[5] Cf. Irene Taeuber, "Family, Migration and Industrialization in Japan," *American Sociological Review*, 1951, 16:149–157.

family would itself adopt an heir. Because the family line remained in a single household, it provided a stable unit for village organization. Not only did the kinship system lend stability to rural organization, but it permitted independence for the family which moved to the city.

The movement of second and third sons to the city made it possible for the family to avoid the dissipation of family wealth through multiple inheritance that occurred, for example, in China. It also avoided the confusion that many Chinese families experienced deciding how much each son would receive. The *ie* system required that the parents select a single heir, and since they made this decision while the children were fairly young, they avoided the prolonged adolescence and the tension of the Irish family where the heir was selected at a much later stage. The fact that parents and village elders were instrumental in placing the young children in the city reinforced the authority of the older generation and prevented uncontrolled movement of young people to the city whenever they might feel dissatisfied with their elders' decisions.

The sons who moved to the city knew that they would not receive any inheritance from their parents, and that they would be accepted back into the rural areas only temporarily in time of emergency. The young sons going to the urban areas therefore were fully committed to finding long-term work. They were willing to undergo long apprenticeships and to acquire skills useful at a later stage of life. Again this is in contrast to the migration in many countries where the migrating sons hoped to acquire money quickly and then return to their original home. Even if such migrants remained in the city indefinitely, they seldom had the perseverance to acquire the skills that would compare with the young Japanese migrant.

The younger sons who moved to the city essentially were free of family traditions. The care of elderly parents and the preservation of family property and traditions were left to the elder son who remained at the farm. The younger son came to the city at a time of life when he was able to learn new urban patterns, and there was no strong kinship or provincial association in the city which interfered with his rapid adaptation. Even close supervision from paternalistic employers in the city usually did not interfere with the essential autonomy of the nuclear family of parents and children.

The Group Control of Mobility

Although there has been considerable mobility in Japan in the past century, it has been a movement from one tightly-knit group to another through prescribed channels. This control over mobility has depended in large part on the fact that the labor supply consistently has exceeded the number of positions available.[6] Yet, with the exception of the period of the world depression in the 1930's, there has been a steady expansion of employment opportunities. As a result, people have felt optimistic enough about getting some kind of work in the city to be willing to exert themselves to obtain these limited opportunities. This has taken the form of laying careful groundwork in placing the second or third son who migrated to the city. The constant labor surplus has also permitted employers to take great care in hiring. Because groups have remained fairly tightly-knit, firms have been reluctant to take in people who are not properly sponsored. The widespread requirement of personal introductions has made it possible for local community leaders to maintain control over the emigration to the city. A person from the rural areas who has wanted a job in the city has had to go through channels in his local community in order to get a proper placement in the city.

Even in the cities today, although the crucial factor in gaining admittance to a good school or a large enterprise is the score on the entrance examination, introductions are also desirable. This insures that the child has the proper sponsorship of his family, his community, and his previous school and serves as a powerful sanction for an individual to avoid incurring the disapproval of his own group. Since the person who manages the introduction is in the position of a guarantor for the behavior of the person he introduces, he ordinarily introduces only young people whose families have shown proper allegiance in their original community. Who is hired and under what conditions still depends on market conditions relating to the individual's competence and the labor supply even though carefully controlled by one's original and new groups.

---

[6] Indeed, many characteristics of Japanese social structure seem to follow from the surplus of labor: the fact that large organizations have more men than can efficiently be used, that women have no work, that well-to-do boys do not take part-time work in vacations for fear of taking jobs from poorer boys, and that the desire to gain security in place of work is so strong.

Although firmly attached to the new group once a person moves, his original group remains his refuge in times of difficulty. If, for example, a boy is discharged by an employer or if the employer goes out of business and is unable to offer support, the boy must then turn back to his family and to the person who originally helped him find the job in order to obtain a new situation. If a girl has marital difficulties, she must go back to her original family for assistance in finding a new livelihood. Until recently, the same pattern held true even for an older woman who had trouble in marriage or for an older man who had trouble in his work. If the parents who had originally been responsible for making the placement had died, then the person who inherited the family headship would assume the same responsibility. Today, with such group responsibility somewhat diminished, the passing of years and the death of the person who made the placement may mark an effective end of the attachment to the previous group. However, immediately after the war, many people returning from overseas made claims for help on families from whom they had been separated for a generation or two, and, weakened as the claims were with the passage of time, help was often grudgingly given.

Hence, a person must remain on good terms with the group from which he originally came, even after he has been placed elsewhere. To burn one's bridges destroys security in case of difficulty in the new group. To some extent the person sent back to his original group is always regarded as a *yakkaimono* (a dependent and a nuisance), but as long as he has maintained good relationships with his group and has performed diligently in the group in which he was placed, every effort will be made to provide him with new opportunities and to give him proper care in the meantime.

To maintain good relationships with one's previous group one must also perform well in one's present group. If a girl goes back to her parental home as a result of marital difficulties, her family wants to know if she has done everything possible to make the marriage a success. To some extent, she is always regarded as responsible for marital difficulties, but if the evidence shows she really tried her best, the family and go-betweens will make every effort to find her a new opportunity. Hence, she wants to have her family's approval when she first marries so they will share the responsibility in case of difficulty. Furthermore, she keeps her family informed of the problems to make sure they will be willing to help her in an emergency. Ordinarily, she will not consider divorce or separation unless she has her family's support or at least some assurance that they will help out. Hence, even to leave her present group requires evidence that she has done everything possible to make it a success. The same is true for the young man in relation to his place of employment.

A good relationship with one's sponsors can also be a help in improving one's present situation. Even in the so-called "paternalistic" small shops and plants many employers have exploited the workers. But if the worker had been placed by an influential go-between or if the family of the worker had power and influence, he could rely upon their intervention to improve conditions. Similarly, if a girl were mistreated in marriage, her original family and go-between could bring pressure to bear to insure better treatment. The large firm or government office offers such good working conditions and job security that there is little likelihood that an employee will have to call on the family for assistance, but his original family remains his secondary security system. For the man employed in a small firm the possibility of returning to his original group remains an important consideration, as it does for a girl in her marriage.

The group control over mobility and the mechanism of returning to one's previous group in case of difficulties has contributed to the stability of the social order not only because the movement itself is orderly, but because it has reinforced the power of the group in controlling its members. It insures that a group will neither be ruined nor drastically altered by unexpected departures, and the system of returning through channels insures that a person who has failed in work or marriage may still be integrated into a tightly-knit group.

Group Control of Alienation and Change

At least until very recently, the basic cleavages in Japanese society have not been between the different social strata within a given group but between one group and another. The relationships among group members have generally been sufficiently close and humane, and the possibilities for the lower strata to shift their allegiance to another group have been so limited, that class solidarity going beyond a given group has been relatively weak. The cleavages within the rural village generally have been between one kin group and another or between two prominent families with their respective followers or between several landlords with their respective tenants. In intervillage relationships, instead of poor people in one village uniting with poor people of another village, all residents of one village have generally united to compete with other villages. Workers in a company have a strong attachment to their firm, and even today unions which link workers across company lines are weak.[7] It is precisely this pattern that has led so many Japanese social scientists to criticize their own society as feudalistic. But this feudalistic loyalty has also functioned to prevent cleavages between social classes and between age groups. Even those who complain about elders or upper class generally remain loyal to their own superiors.

Ordinarily Japanese have not been motivated to change their status radically but to rise within the confines of certain groups or through arrangements made by other members of their group.[8] People ordinarily have not seriously considered giving up their way of life for another. Merchants, for example, have not aspired to give up business for another way of life, nor have artisans aspired to give up their crafts.[9] Even though within the last decade large numbers of farmers have turned over the farming to their wives and children while they work in nearby factories or shops, a family with a plot of land rarely expects to leave the farm.

Although Japanese have not been motivated to effect a radical change in their personal status, they have been very much motivated to effect changes within their group. They have been willing and eager to take on new techniques and develop new organizational

[7] Solomon B. Levine, *Industrial Relations in Postwar Japan*, Urbana, Ill.: University of Illinois Press, 1958.

[8] In comparing work that Herbert Hyman did in the United States with Japanese data, Baker finds that even today lower-class Japanese are less likely to have as high aspirations in their society as lower-class Americans do in their society. Wendell Dean Baker, *A Study of Selected Aspects of Japanese Social Stratification*, doctoral dissertation, Columbia University, 1956.

[9] Marion Levy has compared these factors in Japanese development with the different situation in China. "Contrasting Factors in the Modernization of China and Japan," *Economic Development and Cultural Change*, 1954, 2:161–197.

practices which would improve their group's position relative to other groups. Many of the early pressures for modernization and rationalization came from members of an *ie* or of a firm who were trying to improve their competitive position.[10]

For the same reason, groups also desired to take in competent employees. A business family which was to adopt a son or son-in-law regarded the competence of the young man to carry on the business as one of the most important considerations for selection. Because the owner of the small enterprise expected to be in business indefinitely and was concerned with the future of the enterprise, he was ordinarily willing to take in able young people, provide them with training, and give them opportunities to use their talent. In any field the able employee was a recognizable asset and was treated accordingly.

The paternalistic link between a tenant and the landlord or the worker and his employer have generally contained the alienation of the worker.[11] Even after World War I when many tenants and employees were beginning to have a sense of alienation against their superiors,[12] much of it was expressed simply in the form of protesting for better conditions within a given organization. Just when alienation was becoming most severe, the seriousness of the disputes was minimized by the spirit of virulent nationalism which served to unite worker and capitalist in the same effort. Later radical societal changes, especially in the rural areas, were kept in bounds by the control of the Allied Occupation.

As a result of the willingness of groups to make changes in the interest of the group, the containment of alienation by paternalistic patterns and later by nationalistic sentiments, and the introduction of major changes under tight organizational control, it has been possible to have major changes in the society without destroying the power of the local groups. The rural community and the urban business enterprise have remained sufficiently strong to absorb the changes and keep them within bounds. However painful the process

---

[10] This point has been developed in some detail in an as yet unpublished manuscript by Kazuo Noda.

[11] Cf. John C. Pelzel, *Social Stratification in Japanese Urban Economic Life*, doctoral dissertation, Harvard University, 1949.

[12] Cf. George O. Totten, "Labor and Agrarian Disputes in Japan Following World War I," *Economic Development and Cultural Change*, 1960, 9:187–212.

of change within groups, massive disorganization and anomie have not developed. Changes have been mediated by group consensus so that the basic social units have remained relatively solid in a time of radical changes in internal organization.

Child-Rearing, Personality, and Values

Child-rearing and certain characteristics of personality structure have lent support to the orderly process of change. The child-training techniques make the individual dependent on the group. Even in modern urban society, the concept of expelling a member from a family (*kandoo suru*) or from a village (*mura hachibu*) continue to evoke strong sentiments, and members are motivated to remain in good standing in their own group. The individual is typically group-dependent and is cautious in departing from the wishes of the group; even in moving to a new group he prefers the formality of *o-zen date* (literally, that the table be all set), whereby all arrangements are made previously and he is invited to move in. The value system which stresses the individual's loyalty to the group has given full support to the fundamental allegiance of the individual to the group and has tended to reinforce the ability of groups to control the process of change.

THE NATURE OF THE NEW ORDER

Until recently, social order within a group was maintained primarily by the paternalistic relationship between employer and employee, sponsor and sponsored, benefactor and recipient. With rapid social change and the concentration of power in large organizations, these small units are no longer capable of controlling the rewards and providing the security they once did. Although this pattern of relationship continues to provide some order in the local community, in the urban area it has receded in importance and is being replaced by a new pattern centering on the large organization.

The new order, made possible by the large bureaucratic organization, is most striking among the new middle class. Because of its size, the large organization has had to develop standardized methods of recruitment, salary, promotion, and distribution of auxiliary benefits to the workers. This new order has been subject to rationalizing processes which have made it radically different from the old paternalistic order. The section chief in the large organization has none of the independence in imposing arbitrary patterns upon his underlings that the old middle-class boss had in his narrow social microcosm.

Yet the rationalizing process in large Japanese enterprises has not resulted in the same patterns of social organization that one finds, for example, in the United States. The basic mode of integration of the man into the economic order is not through his occupational specialty, but through his firm. His commitment to the firm is ordinarily more basic and longer lasting than to any occupational specialty. The individual's security and his sense of identity derive from membership in a particular firm or government bureau. If a man is asked what work he does, he is likely to reply not by giving his occupation but by giving the name of his firm. Within the firm, an individual will be given the necessary training or retraining that the firm considers to its best interests. Employees are not committed to any occupational procedures which would interfere with the practices of the firm, and the firm is able to change them to new positions and provide new training as new technological and organizational procedures require. Just as in the United States men often remain in the same organization, so in Japan people often remain in the same occupational specialization, but, in a conflict, in Japan the deeper commitment is to the firm or government bureau.

The rationality of the Japanese firm derives not so much from specific set procedures and social roles as from the subordination of all to the goals of the group. The members of the firm are highly motivated to take any steps for the group to achieve its goals.[13] The firm cannot ordinarily discharge members for inefficiency and must occasionally make decisions on the basis of personal rather than technical considerations, and considerable energy must be expended in keeping members happy and soothing tensions. Yet the entrance examinations insure that employees have at least a minimum level of competence, the informal system within the firm provides a flexibility for the person of ability to affect policy and its imple-

---

[13] Takeshi Ishida has cogently argued that Japanese rationality is a rationality of means rather than ends and that a group's ends are ordinarily never brought into serious question. Takeshi Ishida, "The Pattern of Japanese Political Modernization." Paper presented to the Association for Asian Studies, March 1963.

mentation regardless of his position, and the firm is not troubled by the problems of heavy labor turnover. Low mobility between firms makes the process of introducing changes from outside somewhat more difficult, but it permits a higher degree of integration of changes in the firm. Furthermore, the early retirement age means that new blood will be entering the company rapidly and that control passes more quickly to younger people who are less influenced by traditional practices. How long the low mobility between firms and the primary commitment to the firm rather than to occupational specialty will continue is an open question. While these practices are being challenged in areas of labor shortage or where a high degree of technical skill is required, they remain firmly institutionalized for most salary men.

The life of the modern Japanese family with a husband in the new bureaucratic organization has changed greatly from Japanese family life of an earlier era but it remains different from the common patterns in the United States and many European countries. The unique features of the salary-man family discussed in the body of this work (the insulation of the family from the firm, the lack of participation of husbands in household tasks, the narrow range of the wife's social participation and her very close relationship with the children) show no signs of radical change.

The salary man has not surmounted all difficulties. The room for independent free movement apart from the wishes of the group is considerably less than in most Western countries, the amount a person must give up to group unity much greater, and the amount of group solidarity required to maintain such sacrifices much greater than the solidarity existing in most Western organizations. Many salary men whose ambitions are frustrated within the firm or who are not accepted by the dominant company cliques are likely to develop a sense of apathy and may complain bitterly to friends or identify with the unfortunate self-sacrificing heroes in movies, novels, and short stories.[14] Despite these frustrations, however, the salary man is basically pleased with his way of life. Although the salary man's wife may feel that she sacrifices herself and has a more

---

[14] Professor Howard Hibbett informs me that the themes of modern novels, stories, and movies are filled with such unfortunate situations, and that the life of the salary men portrayed in fictional form is filled with frustrations.

difficult life than her husband, the world outside her own narrow sphere is so stiff and the inside of her world so relaxed and so subject to her control, that she prefers to stay at home cultivating the wifely arts and caring for the children.

THE DIFFUSION OF THE NEW ORDER

The contrasts between the salary man and other groups in Japan have been drawn sharply in this study in order to highlight the pattern of the salary man. The contrasts may have been drawn overly sharp because there is considerable variation among salary men, and even more because the patterns described have already spread beyond the confines of the group of the salary men.

With the managerial revolution, most of the Japanese elite have now been incorporated into large organizations, and their pattern of life has become essentially that of high-level salary men.[15] The great industrial, business, and political leaders increasingly arise from the ranks of the large organizations. They are not placed in high position merely by having influential family and friends. Even the "well born" who rise to high positions have been subjected to competition with boys of lower standing, especially during the period of entrance examinations.[16] They follow the same pattern of regular hours, regular pay, regular vacation. Although they have higher standards of consumption and participate more actively in political and community life than the average salary man, they do not have the independence in action that the independent entrepreneur had. Their activities, like those of lower-level salary men, are subject to their groups' consensus about the interests of the firm.

With the proletarization of industrial workers into large organization, their lives have become increasingly similar to those of salary men. Their salaries are much higher than those of industrial workers

---

[15] In his work on Japanese executives, Kazuo Noda has called these men "super salary men." Cf. Kazuo Noda, *Nihon no Juuyaku* (Big Business Executives). Tokyo: Diamond Sha, 1960.

[16] Although a much higher percentage of Japanese elite come from families of higher social status than would be expected on the basis of statistical probability, university training (which depends on success in entrance examinations) is even more crucial for entrance into the elite than in the United States. Cf. Hiroshi Mannari, "Nihon no Keieisha no Shakai-teki Seikaku" (The Social Characteristics of Japanese Business Leaders), *Shakaigaku Hyooron*, 1961, 12:7–19.

in smaller enterprises, and, in contrast to what one might have expected from Marxian theory, there is not only little revolutionary spirit among such workers, but there is a very high degree of satisfaction of being able to work in their present organization.[17] In their consumption patterns, in their political attitudes, in the patterning of leisure time and work time, they are similar to the lower-level salary men, and even their salaries are not too different.[18] The regularity of salary and the rationalization of various procedures within the firm have had the same effects on the factory worker as they had on the salary man.

Finally, because the pattern of the salary man has achieved such prominence and because it has become a symbol of the desirable life, it has an important effect even on those who are not part of large organizations. The way of life of the salary man dominates the mass media, the popular stories, the "how to" books. The advertising and the standard package for the consumer are probably geared more to the level of the salary man than to any other group. The educational system is dominated by the spirit of the salary man, and anyone who hopes to advance beyond the junior-high-school level must take entrance examinations whose tone is set by those who aspire to be salary men. The independence of the salary-man's wife from the cares of earning a living and her opportunity to devote herself to her children without the interference of a mother-in-law are becoming a powerful model for wives of farmers and small shopkeepers. Small business associations have been clamoring for government help so they could provide the same welfare benefits provided by the larger organizations. Many rural co-operatives and mutual-benefit organizations of professionals attempt to provide a salary-man kind of security to their members. In some rural communities, farmers now turn over their income to the co-operative,

---

[17] Survey data on this problem are presented by Kenichi Tominaga, "Nihon no Keiei to Nihon no Shakai" (Industrial Organization and Social Structure in Japan), *Shakaigaku Hyooron*, 1961, 12:30–45.

[18] Survey data on this problem are presented by the Group for the Study of Japanese Social Structure (Nihon Shakai Koozoo Choosa Kai), in *Howaito Karaa no Ishiki Koozoo* (The Structure of White-Collar Ideology), Tokyo: March 1962. In analyzing their questionnaire data, these authors also note the striking similarity between lower-level salary men and workers in large factories.

draw it out in the form of "sarari" (salary) and proudly claim that they are just like salary men.[19] As in Western countries, the powerful influence of the middle class does not mean that society will be completely homogenized and that individual and group differences will disappear. It does mean that the new order of the salary man is not only a way of life for people in large organizations, but a model affecting the life of others. For the rest of society the salary man mediates the direct impact of Westernization and industrialization by offering a model of life which is modest enough to be within the range of realistic hopes and modern enough to be worthy of their highest aspirations.

---

[19] For this information I am indebted to Dr. David Plath, an anthropologist who did his field work in Nagano prefecture.

Part Five

MAMACHI REVISITED

Chapter XIV

A New Confidence in Old Mamachi

In 1969, ten years after our initial study, my wife and I returned to Mamachi. Unlike many suburban areas studded with new stores and recreation centers, Mamachi remains much as it was. During the same ten years entirely new suburbs have been created further from the center of Tokyo and many downtown areas of Tokyo have been completely rebuilt; by comparison, the physical appearance of Mamachi, like that of other older suburbs, is relatively unchanged. To be sure, streets are better paved, stores are better built and better stocked, homes have been renovated, and a new school building has replaced the old. Yet the homes, the gardens, the fences, and the little shops in Mamachi all look familiar. Surprisingly, almost all families live where they did a decade ago, and as before, the breadwinners are almost all salary men.

A decade ago the families we saw were eager to learn about America. They were trying to understand all the essentials of private life, business and society in America. They were already imitating many aspects of America, but they were still learning. Today they are still interested in America and Europe, but the eagerness is gone because they have mastered the essential characteristics of life in the West. Ten years ago when Mamachi citizens compared Japan with America it was with uncertainty and it usually ended with a question about America. Now when they make the comparison, they are more sure of themselves. In a sense, ten years ago they were still part-time pupils of the west; now they have not only completed their training with flying colors, but they have finished their apprenticeship also. Where they have kept Japanese customs it is not because they have not yet learned Western patterns, but because they prefer Japanese.

271

The phenomenal economic growth rate, the new material prosperity, and the greater understanding of the West have given Mamachi citizens, like other Japanese, a new sense of pride. A decade ago Mamachi residents were worried about economic stability; there was a sense that daily livelihood was precarious, and they talked of the dangers of a new recession. Now with more money in the bank, more material possessions, and a national consensus that the economic prospects of Japan are, if anything, brighter for the future, anxiety about material welfare has almost disappeared.

SALARY WITHOUT VISIONS

This new confidence has led to a new evaluation of the life of the salary man. Ten years ago, to be employed by a large company was considered highly desirable by most of these families, as well as by most of the other people in Japan. The large companies and government bureaucracies could provide security, regularity, and assurance of advancement with age. At a time when acquiring the new kitchen and electrical machines for the household and insuring an education for the children was problematic and not possible for many families, this security was obviously desirable. The salary man's family could purchase new goods with predictable regularity and without anxiety. Their "bright new life" set a standard which Japanese from other walks of life envied and emulated.

By now all these aspirations for security, material possessions, and regular hours have been realized not only by the salary man, but by most of the population of Japan. The model and the vision that were provided by the salary man a decade ago have been essentially achieved already.

This very success has led the Mamachi citizen to raise new questions about his life, to question assumptions that a decade ago were taken for granted. Why should one sacrifice for the good of the company? Why should one labor so assiduously for so many years at the same place? Are there not other, more interesting things to do? Why should the youth study so hard to be admitted to the good colleges and the the good firms? Are there not other values of greater importance?

Despite the questioning, Mamachi men still work in the large companies or government offices. In fact, the proportion of Japanese citizens who are salary men has actually increased as large companies have grown more rapidly than small ones. They remain salary men, but they wonder if this is still so desirable.

For no one has the new questioning become more acute than among teenagers and young adults. Junior high school students still work hard in preparation for high school entrance examinations, and high school students still work hard in preparation for university examinations, but many students admitted to the university now wonder why they have worked so hard and whether it was worth it. Students preparing for examinations are still very concerned with getting into the better institutions and companies, and those who fail are disappointed. The feelings of ambition and of wanting to do well remain strong, but the anxiety that failure might lead to serious economic hardship is now gone. Students studying for examinations are increasingly reluctant to undergo the excessively long hours of training, and their parents now have more doubts about the necessity or even desirability of pushing their children so hard in preparation for the examinations.

The number of Japanese students actually involved in barricades, occupation of university buildings, and armed clashes with police is only a tiny minority of the total university population, and virtually no Mamachi youths were among these radical activists. Yet they share much of the radical criticism of the universities and feel that the university system is in need of radical reorganization. They object to the fact that their teachers often are not well-informed on their topics and that the lectures are in terms of abstract theories which seem to have little relation to current realities; they object to the fact that their classes are not intellectually challenging and do not prepare them either for the work which they will do later or for the society in which they will live; they find that many programs on television and many current magazines are more informative and more interesting than their classrooms, and they do not feel involvement or identification with the universities they attend.

Universities in turmoil created an additional hurdle for the youth. The student and his family had to decide what to do when the uni-

versities closed down for a few months or a year, and the youth selecting a university had to make some estimate of whether a given
institution will be open during the next several years. The problem
of the universities thus exacerbated the problem of youth confronted
with the basic questions of where to work and what kind of life to
lead.

Most of these teenagers and young adults continue to live at home
while attending the university. Since family life remains stable it
provides a haven for the perplexed teenager. But parents cannot always understand the adolescent in turmoil. Even parents who are
close to their children cannot answer the basic questions about what
kind of work the children should do and what kind of life they should
lead because they, too, are uncertain about what is desirable in the
future.

Many young men in Mamachi now specifically say that they do
not want to become salary men. They hope for a more interesting
and challenging life—perhaps one connected to the literary or artistic world—one that provides more challenge and excitement. Although new possibilities are opening up in these new fields, the
economic structure of the society is such that most young men will
eventually become salary men and most of the young girls will eventually become wives of salary men. In most cases their search for
more interesting lives leads not to a different kind of job: at best it
leads to the pursuit of new interests outside the job.

The transition from university life, where talk of adventure is big
and restraint on personal freedom small, to highly disciplined company life is difficult. Yet even those youths who have weathered the
stormy transition accept company discipline almost immediately.
They are much more reluctant than are their American counterparts
to raise basic questions or criticize their superiors in their firms. The
reservations they have about accepting this new and, in their view,
mundane life are reserved for their private thoughts, their families,
and their closest friends.

In contrast to the young man in the first few years with his company—who complains in private that he is given few responsibilities,
that the work is boring, and that he must subordinate himself to a
horribly disciplined life,—the young salary man in his late twenties

or early thirties has a distinctly different attitude. He has already begun to share the excitement of the company life. The sense of solidarity within the company, the vitality of most Japanese companies, which are growing at an astonishing rate, and the young man's participation in the meaningful responsibilities of a new family mollify his desires for new adventure. Questions about the desirability of this kind of work do not disappear, but most of the young married couples in their late twenties and early thirties have accepted their fate in life. The adjustments they make in finding or creating more interesting activities do not disrupt the framework of their company, their community, and their family.

The attitudes toward work and life of a particular salary man are bound closely to his work position. If he is in a small company, or an unsuccessful company, then he may be looking for opportunities to change to a better situation. If he is in a large company but has an unsympathetic superior, if he has been passed over in promotions or assigned to relatively uninteresting work, or if his prospects within the company are not very bright, he is likely to be acutely frustrated. But the young man with a promising future who moves into positions of responsibility feels an excitement and devotion to his work that is comparable to older high-level executives in the United States.

No new, clear vision has emerged to compare with the clarity of the vision of the salary man of a decade ago. To the extent that there is a new vision, it is a many-sided vision which centers on leading a richer fuller life. Some are taking to new hobbies and spending more time in recreation; some watch television or read or travel more; some men spend more time with their families; some are busy planning to remodel their homes or to purchase a new car. But none of these goals provides the sense of purpose or requires the discipline that was required only a decade ago to become and remain a salary man.

APPROACHING AFFLUENCE

The unprecedented economic growth in Japan brought new prosperity to Mamachi. Men wear neatly-pressed dark suits of materials that compare favorably with those in middle-class America. Women dress in accord with world fashion. Many families have new cars.

Most families have made major home repairs, and many have torn down their old homes and put up new ones on the same site. The homes are now equipped with modern electric equipment and kitchens which resemble those in middle-class America. Many of the homes have new Western-style living rooms, and, not uncommonly, traditional tatami mats have been replaced by carpets.

With this progress the excitement about acquiring new material belongings has begun to fade, but it has by no means ended. Families that a few years ago were acquiring their first refrigerator or washing machine are now planning to buy their first color television, or to add on a new room, or to lay wall-to-wall carpets. Those who lack cars are likely to be planning to buy one, and those who have cars are likely to be thinking of a new one. The chance to acquire all these new objects is still sufficiently fresh that these families are not as indifferent to new purchases as are their counterparts in America.

A decade ago families made a sharp distinction between what they showed to the outside (the *omote*) and what they kept to themselves (the *ura*.) The part of the house they showed to guests, the clothes they wore outside, and the food they served others were very different from what they had for themselves alone. They were extremely generous before others but penurious with regard to their own daily material belongings and to financial affairs within the home. The distinction between omote and ura has not disappeared, but the omote area has greatly expanded with the rise in material wealth, and the proportion of life and belongings which the family would be reluctant to show visitors has greatly declined. Families still eat plainer food for their daily meals than they would eat outside, and they still have poor material belongings which they are reluctant to show to others. The area of the ura has decreased, however, and even the distinction itself is less important than when frugality was essential for making ends meet.

It is a testimony to the rise in expectations that families are so seriously concerned about the rise in prices. Although salaries have risen more rapidly than prices, expectations have risen still more rapidly, so there is often frustration at being unable to buy more than actually can be purchased. Because desires have risen so rapidly and money does not go far enough, some husbands still complain bitterly that their wives do not give them enough allowance for daily spending money, while wives complain that their husbands spend too much and do not leave enough for them to use for the home and the children.

The advent of the car has greatly increased family travel, making it even more common than the company outing. The increase in seashore resorts in the last several years has, in a short space of time, given rise to summer activity at the seashore comparable to that in the United States, except that crowding is more severe. But even with greater income and security there is still a feeling that one should not lock up one's home for more than a day or so. Families are reluctant to take trips for more than two or three days at a time, especially if no one is left to look after the home. Individual family members may take longer trips to see relatives or to visit friends or see some new scenery, but family trips are generally very brief. Still, an increasing number of Mamachi families have by now been able to send one or more members abroad to Hawaii, Hong Kong, Taiwan, or elsewhere on vacations. Many others in Mamachi are beginning to think of their first trip abroad. While approaching affluence, Mamachi dwellers have not yet arrived, and there are still many things they look forward to acquiring or doing for the first time.

THE GROWTH OF NATIONAL PRIDE

Fantastically rapid economic recovery has led to a new view of Japan and the world. Twenty-five years ago, amidst defeat and food shortages, Japanese had a sense of inferiority to the modern West. Even a decade ago they felt that Japan as a whole was less advanced than Western European countries in its general standard of living. Since Japan has now passed all countries except Russia and the United States in gross national product, and since its rate of economic growth is clearly much faster than any other country in the world, Japan's position in the world is undergoing a new appraisal. The fact that the American government has to make special appeals to the Japanese government to overcome its unfavorable balance of trade helps reduce the vestiges of inferiority which some still feel toward the United States. The fact that the Japanese have been able to achieve all this despite poor natural resources, a very small geographical area, and the devastation of World War II gives them a feeling of enormous vigor and achievement. In contrast, the United States looks slightly decadent and soft, and American cities look run-down. The internal dissensions in the United States because of race and Vietnam give the Japanese a feeling that they are fortunately spared some of America's debilities.

The citizens of Mamachi are not more nationalistic than a decade ago, but they are prouder. They feel an intensely close identification with Japan on the international scene, and they repeat what they have heard on television or read in the popular press about the relative competitive position of Japan on the world economic scene or the world sports scene. Their sense of international competition in sports reached a peak at the time of the Olympics in Japan, but it was revived for Expo 1970. Their identification with Japan's international status is concentrated on peaceful competition—Japan's standing in international sports meets, Nobel prizes, international musicians, productivity, and standard of living. In contrast to Americans, they are not preoccupied with national security; they deem it highly unlikely that any nation will attack Japan.

A new sense of confidence and the new perspective about Japan's position in the world at times promotes vaulting ambitions. People talk of surpassing Russia in gross national product within a decade and of surpassing America in the average standard of living before the end of the 1980's. Indeed these are the conclusions which follow if one projects into the future present economic growth levels of various countries.

This new perspective on the position of Japan in the world has given rise to a desire to correct those situations in which Japan is perceived and treated as a junior partner. American bases in Japan still symbolize American occupation and Japanese subordination to America, and most Mamachi residents would like to see these removed. The return of Okinawa by America and of the northern islands by Russia seem to be natural reflections of Japan's new, increased power. A commitment to peace and a feeling against rearmament remain very strong, but the Japanese expect Russia, America and the other nuclear powers to make concessions about Japanese possession of nuclear weapons—and perhaps about the destruction of many nuclear weapons if Japan were to completely forego them.

Although they are proud of their domestic productivity, they feel that the level of Japanese investment and ownership abroad is not in keeping with Japan's new economic power, and most citizens consider it natural to invest more heavily abroad. However, the residents of Mamachi are overwhelmingly opposed to Japanese involvement in political and military disputes abroad like the one that has recently entangled the United States in Southeast Asia. They do not feel a responsibility for keeping order and promoting development abroad; indeed they consider it beyond their capacity.

For all the enormous progress that Japan has made in the last few years, the residents of Mamachi have a very low opinion of Japanese political leaders. They remain cynical and skeptical of their own leaders, and they have no political heroes. The elected leaders of the Liberal Democratic Party are accepted with resignation, for Mamachi residents are no more hopeful that Socialist or Komeito leaders would deal effectively with national problems. But the officials are seen as politicians, not statesmen, and none of them has become a living symbol of the new Japan.

In their own community Mamachi residents are becoming freer in expressing their political attitudes. Local housewives are more willing to complain about public nuisances or to call to the attention of the local officials the inadequacies of neighborhood public facilities. Some are willing to join support clubs for local politicians, but even then their perspective is more that of a practical citizen interested in certain goals, than one spell-bound by the idealism and the talent of the local leader.

"MY HOME-ISM:" OLD WINE IN NEW BOTTLES

A new concept, "my home-ism" (*mai homu-shugi*) is the current fad for describing the widespread commitment to family life. In some cases, husbands who are no longer thrilled by the excitement of company life devote themselves more to their families. However, "my home-ism" is essentially a new concept for what has existed for a long time. Family life is much the same as it was a decade ago; even the close relationship with grandparents and the frequency of young married couples visiting their parents has not greatly declined. It is not uncommon for a young wife to return to her mother's home to recuperate after having given birth to a baby. It is not uncommon for a young married couple to live with or near their parents. Even if the old kotatsu, the old family hearth in the middle of the floor, has been replaced by a new gas stove, the sense of the warm family circle joining together in discussion remains much the same.

The increased material comforts make homelife easier and relieve the wife of some of the greatest drudgeries, thus giving her greater freedom to pursue hobbies, social visiting, or other interests of her own. Children acquire more freedom earlier and parents, convinced that they need to adjust to the greater freedom and the higher standard of living demanded by their children, are reluctant to oppose the children's desire for more independent activities and more travel. Still, high-school-aged Mamachi youth are much more protected than their American counterparts, and dating and marriage occur at correspondingly later ages.

Just as traditional samurai compared their competing loyalties to their lords and their families, present-day salary men sometimes joke about their mixed loyalties to their companies and to their families. If he were transferred to an out-of-the-way city, and the family refused to go, for example, would the man give up the company or the family? If a company trip and a family trip occur on the same day, which one will a man choose? In general, however, the husband keeps up with both. He still goes out with the company gang after work and occasionally goes on company trips. But he also spends a moderate amount of time, especially on weekends, with his family. Although the wife may join the husband with another young couple from the firm for occasional outings, as a whole, the family life still remains sharply separated from the life of the company. In some families the husband has become a full participant in the warm family circle, but in most he does not share all the intimacies of the wife and the children.

It is too early to predict what will result from the increased questioning of the salary man's way of life and the search for new patterns which bring greater personal satisfaction. The dynamism, the vitality, and the sensitivity to national and international trends make it impossible to predict whether frustrations will become more acute. However, despite the serious disruptions in late adolescence and early adulthood, despite the problems with public nuisances and the re-evaluation which is taking place, most people in Mamachi still have a strong sense of purposiveness and public discipline. The purposiveness which underlies the questions and doubts comes not from ideology, and not even from the material prosperity, but from close ties in the most fundamental groups: family and place of work. Despite the more rapid changes of the last decade, and despite the search for a richer life beyond salary, these social bonds still provide a framework of meaning for those who live in Mamachi.

APPENDIX

Appendix

A REPORT ON THE FIELD WORK

At the outset of the field work my wife and I were interested in the middle-class family, but not particularly in the salary man. Our interest in the salary-man family emerged gradually during the field work and analysis of data as we were struck by its uniqueness and importance in modern Japan. We had originally gone to Japan to get information on middle-class Japanese families to compare with the results of a study of Irish-American, Italo-American, and old-American families, in which I had participated.[1] Our research problem had two parts: (1) the determination of Japanese family patterns to contrast with these other ethnic groups; (2) the contrast between families of emotionally disturbed and "normal" children. It is the first problem which is reported in the present work. In order to make our research design comparable to the earlier study we decided to find six families with an emotionally disturbed child and six families with "normal" children,[2] and to see these families intensively, at least once a week for a year or more. Furthermore, we hoped to be participant-observers in middle-class Japanese life and

---

[1] This study was under the direction of Dr. John Spiegel and Dr. Florence Kluckhohn of the Department of Social Relations, Harvard. Among the research reports are: John P. Spiegel, "The Resolution of Role Conflict Within the Family," *Psychiatry*, 1957, 20:1–16; Florence Kluckhohn, "Family Diagnosis: Variations in the Basic Values of Family Systems," *Social Casework*, 1958, 39:1–11; Ezra F. Vogel, "The Marital Relationship of Parents of Emotionally Disturbed Children: Polarization and Isolation," *Psychiatry*, 1960, 23:1–12; Ezra F. Vogel and Norman W. Bell, "The Emotionally Disturbed Child as a Family Scapegoat," *Psychoanalysis and the Psychoanalytic Review*, 1960, 47:21–42.

[2] An emotionally disturbed child was defined as one sufficiently ill to be judged as needing treatment by clinicians at the Japanese National Institute of Mental Health. "Normal" was defined as the absence of any pathology obvious enough to be judged worthy of psychiatric treatment by the family, school, and clinical psychologists who administered the projective tests.

to familiarize ourselves with relevant research by Japanese scholars.

Our approach to field work was a result of our graduate training in sociological and psychoanalytic theory, our experience doing clinical and home interviewing under psychiatric supervision, and our participation in interdisciplinary projects. My wife had worked for several years as a psychiatric social worker and had done home interviewing as part of an interdisciplinary research project. I also had had experience in clinical work with psychiatric patients and with parents of psychiatric patients. Consequently our approach to anthropological field work was heavily influenced by an interest in subtleties of relationships which comes from intensive personal contacts.

In Japan, we tried as much as possible to develop close relationships with people in our community. We lived in Japanese-style homes in Japanese neighborhoods in which we were the only foreigners. To have intimate contacts with the Japanese we felt it essential to conduct our work in Japanese. We had some language-training before going to Japan, and most of our first year there was spent in intensive language study. We had developed contacts in Mamachi during this first year and made a number of visits there before moving to Mamachi in June, 1959, where we then lived as participant-observants for slightly more than one year. We conducted our field work in Japanese from the beginning, regardless of communication problems. However, we tape-recorded many interviews in order to go over the material later with Japanese assistants to insure accurate understanding. Even when our command of Japanese was elementary, most people made an effort to talk in simple Japanese and to elaborate when we did not understand. Although the process was sometimes time-consuming, it is our feeling that much was communicated even when our language ability was minimal. Language difficulties made it difficult for us to catch subtleties of meaning, but it also caused us to be more sensitive to nuances of facial expressions, gestures, and tone of voice. When studying taped interviews with assistants we learned we had frequently misunderstood words and phrases, or at times even entire sentences, but we rarely had misunderstood a person's feelings or the general import of the conversation.

From the beginning, we presented ourselves to Mamachi residents as social scientists. But in our own minds our model was not the detached scientist who keeps his feelings out of his work. We felt we could learn more by participating in the life of the local community than by trying to remain aloof. We defined ourselves as foreigners interested in forming friendships and learning about Japanese life. To the extent that we retained scientific detachment, it was not in restricting our participation but in later analyzing the nature of this participation and what it meant for an understanding of the studied families.

Some fellow American social scientists have asked us how we can be certain our informants told us "the truth." I would prefer to phrase the question not "Did they tell us the truth?" but "What truth did they tell?" For example, when I asked one man why he moved to his present residence, he explained it was convenient to his office and nearby relatives. His wife told my wife confidentially that they moved because a fortune teller had told them that their old home was facing the wrong direction and might bring them bad luck. Some people might call the husband's answer a cover-up. I prefer to interpret it as one part of the truth, a reflection of genuine embarrassment about believing a superstition and a desire to be modern and scientific, especially when talking with a representative of the modern West.

We had expected that questions about sex or personal finance would meet with the greatest resistance, but these topics seemed easier for the Japanese to discuss than their superstitions or information which might adversely reflect on their status in the community. When we asked questions about folk beliefs and superstitions, most denied any interest and said they no longer believed or practiced superstitions. It was only by observations of shrines, ceremonies, and by chance remarks that we were able to find some of this information. For example, when I inquired what was around a boy's neck, the mother looked embarrassed and replied that it was an amulet for luck. She spontaneously continued by explaining that it was only a toy and that they did not really believe it brought good luck. Her embarrassment and apologetic tone, as well as the man's failure to acknowledge the family's going to a fortune teller, convinced us that superstition is more widespread than people verbally indicated. However, what is considered folk belief varies from country

to country, and just as some Western practices would seem superstitious to Japanese, so they talked freely about some practices that
appeared to us as folk beliefs. For example, they believe that a number of diseases can be helped by hot springs, and medical specialists
advise wearing a *haramaki* (special cloths to cover the stomach) at
night even in the hottest weather to avoid *nebie* (a cold caught
while sleeping).[3] However, we are not in any position to give a
quantitative estimate of the extent of superstition except to say that
it is more common than people report.

Similarly with regard to matters which might adversely affect a
family's community reputation, we suspect that a number of things
were not fully reported. No family told of any relative who had
been involved in any kind of crime, but many told of rich and
famous relatives. Even the few cases of marital problems and divorce we heard about from normal families were usually told only
after we had developed a close relationship. Several families were
reluctant to tell us about their ancestors, and while this may reflect
a conviction that the past should not be considered important, it is
our feeling from other incidental information that these families
were not proud of their background. Hence, without making independent investigations about their relatives, which would have been
extremely time-consuming, we do not feel we can talk with confidence about certain aspects of their backgrounds or to discard the
possibility that some relatives might have more problems and less
fame than we heard about.

On the whole, however, we felt that Mamachi residents were as
willing to talk about their lives as Americans we had previously
interviewed. Americans were also reluctant to talk about their own
violations of law or of mental illness in the family. However, the
areas of sensitivity were slightly different. Although the Americans
felt sufficiently removed from peculiar relatives to talk of them in a
completely detached way, the Mamachi residents felt closely identified with relatives and were therefore ashamed of any misconduct.
American sensitivities centered on the invasion of privacy (especially sex and family finance) which was not the object of particular

---

[3] Many Americans similarly believe that feet are unusually sensitive to cold, but
this would appear as folk belief to Mamachi residents who go barefoot at home even
in very cold homes in winter without catching cold.

sensitivities in Mamachi once a relationship of trust had been established.

There is no simple answer to the question of "What truth?" because it depended on context and situation. To be sure, we watched for the standard clinical clues, the slips of the tongue, the spontaneous expressions of feeling, the latent meanings in the association of one idea with another. In addition to this, we felt it important to see the persons in a variety of situations.

Most people behaved differently when seen by a man than by a woman; they behaved differently when a third person was present than when interviewed alone; they behaved differently in different groups; they behaved differently when first introduced than after further acquaintance. But people we met for the first time early in our stay behaved differently on that meeting from people we met for the first time later during our stay when we knew better how to behave and could relax and talk with them more freely. People behaved differently in formal and in informal situations. Men behaved differently when drinking, when at home, and when in their office. Children behaved differently at home and at school.

We saw people privately and in groups, in their homes and ours. My wife visited tea-ceremony and flower-arrangement groups and attended meetings for mothers of nursery-school children. I saw men in their offices as well as in their homes. We visited the schools, greeted people in the streets. We attended formal parties on special occasions. We saw people when their children were present and when they were absent, and at different hours of the day.

Many of the opportunities to see people in a variety of circumstances was provided by our very intensive contact with the six well families who had specifically agreed to have us visit at least once a week for more than a year. It is perhaps characteristic of Japanese society that we were introduced to these families by the local grade-school principal, who was introduced to us through an acquaintance of a friend of ours. The wives in the six families formed a little club for such varied purposes as discussing problems of coping with us, giving us parties, learning Western cooking from my wife, and teaching her how to cook Japanese delicacies in return. This group of six ladies, which calls itself the "Vogelkai" (the Vogel club), has had several meetings since our return to the United States.

But in addition to these families whom we saw on a regular formal basis, we had numerous contacts with many families through our neighborhood, the local school, shopping, places of work, and friends and relatives of people we met in these places.

It is our feeling that an accurate picture of Japanese life comes not through any sudden or semimagical penetration into their inner secrets but through the patient accumulation of observations in a wide variety of situations. Of course, in interviewing, getting a straight forward account of the informant's experiences is essential, and it is our impression that this is most likely to come from a relationship with the informant based on mutual trust. In any conflict between information-gathering and the development of a good relationship, we gave priority to the development of the latter. If a person seemed reluctant to talk on a subject, we did not press him. If someone wanted us not to see them at a certain time or did not show us certain parts of their house, we did not insist, nor did we attempt tricks or pressure to see what we might not otherwise be shown. We raised questions and expressed an interest in seeing or hearing about virtually everything and tried by winning their confidence to overcome their reluctance to tell us or show us something. It is our conviction that this basic trust was repaid in the long run by a willingness to relate their feelings freely and honestly. We tried to show by our actions as well as our words that we were deserving of their trust. Early in our research we said that information would be treated confidentially, but this was less convincing than our refusal to pass on gossip when asked questions about other families.

In general, we felt that we received more reliable information when people discussed concrete instances than when they answered on a general level. Hence, in our questions and in our responses to their comments, we indicated an interest in their concrete experiences. Most people responded to our interest in them, and many even seemed to enjoy and look forward to having someone listen to their problems. This kind of relationship also required our willingness to tell about ourselves, and often people responded to our self-revelations with spontaneous revelations about themselves.

At first we underestimated their interest in us, not as social scientists, but as Americans. The first time we entertained friends in

Mamachi we were anxious to show how completely we were living Japanese style; only toward the end of the visit did it become clear to us that they had been disappointed not to have a chance to see what an American home was really like. Some of the clearest expressions of their attitudes came from their questions or expressions of surprise about our American habits.

As a whole, we feel we were successful in establishing close personal relationships with Mamachi families and in receiving an opportunity to observe their lives. The fact that we were foreigners trying to understand their culture made it natural for them to explain to us how they did things, what they believed, and what their family and community was like. Some even said they felt freer in talking to us than to their friends and neighbors since we would never be involved in community gossip and evaluation. Some were reluctant to explain the mundane common experiences of their lives, apparently thinking it not worthy of "research" by an American associated with Harvard University—a university with high prestige among educated residents of Mamachi. We feel, however, that we were able to overcome this resistance by our obvious interest in ordinary details. However, the process of developing close relationships was more taxing for Mamachi residents and for us than we had anticipated. For one thing the process of mutual understanding that goes beyond surface pleasantries and comes to terms with differences in attitudes and patterns of living requires considerable adjustment. Moreover, Mamachi families were extremely generous in entertaining us and extremely patient in answering our questions. They entertained us more elaborately and with greater expense and trouble than we felt comfortable in receiving. We tried to return their kindness by giving presents, by offering return entertainment, and perhaps most of all by giving English-conversation lessons to their children. For many, it was the first time they had come into direct contact with Americans. Some eagerly sought out our acquaintance, either to practice English conversation, to find out how Americans handle child-rearing or business problems, to find out how a child or relative of theirs might visit America, or just for the exciting experience of getting to see and know some Americans. In almost every group discussion, when an issue arose, someone would turn to us to find out how it would be handled in America.

A few seemed somewhat frightened of us at first and later somewhat relieved that we did not fit their image of Americans, which they had derived from stories of American soldiers in Japan. A few people remained cautious in talking with us, but they were invariably polite in answering our questions. Many found it easier to relate to our three-year-old son, who quickly acquired the Japanese language, than to us, and our son's presence often softened the stiffness of conversation with other adults. Most people were impressed by our seriousness and willingness to learn the Japanese language, but some, not completely comfortable with the thought that we were studying them, were concerned about presenting what they thought was the good side of Japanese life. Most, however, after getting to know us, spontaneously talked of their own lives and asked questions about ours.

We soon found that if we presented our opinions first, they would find some way to agree with us. If we started a question by saying, "We have been impressed that . . . ," they would usually answer in a way that would support our observations. Only the frankest and closest of friends directly corrected our misunderstandings. We soon realized that we should ask questions in such a way that would give them an opportunity to answer in a variety of ways without causing them embarrassment. We also learned, however, that they were very responsive to our definition of the situation. If we were stiff in asking a question, they were usually stiff in answering, but if we were jovial and light, though frank, they tended to respond in the same way.

When we went to Mamachi, we had certain general questions about family life to which we hoped to get answers, but we had no formal questionnaire. In addition to the questions which we were seeking to answer, we determined to be sensitive to clues that would indicate strong feelings about problems that we had not anticipated. The process of drawing generalizations was one of following up observations with detailed questioning about the meaning, context, and extent of the practice. We conducted roughly six hundred hours of scheduled visits in people's homes specifically for the purpose of research. Altogether we accumulated several thousand pages of typed notes based on these interviews. Although we had discussions during these visits, the fact that we were in private homes gave us the opportunity to see a wide variety of situations, many of which arose spontaneously during our visits.

In families of disturbed children, the weekly therapy was conducted by staff members of the National Institute of Mental Health, except for one family where my wife treated the mother. In addition, I conducted one or two lengthy home interviews per family. The well families were visited primarily by my wife and me, but a few brief interviews were conducted by a Japanese assistant; besides, the projective test material was given by Japanese psychologists. Once we had made an observation or learned something of interest, we then followed it up by asking relevant questions of other families with whom we were in contact. The use of intensive interviewing techniques makes it more difficult to count precisely how many people engage in a certain practice, but it makes possible a thorough check on the context and meaning of a practice or attitude when it arises. It does make it necessary to rely on a variety of informants to achieve an estimate of how widespread practices are. On this matter, obviously some people are much abler than others. Many wives, for example, had a very limited range of social contacts and did not prove reliable but some wives with a wide range of contacts and acute sensitivity to others' attitudes were extremely useful for our aim to obtain a picture of the extent to which certain practices are followed. Fortunately, there are many studies based on larger samplings now available in Japan, and it was possible to compare specific items obtained in our work with the results of larger surveys. Although our better informants could not give precise statistics on the extent to which certain practices were observed, on items covered by surveys we were pleased to find a high level of agreement between the results of the surveys and the opinions of our informants.[4]

In addition to questionnaires available from other researchers, we developed some questionnaires of our own to supplement our intensive material on basic information about family relationships and child-rearing practices. Also we used a sentence-completion test,

---

[4] The results of some of these larger sampling surveys are included in the footnotes accompanying the text.

essentially a translation of the one developed by Robert Hess and Gerald Handel.[5] We felt that it would unduly stiffen our relationships with Mamachi friends if we distributed these questions in Mamachi, but we distributed them to about sixty families in each of seven other communities. These communities included one salaryman neighborhood, one small shopkeeper neighborhood, three agricultural villages, one deep-sea fishing village where fathers were away for eleven months a year, and a nearby off-shore fishing village where fathers returned home every day.

I also interviewed a number of expert informants in various cities throughout Japan. For the most part they were either marriage arrangers (who had investigated various family backgrounds, brought together suitable couples, and obtained parental consent for the wedding) or social scientists. We have also had the opportunity, both while in Japan and after returning to the United States, to consult with Japanese and American scholars interested in the Japanese family. Although we have not used this information directly in the writing of our Mamachi material, it has permitted us to correct some mistaken impressions, to see new dimensions in some of the things we observed, and to alert ourselves to the specific context in which we conducted our interviewing. In general these experts have lent considerable support to our feeling that the patterns we have described in Mamachi are widespread in many parts of Japan.

To spell out in detail how we arrived at each of our conclusions presented in the text would require several thousand pages. The conclusions presented reflect not only a simple recording of facts which we heard and observed but occasional leaps in interpretation. In order to convey our general approach to the problem of getting information and drawing conclusions, I present the following examples:

The uniqueness of the salary-man pattern.—Of the twelve families which we studied intensively, it happened that six were salary-man families, one was an independent professional family, two were businessmen families, and three were families of white-collar workers in small enterprises. We soon noticed patterns of difference

---

[5] Cf. Robert Hess and Gerald Handel, *Family World,* Chicago: University of Chicago Press, 1959.

between these groups of families, but our attention to the problem of the salary man first came from the contrasts which the professional family and one of the business families drew between their way of life and the way of life of the salary man. The descriptions they gave were even more detailed than the observations we had made to that point. From that time on, I began exploring the sociological factors that might be associated with these differences. With every salary man, I began exploring the relationship with his family and outside in terms of the relationship with the firm. With all nonsalary men, I began comparing their lives with those of salary men. Through medical colleagues at the National Institute of Mental Health and elsewhere, I could get more detailed information about how friends of theirs had entered private practice. However, I did not decide to focus on the salary man in the write-up of the material until after returning to the United States and analyzing the questionnaire responses of the salary men and the small shopkeepers. There were many consistent differences between shopkeepers and salary men which seemed to sharpen the distinction between the salary man and other occupational groups. We had not had any formal interviewing experience with small shopkeepers, but our daily contacts with them and what we had heard about them was fully consistent with what we learned from the questionnaires. Once I had decided to organize the material around the topic of the salary man, it was then necessary to go through all the interview material which we had collected to trace the implications of this pattern in various social spheres.

The patterning of community relationships.—Many of our early observations about the community grew out of our concern with our own relationships with Mamachi residents. For example, we found that we were treated very differently by high-status people in the community than by those of low status. We were concerned as to how to develop smoother and easier relationships, but we noticed that in general high-status people seemed relaxed and were not overly polite. Low-status people were extremely polite and seemed anxious to prove that they came from respectable families. This sensitized us to certain clues to look for in groups of people in higher and lower status. We noticed, for example, that in the meetings of the six well families the higher-status families behaved to the lower-status families much as they had toward us. The reserve, caution, and anxiety felt by the lower-status families toward us was also reflected in their relations toward higher-status families but not toward other lower-status families. We noticed that people of high status were polite but seemed wary about deep involvement. Having received a number of vague requests and presents from people who wanted favors, we sympathetically asked the higher-status families how to deal with such requests, and they replied with a spontaneous and lengthy outpouring of feeling and information reflecting their deep concern with this issue. Once we had made concrete observations, we could use them without mentioning names as a basis for seeking explanations and for eliciting related experiences of other families.

Immediately before moving to Mamachi, I asked various people there how we should go about finding a place to live and whether there were any special problems we should expect in moving. Many people thought it would be somewhat lonely for us, and they continued further by relating some of the feelings they had when they first moved. It is our belief that these spontaneous expressions of feeling provided us with a fuller understanding of the subtleties and strength of their feelings than more formal and rigid interview procedures.

General knowledge of community practices.—On some topics people talked about their own experiences but knew little about the activities of their friends. For example, men talked fairly freely to me about their friends' sexual experiences as well as their own, but women, although willing to talk to my wife about their own experiences, were so poorly informed about other women's activities that they could not be useful informants about wider community patterns. Hence, our information on women's sexual activities is based on only a small number of cases and we would not have had confidence to report our own findings had it not been for the fact that they generally coincided with the findings of Japanese scholars who have conducted much more extensive research into the field of sexual behavior.

Interpretation of material.—Some problems do require a leap in interpretation. For example, I have concluded that one important reason why Mamachi residents do not go back to their rural villages is their fear of requests which would be difficult to handle, yet no person in Mamachi specifically gave this as the reason. They said they felt they should go back more often, but many gave no reason or explained that it was due to having only a short time off from work or congested traffic during the special holidays when they have time off. Although these are undoubtedly important considerations, on two occasions we went with Mamachi residents to visit their rural relatives, and both times large numbers of villagers came bringing presents to the Mamachi residents with requests to find homes and be of assistance in the city. Supplementing these observations were the many accounts given us in Mamachi of difficult requests from rural friends or relatives. Since many felt guilty about not going back more to rural villages, and since many expressed concern about requests from rural acquaintances, we felt it was reasonable to relate these two observations even if they did not.

Child-rearing practices.—Most parents with whom we had close contact were in their thirties or early forties and their children were already in school. Because they seemed vague on precise details of handling small children, toward the end of our stay my wife made a concerted effort to study the techniques of mothers who had small children. The director of our son's nursery school assisted this study with introductions to ten mothers who each had a child in nursery school and an infant at home. My wife then conducted a two-to-three-hour interview in the homes of each of these mothers which also gave her an opportunity to observe mother-infant interaction. The director of the nursery school supplied us with additional information about the families and about the behavior of the children in the nursery-school setting. We also had opportunities to observe groups of young children playing on the school playground and in the alley in front of our home. Our interpretation of child-rearing practices was heavily influenced by the concrete cases presented to us by Japanese child psychiatrists and child psychologists even though our different cultural perspective sometimes led us to different interpretations of the child's behavior and the mother-child relationship.

Any attempt to understand one's own behavior, or one's friends' behavior, or a stranger's behavior is subject to special hazards resulting from one's inadequate objectivity and lack of adequate understanding. We took as many precautions as we knew to assure a many-sided sympathetic understanding of Mamachi residents, and in analyzing the material we have attempted to consider how our own position and bias might have interfered with our interpretations. We can only hope that our conclusions, though inadequate in giving the full flavor of life in Mamachi, will be of some help in furthering Western understanding of Japanese society.

SELECTED BIBLIOGRAPHY

SELECTED BIBLIOGRAPHY

For bibliographical information on Japanese-language behavioral-science studies, see Kunio Odaka, "Sociology in Japan," in Howard Becker and Alvin Boskoff, eds., *Modern Sociological Theory in Continuity and Change*. New York: Dryden Press, 1957; Takao Sofue, "Anthropology in Japan: Historical Review and Modern Trends," in Bernard J. Siegel, ed., *Biennial Review of Anthropology*, 1961; Ronald Dore, "Sociology in Japan," *The British Journal of Sociology*, 1962, XIII:116–123; *A Guide to Exhibition of Japanese Sociological Books*, Fifth World Congress of Sociology, September 2–9, 1962, published by The Japan Sociological Society.

More specialized bibliographies are available in many of the following English-language works.

English-Language Works on Japanese Society

Abegglen, James G., *The Japanese Factory*. Glencoe, Ill., The Free Press, 1958.

Baker, Wendell Dean, "A Study of Selected Aspects of Japanese Social Stratification." Doctoral dissertation, Columbia University, 1956.

Beardsley, Richard, John W. Hall, and Robert E. Ward, *Village Japan*. Chicago: The University of Chicago Press, 1959.

Bellah, Robert N., *Tokugawa Religion*, Glencoe, Ill.: The Free Press, 1957.

Benedict, Ruth, *The Chrysanthemum and the Sword*. Boston: Houghton-Mifflin, 1946.

Borton, Hugh, ed., *Japan Between East and West*. New York: Harper, 1957.

Burks, Ardath W., *The Government of Japan*. New York: Thomas Y. Crowell, 1961.

Cohen, Jerome B., *Japan's Postwar Economy*. Bloomington: University of Indiana Press, 1958.

Cole, Allan B., ed., *Japanese Opinion Polls with Socio-political Significance, 1947–1957*. Medford, Mass.: Tufts University, 1958.

Cole, Allan B., *Japanese Society and Politics*. Boston: Boston University, 1956.

Dore, Ronald P., *City Life in Japan*. Berkeley and Los Angeles: University of California Press, 1958.

Dore, Ronald P., *Land Reform in Japan*, London: Oxford University Press, 1959.

Embree, John F., *A Japanese Village: Suye Mura*. London: Kegan Paul, French-Trubner, 1946.

Enright, D. J., *The World of Dew: Aspects of Living Japan*. Rutland, Vt.: Charles E. Tuttle, 1956.

Fukutake, Tadashi, *Man and Society in Japan*. Tokyo: University of Tokyo Press, 1962.

Haring, Douglas G., ed., *Japan's Prospect*. Cambridge, Mass.: Harvard University Press, 1946.

Ike, Nobutaka, *Japanese Politics*. New York: Alfred A. Knopf, 1957.

Koyama, Takashi, *The Changing Social Position of Women in Japan*. UNESCO, 1961.

Lanham, Betty Baily, *Aspects of Child Rearing in Japan.* Doctoral dissertation, Syracuse University, 1962.

Levine, Solomon B., *Industrial Relations in Post-War Japan.* Urbana: University of Illinois Press, 1958.

Lockwood, William, *The Economic Development of Japan.* Princeton: Princeton University Press, 1954.

Maki, John, *Government and Politics in Japan.* New York: Frederick A. Praeger, 1962.

Maruyama, Masao, *Thought and Behavior in Modern Japanese Politics.* New York: Oxford University Press, 1963.

Matsumoto, Yoshiharu Scott, *Contemporary Japan: The Individual and the Group.* Philadelphia: The American Philosophical Society, 1960.

Mendel, Douglas H., Jr., *Japanese People and Foreign Policy.* Berkeley and Los Angeles: University of California Press, 1961.

Morris, Ivan I., *Nationalism and The Right Wing in Japan.* London: Oxford University Press, 1960.

Nakamura, Hajime, *The Ways of Thinking of Eastern Peoples.* Tokyo: Japanese National Commission for UNESCO, 1960.

Norbeck, Edward, *Takashima: A Japanese Fishing Community.* Salt Lake City: University of Utah Press, 1946.

Pelzel, John C., "Social Stratification in Japanese Urban Economic Life." Doctoral dissertation, Harvard University, 1949.

Plath, David W., "The Strung and the Unstrung: Holidays in Japanese Life." Doctoral dissertation, Harvard University, 1962.

"Post-War Democratization in Japan," *International Social Science Journal,* 1961, XIII: 7–91.

Reischauer, Edwin O., *The United States and Japan.* Cambridge, Mass.: Harvard University Press, 1950.

Reischauer, Edwin O., *Japan: Past and Present.* New York: Alfred A. Knopf, 1946.

Rosovsky, Henry, *Capital Formation in Japan, 1868–1940.* Glencoe, Ill.: Free Press, 1961.

Scalapino, Robert A., and Junnosuke Masumi, *Parties and Politics in Contemporary Japan.* Berkeley and Los Angeles: University of California Press, 1961.

Smith, Robert J., and Richard K. Beardsley, eds. *Japanese Culture.* New York: The Viking Fund, 1962.

Smith, Robert J., and John B. Cornell, *Two Japanese Villages.* Ann Arbor: The University of Michigan Press, 1956, Center for Japanese Studies, Occasional Paper No. 5.

Smith, Thomas C., *The Agrarian Origins of Modern Japan.* Stanford: Stanford University Press, 1959.

Smith, Thomas C., ed., *City and Village in Japan. Economic Development and Cultural Change,* IX:1, part ii, October, 1960.

Stoetzel, Jean, *Without the Chrysanthemum and the Sword: A Study of the Attitudes of Youth in Post-war Japan.* New York: Columbia University Press, 1955.

Taeuber, Irene B., *The Population of Japan.* Princeton: Princeton University Press, 1958.

Von Mehren, Arthur Taylor, ed. *Law in Japan: The Legal Order in a Changing Society.* Cambridge, Mass.: Harvard University Press, 1963.

Yanaga, Chitoshi, *Japanese People and Politics.* New York: Wiley, 1956.

Japanese-Language Bibliography on the Japanese Family

Kenneth Morioka has compiled an excellent bibliography of Japanese works on the family: "Kazoku Shakaigaku Sankoo Bunken Mokuroku" (A Bibliographic Guide to Works on Family Sociology), *Shakai Kagaku Jaaneru,* International Christian University, 1960, 185–254. (Revised English translation available from the Family

Study Center, University of Minnesota.) The following is a selected list containing some of the major Japanese family studies.

Aruga, Kizaemon, *Nihon Kazoku Seido to Kosaku Seido* (The Japanese Family System and Tenancy System). Tokyo: Kawade Shoboo, 1943.

Asayama, Shinichi, *Sei no Kiroku* (Report on Sexual Behavior). Osaka: Rokugatsusha, 1957.

Isomura, Eiichi, Takeyoshi Kawashima, and Takashi Koyama, eds., *Gendai Kazoku Kooza* (The Structure of the Contemporary Family). 6 volumes. Tokyo: Kawade Shoboo, 1955–1956.

Isono, Seiichi, and Fujiko Isono, *Kazoku Seido* (The Family System). Tokyo: Iwanami Shoten, 1958.

Kawashima, Takeyoshi, *Ideorogi to shite no Kazoku Seido* (The Family System as Ideology). Tokyo: Iwanami Shoten, 1956.

Kawashima, Takeyoshi, *Kekkon* (Marriage). Tokyo: Iwanami Shinso, 1954.

Kawashima, Takeyoshi, *Nihon Shakai no Kazokuteki Koosei* (The Familistic Structure of Japanese Society). Tokyo: Nihon Hyooron Shinsha, 1950.

Kekkon Zenshu (How to Plan Your Marriage). Toyyo: Fufu no Tomosha, 1960.

Kitano, Seeichi and Yuzuru Okada, eds., *Ie: Sono Koozoo Bunseki* (An Analysis of the Structure of the *Ie*). Tokyo: Soobunsha, 1959.

Koyama, Takeshi, *Gendai Kazoku no Kenkyuu* (An Investigation of the Contemporary Family). Tokyo: Koobundoo, 1960.

Rural Welfare Research Institute, *Soozoku Sei no Kenkyuu* (A Study of Inheritance). (Includes lengthy English summary.) Mitaka: International Christian University, 1958.

Shinozaki, Nobuo, *Fufu Sei Seikatsu no Jittai* (The Sexual Life of Married Couples). Tokyo: Muramatsu Shoten, 1949.

Tamura, Kenji, and Makie Tamura, *Anata wa Dare to Kekkon Shiteru ka* (Who Is Your Partner in Married Life?) Tokyo: Sekkasha, 1961.

Toda, Teizo, *Kazoku no Kenkyuu* (Family Studies). Tokyo: Koobundoo, 1926.

Tsuru, Hiroshi, *Nihon no Boshi Kankei* (Mother-Child Relationship in Japan). Nagoya: Reimei, 1958.

Selected Bibliography of English-Language Articles and Pamphlets on the Japanese Family

Ariga, Kizaemon, "The Family in Japan," *Marriage and Family Living*, 1954, XVI: 362–368.

Asayama, Shinichi, "Comparison of Sexual Development of American and Japanese Adolescents," *Psychologia*, 1957, I:129–131.

Baber, Ray E., *Youth Looks at Marriage and the Family.* Tokyo: International Christian University, 1958.

Beardsley, Richard, "The Household in the Status System of Japanese Villages," *Occasional Papers.* Center for Japanese Studies, University of Michigan, 1951, I:62–72.

Bennett, John W., and Michio Nagai, "The Japanese Critique of the Methodology of Benedict's Chrysanthemum and the Sword," *American Anthropologist*, 1953, LV:404–411.

Caudill, William, "Maternal Care and Infant Behavior in Japan" (mimeographed), National Institute of Mental Health, 1962.

Caudill, William, "Japanese-American Personality and Acculturation," *Genetic Psychology Monographs*, 1952, XLV:3–102.

Caudill, William, and George De Vos, "Achievement, Culture and Personality: The Case of the Japanese-Americans," *American Anthropologist*, 1956, LVIII:1102–1126.

Caudill, William, and Harry A. Scarr, "Japanese Value Orientations and Culture Change," *Ethnology*, 1961, I:53–91.

Caudill, William, and Takeo Doi, "Interrelations of Psychiatry, Culture and Emotion in Japan" in Thomas Gladwin, ed., *Medicine and Anthropology*. New York: Werner Gren Foundation, 1962.

De Vos, George, "A Comparison of the Personality Differences in Two Generations of Japanese-Americans by Means of the Rorschach Test," *Nagoya Journal of Medical Science*, 1954, XVIII:153–265.

De Vos, George, "The Relation of Guilt Toward Parents to Achievement and Arranged Marriage among the Japanese," *Psychiatry*, 1960, XXIII:287–301.

De Vos, George, and Hiroshi Wagatsuma, "Variations in Value Attitudes Related to Women's Status in Japanese Rural Villages," *American Anthropologist*, 1961, LXIII:1204–1230.

De Vos, George, and Hiroshi Wagatsuma, "Psycho-Cultural Significance of Concern Over Death and Illness Among Rural Japanese," *The International Journal of Social Psychiatry*, 1959, V:5–19.

Doi, Takeo, "Amae—A Key Concept for Understanding Japanese Personality Structure," *Psychologia*, 1962, V:1–7.

Goodman, Mary Ellen, "Values, Attitudes and Social Concepts of Japanese and American Children," *American Anthropologist*, 1957, LIX:979–999.

Haring, Douglas G., "Aspects of Personal Character in Japan," *Far Eastern Quarterly*, 1946, VI:12–22.

Ishino, Iwao, "The Oyabun-Kobun: A Japanese Ritual Kinship Institution," *American Anthropologist*, 1953, LV:695–707.

Lanham, Betty B., "Aspects of Child Care in Japan: Preliminary Report," in Douglas Haring, ed., *Personal Character and Cultural Milieu*. Syracuse: Syracuse University Press, 1956.

Lifton, Robert Jay, "Youth and History: Individual Change in Postwar Japan," *Daedalus*, 1962, XCI:172–197.

Masuoka, Edna Cooper and Jitsuichi Masuoka and Nozomu Kawamura, "Role Conflicts in the Modern Japanese Family," *Social Forces*, 1961, XLI:1–6.

Nagai, Michio, "Dozoku: A Preliminary Study of the Japanese 'Extended Family' Group and Its Social and Economic Functions," Report No. 7, Project 483, Ohio State University (mimeographed).

Nagai, Michio, and John W. Bennett, "A Summary and Analysis of 'The Familial Structure of Japanese Society by Takeyoshi Kawashima,'" *Southwestern Journal of Anthropology*, 1953, IX:239–250.

Norbeck, Edward, and Harumi Befu, "Informal Fictive Kinship in Japan," *American Anthropologist*, 1958, LX:102–117.

Norbeck, Edward, and Harumi Befu, "Japanese Usages of Terms of Relationship," *Southwestern Journal of Anthropology*, 1958, XII:66–36.

Norbeck, Edward, and George De Vos, "Culture and Personality: The Japanese," in F. L. K. Hsu, ed., *Psychological Anthropology*. Homewood, Ill.: Dorsey Press, 1961.

Norbeck, Edward, and Margaret Norbeck, "Child Training in a Japanese Fishing Village," in Douglas G. Haring, ed., *Personal Character and Cultural Milieu*. Syracuse: Syracuse University Press, 1956.

Norbeck, Edward, "Postwar Cultural Change and Continuity in Northeastern Japan," *American Anthropologist*, 1961, LXIII:297–321.

Olsen, Lawrence, "Japanese Small Industry," American Universities Field Staff Letter, October 10, 1955.

Olsen, Lawrence, "Human Relations in a Japanese Factory," American Universities Field Staff Letter, November 27, 1955.

Olsen, Lawrence, "Four Family Budgets," American Universities Field Staff Letter, February 15, 1959.

Olsen, Lawrence, "Takehara: A Good Place to Be From," American Universities Field Staff Letter, May 7, 1961.

Olsen, Lawrence, "How the Japanese Divorce," American Universities Field Staff Letter, July 1961.

Pease, Damaris, "Some Child Rearing Practices in Japanese Families," Journal Paper No. J-3872 of the Iowa Agricultural and Home Economics Experiment Station, Ames, Iowa.

Pelzel, John C., "Some Social Factors Bearing upon Japanese Population," *American Sociological Review*, 1950, XV:20–25.

Population Problems Research Council, Mainichi Newspapers, Tokyo, *Family System and Population of Farming Communities in Japan*, Series No. 6, 1952.

Population Problems Research Council, Mainichi Newspapers, Tokyo, *Public Opinion Survey on Birth Control in Japan*, Series No. 7, 1952.

Population Problems Research Council, Mainichi Newspapers, Tokyo, *Some Facts about Family Planning in Japan*, Series No. 12, 1955.

Population Problems Research Council, Mainichi Newspapers, Tokyo, *Fifth Public Opinion Survey on Birth Control in Japan*, 1959.

Shinozaki, Nobuo, *Report on Sexual Life of Japanese*, Institute of Population Problems, Welfare Ministry, Tokyo, 1957.

Steiner, Kurt, "A Japanese Cause Célèbre: The Fukuoka Patricide Case," *American Journal of Comparative Law*, 1956, V:106–111.

Steiner, Kurt, "The Revision of the Civil Code of Japan: Provisions Affecting the Family," *Far East Quarterly*, 1950, IX:169–184.

Vogel, Ezra, "The Go-Between in a Developing Society: The Case of the Japanese Marriage Arranger," *Human Organization*, 1961, XX:112–120.

Wagatsuma, Hiroshi, and George De Vos, "Attitudes Toward Arranged Marriage in Rural Japan," *Human Organization*, 1962, XXI:187–200.

Wagatsuma, Sakae, "Democratization of the Family Relations in Japan," *Washington Law Review*, 1950, XXV:405–426.

INDEX